LANGUAGE OF THE LAND

The Mapuche in Argentina and Chile

Leslie Ray

Copenhagen 2007 – Document No. 119

LANGUAGE OF THE LAND
The Mapuche in Argentina

Author: Leslie Ray

Copyright: The author and IWGIA (International Work Group for Indigenous Affairs) 2007 – All Rights Reserved

Editorial Production: Alejandro Parellada

Cover and layout: Jorge Monrás

Prepress and Print: Centraltrykkeriet Skive A/S
    Skive, Denmark

ISBN: 97-88791563379
ISSN: 0105-4503

*This book has been produced with financial support from
the Danish Ministry of Foreign Affairs*

**INTERNATIONAL WORK GROUP
FOR INDIGENOUS AFFAIRS**
Classensgade 11 E, DK 2100 - Copenhagen, Denmark
Tel: (45) 35 27 05 00 - Fax: (45) 35 27 05 07
E-mail: iwgia@iwgia.org - Web: www.iwgia.org

Acknowledgements

This book has come into the world thanks to the belief and involvement of many friends and colleagues, whom I list below, certainly not in order of importance, but in more or less chronological order of their involvement in this project.

My thanks go to Pete Larson, who showed me the road from Buenos Aires to Patagonia, to Hernán Scandizzi, who travelled with me much of the way, to Evis, Graciela and María Luisa, who stirred me to action, to Mauro Millán, for his righteous anger, to Ana Prane, for her patience, and to Reynaldo Mariqueo, for his calm determination.

I am very grateful to Richard Paton and Holly Bembridge for their invaluable help, to Huguette Chatterton, Harry Goode and Cambridge Writers, for their gentle critiques, to Anahí Meli, Nelson Cayuleo and Kumelen Newen Mapu, to Lorena Norín, to Adrián Moyano, to Sandro and La Changa at the Mapuche Centre, Bariloche, to Jorge Nahuel and the Coordinadora in Neuquén, to Beatriz Pichi Malen and to Dario Duch, to José Bengoa, to Sara McFall and to Roberta Bacic at WRI.

Many thanks also to Marcela López-Levy, for taking that leap of faith, to Roman Krznaric for his precious reading lists, to Dr Charles Jones and Julie Coimbra of the Centre for Latin American Studies, Cambridge University, for their support, and to Mark Brown and the Legacy of Colonialism list, for providing such an inspiring resource, and to Martin Pennock and Cynthia Stephens for their encouragement.

I am also deeply indebted to Alejandro Parellada, my facilitator in the nick of time.

Last but by no means least, I must thank Gladys, Nick and Natalie for putting up with me through the long process of researching, writing and publishing this book.

CONTENTS

Introduction 10

Part I: Recovery and Resistance

People of the Land: the dilemma
of the urban Mapuche today 20

No Man's Land: First encounters between the
Original Peoples and the Europeans 32

Reluctant Compatriots:
The Mapuche and the new states 50

Savages and Statecraft: Preparation and execution
of the Pacification of Araucanía and
the Conquest of the Desert 64

Part II: Reduction and Repression

Land for sale:
Populating Mapuche land after the Conquest 84

Fraternalism or Paternalism: Relations between the pacified
Mapuche and the State until the coups 100

The jackboot returns:
The Mapuche under the Dictatorship 118

New treatment or the same old trick?
The Mapuche in the restored democracies 132

Part III: Resources and Resurgence

    Puel Mapu: Conflict today in Chubut, Neuquén
    and Rio Negro, Argentina 148

    Gulu Mapu: Conflict today in Bío-Bío, Araucania
    and the Lakes, Chile 174

    This land is our land: exploitation of the *Wallmapu* 206

    "*Cabecita Negra*": stories of everyday racism
    and religious intolerance 226

    Seeds of Hope: Mapuche success stories today 248

Conclusion
    El Lenguaraz 272

Epilogue 276

Glossary 280

"Now hear this. You are mountain people. You hear me? Your language is dead. It is forbidden. It is not permitted to speak your mountain language in this place. You cannot speak to your men. It is not permitted. Do you understand? You may not speak it. It is outlawed. You may only speak the language of the capital. That is the only language permitted in this place. You will be badly punished if you attempt to speak your mountain language in this place. This is a military decree. It is the law. Your language is forbidden. It is dead. No one is allowed to speak your language. Your language no longer exists."

Harold Pinter, *"Mountain Language"*

INTRODUCTION

Bío Bío calls her sisters the clouds and tells them of her hollowed out body, prisoner of the dam. Pewen Ñuke and Pewen Wentru, the monkey-puzzle trees, call their sisters the clouds and tell them of their bodies, cut down by modern machines. Mawida, the mountain, calls her sisters the clouds and tells them of the plundering of her bosom. Mapu Ñuke, the Mother Earth, wounded and sick, feels the pain of her daughters and sons whose lives have been taken[1].

This book is about a proud people and their unyielding struggle for identity, for dignity, in their relations with the two states of the southern cone of South America, Argentina and Chile. Their struggle to speak their language, the language of the land.

The Mapuche are a defiant people, who resisted against the Spanish invaders for more than three centuries before finally capitulating, in the latter decades of the 19th century, to a pincer action by the armies of the two new nations.

Since that capitulation they have been reduced. Initially their reduction was a literal one, as the reservations on which they were forcibly placed following conquest were known as *reducciones*. They have since been reduced in other ways: reduced to a struggle for survival in their rural communities, under threat from unscrupulous landowners and multinationals, or reduced to earning a living in the margins of the cities as labourers or domestic helpers.

Along with defiance, distrust of the *winka* (non-Mapuche) has also become an aspect of Mapuche character, for reasons that will become clear through the course of this book. Writing it as a *winka*, I feel privileged that a number of Mapuches have trusted me sufficiently to offer their thoughts and views, their hopes and fears, to be included in it.

Why should we learn the Language of the Land?

"Language of the Land" is the English translation of *Mapudungun*, the Mapuche word for their own language. The word *Mapuche* itself means "people of the land" (*mapu* = land, *che* = people). This might seem odd to us, grappling as we are with the dilemma of which name best suits us; someone living in London but born in Bootle to Caribbean parents, for example, could consider themselves English, British, West Indian, European, a Londoner or a Scouser, or none of these. Our ideas of what labels to attach to ourselves - racial, cultural, religious, geographical or ideological - are almost as various as we are. For the Mapuche, however, the matter is very simple: they are the people, the people of the land, inextricably bound to it, their language springing from their connection to the land. Not the land understood as just the soil, but the territory in a broad sense, and all that was, is and will be associated with it. Phillip Wearne explains this well in his book Return of the Indian:

> "The [American] continents' indigenous peoples define themselves primarily through their relationship to the land. Whereas the names they give themselves - Inuit, Kayapó, Runa (Quechua) - often mean simply 'people', the names they give their territories usually translate simply as 'land'. The two are inseparable. As the World Council of Indigenous Peoples, a global federation based in Canada, noted in 1985, 'Next to shooting indigenous peoples, the surest way to kill us is to separate us from our part of the earth'."
> (...)
> "The land is identity - past, present and future. The earth is literally and figuratively the home of the ancestors, the people who gave the current generations life and who demand veneration in traditional rituals and custom. Land represents, in one indigenous activist's words, 'the living pages of our unwritten history'."[2]

The Mapuche's identity is in the land, with which they have an intimate relationship. We, on the other hand, are modern, sophisticated, citizens of the world. What could their struggle possibly have to do with us? We travel around in metal boxes between air conditioned environments; we see the world through glass and are protected from it by concrete. We are in danger of living most of our lives out of contact with the land from which we came and to which we will inevitably return.

Yet at this very moment, on the other side of the world, Mapuches are fighting to regain their land, land that may have been taken from them a century ago, a decade ago, or just months, weeks or days ago.

In much the same way as we are losing contact with the land, we are losing contact with the rhythms of the land. The cyclical time of dawn to dusk to dawn and the subtle changes of the seasons have been all but lost to us; we have moved from the time of the cock-crow, through the chime of the factory clock, to the digits at the bottom of the PC screen.

In contrast with the cyclical time of nature, with its intrinsic expectation of renewal and return, the modern arrow of time moves not round, but inexorably forward, what we call progress. With the digital clock, now even the turning hands on the clock face have gone: now time is ever increasing numbers.

The Mapuche are among the "heretics"[3] who refuse to accept such notions as time being flat and straight. Their celebration of the New Year, held on June 24th, is called *Wiñoy Tripantu*, "the return of the year", when the cycle recommences.

It is tempting to conclude that we in the "developed" world have lost our sense of connection to the land and our sense of cyclical time afforded by closeness to the land, and with it a sense of our place in time, of our history. Maybe that is of no importance to you, if you are dazzled by all the purchasing opportunities out there in the marketplace, by all the information at your disposal, twenty-four/seven, by the buzz of instant worldwide communication. If, however, you feel that so-called progress may provide a loss for every gain, then you may wish to accompany me as I travel with the Mapuche on their journey of recovery.

In certain periods in Argentina and Chile, the teaching of history has been conducted with a great fervour, the glorification of the state conducted with disciplinarian zeal. At the time when I was mulling over the idea of writing a book on the Mapuche, I came upon a history book by chance on a second-hand bookstall in Buenos Aires; this find undoubtedly helped motivate me to put fingers to keyboard. Turning to the pages discussing the 'need' for the Campaign of the Desert, the name given to the Argentine part of the anti-Mapuche pincer movement, I read the following words:

> "We were practically without possession of a large part of our country. The frontier army units failed lamentably in their mission to contain the savage, who occupied a vast area of the Argentine territory, constituting a menace and a national disgrace."[4]

Such a book, and such sentiments, are by no means exceptional in Argentina and Chile even today, with those considered as savages still being viewed by many as "a national disgrace." Such "history" books, and the preconceptions of those who write them, intend to leave no space for an alternative view. In one sense, this book is an attempt to claim such a space.

We're still alive!

"Murió la ultima ona!" ("The Last Ona has Died!") is the title of an article that appeared in *Clarín*, Argentina's leading daily newspaper, in 1999. The article reported the death of Virginia Choinquitel, aged 56; she was purportedly the last surviving member of the Ona, or Selknam, whose origins in Tierra del Fuego date back 9,000 years. "Virginia was the last pure Indian. She didn't speak a word of Ona, but she was proud of her race. She knew the history of her people and her culture better than anyone", Father José Zink, her Catholic priest friend, was quoted as saying[5]. Unlike the Ona, the Mapuche are still very much alive.

In July 1999 I was in Buenos Aires, and friends who knew of my interest in land rights invited me to go along to a talk by some Mapuches who had travelled up from Esquel, in the Patagonian province of Chubut.

The small trades union meeting hall was full. It was a cold evening outside - July is mid winter in Argentina - and many of the audience of students and activists arrived sporting black and white scarves of the Arafat/Leila Khaled variety, as did one of the speakers. I mistakenly assumed that this was to show solidarity with the Palestinian cause, until someone explained to me that a large job lot of these scarves had recently arrived and they were being sold very cheap all over the city.

The three speakers, all Mapuche women, stepped onto the podium: Evis and Graciela of the "11 October Organisation of Mapuche-Tehuelche Communities", both in their 20s, and María Luisa, an elderly lady from the Gualjaina community, 70km or so from Esquel. Evis and Graciela were *werkens* (spokespersons, literally "messengers", in Mapudungun) of the 11 October Organisation, and I was given to understand that María Luisa was a *machi* (spiritual leader). *Machis* in particular are often verbally abused and victimised by *winkas*, as their centrality to Mapuche religious ceremonies and their arcane knowledge mean that even today they are suspected and accused of being witches. Hence the hushed tones when the name *machi* is mentioned.

The three of them had travelled the 800 miles to the capital from Esquel. Though I had journeyed much further purely in distance terms, their journey had been greater in two important ways: firstly, to gather together three return coach fares to the capital was a real challenge for an organisation long on commitment but very short of funds; secondly, because the mental leap that needed to be made to bridge the distance between Esquel, a provincial town with a population of less than 30,000, a large proportion of whom Mapuche, and Buenos Aires, the sprawling modern cosmopolitan capital with its gaze constantly fixed on Europe and the USA, was enormous, requiring a much greater adjustment of perspective than that required of me.

They had come to the capital to run a workshop on Mapuche ceramics and to talk about the struggles of their people for recognition and respect. These two activities may appear at first sight to have little in common, but this was not the case, as I was to discover.

The Last Day of Freedom

It was in 1992, and through the events surrounding the commemoration of 500 years since 12 October 1492 - the greatest day of mourning for the Original Peoples of the Americas - that many Mapuches in Argentina began to find the inner strength that comes from being part of a common cause, and to become involved in the resurgence of the Mapuche people.

Evis began the meeting in Buenos Aires by talking about how their organisation came to be formed back in 1992:

"It was neither organised nor planned, it took place spontaneously. The official Five Hundred Years celebrations were drawing near and there was no talk of holding a counter-event; it had not occurred to anybody. Yet we could not allow this opportunity to go to waste; we had to do something. So four of us joined together and formed a committee to organise a festival. We called ourselves the 11th of October Committee, using that date to commemorate the last day of freedom in America. That event was attended by 500 people, a massive number, considering the size of Esquel.

Brothers and sisters from the surrounding communities became involved, and the event changed from being just a commemoration of the Last Day of Freedom into a space to denounce injustices and to participate in activities. We had set up a stage in the town square, and people came up onstage and said why they had decided to join in, what was happening in their communities scattered around Esquel; not only that, they also made those present make a commitment to give their support, to look for a way to organise in the struggle."

This process of denouncing injustices was now being taken a stage further, as the audience in Buenos Aires learned from the three women about Futa Huau, where the community school had been expropriated by a local landowner, who had fenced it off and was using the land to graze his animals. We learned about the Prane community, who had been expelled from their land way back in 1938, and who, since their return to reclaim their territory, had been intimidated by the army, who wanted to use the disputed land for military exercises. On one occasion the bully-boys even staged a mock firing squad to frighten the community members into giving up their claim.

Then there is Benetton, those self-proclaimed champions of interracial harmony, who have diverted the water source of the Vuelta del Río community, depriving them of access to the river, causing drought and the death of their animals. They have even had Mapuche families evicted from their homes.

The communities and the groups supporting them had attempted in countless ways to draw the attention of the authorities to the abuses to which they were being subjected. The experiences of their representatives had tended to be remarkably similar: politicians and government bodies would either refuse to meet them, or promise to look into the matter but then fail to act, or - perhaps most insulting of all - leave them waiting in corridors to meet officials who would never show up, forcing them to go home empty-handed.

Evis explained that the article about the death of the last Ona exemplified an attitude typical of the Argentine state and its metropolitan élite towards Argentina's original peoples: to consider them a problem now as good as solved, as those of mixed blood are not pure, and full-blooded Indians are supposed to be dying out fast.

To counter this attitude, 11 October were embarking on a project entitled *Petú Mogeleiñ* (we are still alive). The idea of the project is to draw attention to the problems of Mapuche communities, but also to enable urban Mapuches to rediscover their cultural identity - indeed, often to encounter it for the first time - and also to reveal to *winkas* the depth and vibrancy of Mapuche culture.

After the talk, I was introduced to Evis, Graciela and María Luisa, and was able to find out more from them about their lives and the communities they were involved with. I told them their words had had a powerful impact on me, and I promised to do my best to help them, perhaps by providing a mouthpiece for them in the English language. It has taken me some time, years in fact, but this book is my attempt to deliver on that promise.

This project began with a book found on a second-hand stall, and took concrete shape following my fortuitous encounter with three extraordinary women with an important message to spread about the struggles of their forgotten people and the realisation that I could help spread that message.

Aims, Approach and Structure of *Language of the Land*

This book was written using as its basis information gained and interviews conducted directly during my research visits to the Argentine provinces of Chubut, Río Negro, Neuquén and Buenos Aires in July and August 2001 and in January and February 2003, during which I was given special access to the archives of the following Mapuche organisations: *Kumelen Newen Mapu* in Bahía Blanca, the Co-ordinating Committee of Mapuche Organisations in Neuquén, the Mapuche Centre in San Carlos de Bariloche and the 11 October Organisation of Mapuche-Tehuelche Communities in Esquel.

I also gained valuable insights by participating in the *Futha rume Mapuche Trapemn*, the International Mapuche Conference organised in London in January 2001. I was there at the invitation of Mapuche International Link, the support group that organised the conference, with which I have worked on a continuous basis since the late nineties, as a translator and representative in Eastern England. At the conference I was able to meet and talk to the delegates of Mapuche organisations from Europe, North America and the Southern Cone, and establish contacts and begin correspondence that have continued since then.

I am grateful to Richard Paton and Holly Bembridge, who visited Santiago and Chile's IX Region to conduct interviews on my behalf in January and February 2002. I have also commissioned a number of interviews for exclusive use in this book from my friend and colleague Hernán Scandizzo, a journalist based in Neuquén.

I have e-mail to thank for the fact that I have been able to keep in constant contact with Mapuche friends in the Southern Cone, and to conduct interviews with a number of them "at a distance."

In short, I have written this book not as an academic studying the Mapuche, but as a friend, someone concerned about their cause. It is this fact of being a friend, I think, that has allowed me access to information and opinions often denied by Mapuches to academics, about whose motives - rightly or wrongly - they are inclined to be suspicious; information and opinions given in the trust I will not distort them, but use my translation skills to convey them honestly. Let it be clear that I am not neutral, but unrepentantly partial, suffering from one of the nobler English tendencies, that of being on the side of the underdog. For this I apologise in advance. Having said that, in this book I attempt to provide a balanced perspective, and to present the other point or points of view. Though I have consulted the specialist academic literature in my research, I have attempted to privilege Mapuche views with respect to those of non-Mapuche experts. Therefore, affirmations not cited are my own, or the combined result of opinions repeatedly expressed during numerous informal conversations with Mapuche friends.

Language of the Land is divided into three parts: Part One is entitled Recovery and Resistance, and consists of chapters one to four. Chapter one deals with the theme of recovery, a look at the reality of most Mapuches today, the reality of living in the city when as a people they have traditionally drawn strength from their proximity to the land, the *Mapu*. The chapter offers some initial considerations on the attempts to recover and reinterpret their land-based traditions.

The chronological approach begins with chapters two, three and four, which outline the history of the Mapuche as a free people: chapter two spanning the period from prior to the first contacts with the Spanish up to Chilean and Argentinian independence; chapter three covering the early years of uncomfortable coexistence with the new states, and chapter four the period of preparation and execution of their conquest.

Part Two, Reduction and Repression, comprises the central four chapters of the book. Chapter five considers the immediate aftermath of conquest, with the Mapuche either forcibly removed from their land or placed on reservations (*reducciones*), as the lion's share was divided up as the spoils of war. In chapter six we see the various attempts to legislate on land issues and the formation of the first Mapuche organisations in the 20th century. Chapter seven covers the period that saw the return to the dark days of war, this time the war by the Chilean and Argentine states on their own people, in the dictatorships of the 1970s and '80s. Finally, the painful return to democracy is considered in chapter eight.

The five chapters of the third and last part of the book, Resources and Resurgence, look in detail at the struggles of the Mapuche people today to control their land and resources: chapter nine looks at the issues affecting Mapuche communities in Argentina, and chapter ten those in Chile. Chapter eleven looks at exploitation versus ecology in the use of Mapuche land, while chapter twelve focuses on racism and the lack of respect for Mapuche beliefs. The final chapter is intentionally more upbeat, and looks at the signs emerging of a more positive future for the Mapuche people.

This book is intended to serve as an introduction to the Mapuche, their culture, way of life and history. Having such broad scope, it cannot hope to present the wealth of detail of more specialist works. However, as the first general book on the Mapuche to appear in the English language, it has certainly been long overdue, and I hope it will encourage readers to seek out further information on this complex, resilient people. A people that is still alive and still proud, despite centuries of attempts to annihilate and humiliate them.

Mapudungun for beginners

Necessarily, when discussing the Mapuche, their history, culture and traditions, we must use the words of their language, Mapudungun. Many such words therefore appear throughout this book.

The first attempts to give written form to the Mapuche language were made by the missionaries who entered their land to persuade them of the benefits of Christianity. Subsequently various phonetic versions of the spoken have emerged, of which the two most important are 'Unificado' (Unified) and Ragileo. Neither is ideal; Unified is criticised for being too hispanicised, that is, influenced by the spelling of Spanish, whereas Ragileo, by consciously avoiding similarities with Spanish, is sometimes too obscure and illogical. In this book I have therefore opted to use a compromise between the two.

Regarding the word *Mapuche* itself, some believe that the plural form *Mapuches* should not be used, as this form does not exist in Mapudungun (in which the plural of *mapuche* is *pu mapuche*). For clarity's sake, in the book I have opted to use *Mapuches* as a plural form, and *the Mapuche* when referring to the people as a whole. Anglicised plural forms of other Mapudungun words, such as *winkas*, *machis*, are also used.

The first time a Mapudungun word appears in the text, its English translation is provided in brackets. To further assist the reader, there is also a glossary at the back of the book.

Notes

1 "Palabra abierta de la gente de la tierra" by Mapuche poet Rayen Kvyeh (www.mapuche.nl/publ/camp_rayen_kvyeh.htm).
2 Phillip Wearne, "Return of the Indian", pp. 23-24, publ. Cassell/LAB 1996.
3 To use Eduardo Galeano's preferred term for those who do not conform to the dominant model of "development."
4 "Lecciones de Historia Argentina" by J.C. Raffo de la Reta (1950), on the subject of the Conquest of the Desert: *"Prácticamente carecíamos de la posesión de una gran parte de nuestro país. Las comandancias de fronteras fracasaban lamentablemente en su misión de contener al salvaje, que ocupaba una extensa zona del territorio argentino, constituyendo una amenaza y una vergüenza nacional."*
5 The article appeared in *Clarín* on 3 June 1999.

RECOVERY AND RESISTANCE

PART ONE

*"Our people has lived through different moments.
This is our moment of recovery"*

Graciela,
11 October
Organisation of Mapuche-Tehuelche Communities

PEOPLE OF THE LAND:
THE DILEMMA OF THE URBAN MAPUCHE TODAY

This first chapter looks at the reality of the majority of Mapuches today, the reality of life in the city. Away from the rural communities, they find themselves deracinated. It is the *lofs*, the rural communities, that hand down the stories and songs, that provide the social structure and ceremonies that give a sense of Mapuche identity. Rootless in the city, they are more vulnerable, prey to racism and exploitation. They are in a sense caught between two myths, the myth of the "purity" of traditional rural life and the (illusory?) dream of self-betterment offered by education and the media. These two myths have resulted in generational conflict between old and young, with the former still inclined to cling to the myth of the *lof*, while the latter seek to forge a new urban Mapuche identity.

Certain leading academics have affirmed that a Mapuche culture as such does not exist today. In the second half of this chapter, I attempt to show that this is not the case, thanks principally to the role of the *machi*, who has taken on the burden of keeping the "ancient" knowledge alive in the city. Another key factor is the revival of interest in Mapudungun, the Mapuche language, of which I provide a brief history.

The Urban Mapuche

If I asked you to picture an indigenous person of the Americas in your mind's eye, I imagine this person might be male or female, their dress might vary from ponchos to furs or feathers, and the setting could be forest, mountain or plain. I am betting you would not picture them in the city. Yet that is the reality of the majority of Mapuches today, in both Chile and Argentina.

According to Mapuche sociologist José Ancán Jara, Mapuches who live in the cities are subject to "the triple discrimination of being Mapuche, poor and urban."[1] While discrimination for being Mapuche and for being poor is perceived as coming from others, from those of European ancestry and from those who are wealthier respectively, discrimination for being urban is self-inflicted. Urban Mapuches have a strong sense of being rootless, without identity, inferior with respect to their relatives who live in the rural communities, who are closer to the land. That is why recovery is so important for them; not only in the sense of recovery of land, but also that of the identity than comes from traditions, religious faith and community cohesion.

I became aware of this powerful desire of urban Mapuches to reconnect with their lost identity in a poor suburb of Bahía Blanca, in the kitchen of Ilda Painefilo, an elderly Mapuche and member of the *Kumelen Newen Mapu* (Welcome to the Force of the Earth) group, which was founded in 2000. Since they formed the group, they had visited various rural communities in the west of Neuquén province, such as the Lof Puel, staying there for extended periods, learning their songs and taking part in their ceremonies. Ilda proudly showed me the instruments her son Daniel had learnt to make, the *trutruka*, a wind instrument, and the *kultrun* drum. As a group they are now learning to play and sing the old songs. At sixty years of age, Ilda has at last felt what it means to be Mapuche; she is born again: "now at last I have become what I should always have been", she told me. This is recovery in action.

In Argentina it was called "The Conquest of the Desert", in Chile "The Pacification of Araucania." Both of these brutal military campaigns of the late 19th century served the new states' purpose of driving the original peoples off their fertile lands and paving the way for European colonisation and the exploitation of the land through livestock and agriculture.

Over a hundred years later, while the perpetrators of these genocidal campaigns are feted as the heroes of their respective nations, the descendants of the attacked very often find themselves in the margins of cities.

Indeed, it is estimated that today, out of a Mapuche population in Chile of nearly a million, 44% live in Santiago, with only 15% living in the 9th Region, the traditional Mapuche heartland. The same is true of Argentina, with the majority of Mapuches, approximately 100,000, struggling to eke out a meagre existence in the poor neighbourhoods of Bariloche or Neuquén, or over on the east coast, in Trelew or Bahía Blanca.

Urban Mapuches are the ones who supposedly do not exist. Very often they have lost awareness of their identity, as it has been undermined - some would say systematically - by state-imposed education, religion and the media. Very many Mapuches would not call themselves such, because to be an "Indio" in Chile or a "Negro" in Argentina (the usually derogatory Spanish words used by the non-indigenous to describe indigenous peoples) is to be third class, inferior, dirty, and - ironically - foreign, even in their own land. In Argentina someone with Native American features is quite likely to be taken as Bolivian, though they may very well come from northern, central or southern Argentina. In these tough times, Bolivians - and immigrants generally - are often cynically blamed for the country's woes, as scapegoating the vulnerable lets the responsible of the hook.

Moira Millán, the fiery-tempered *werken* (spokesperson) of the Pillan Mahuiza community in Corcovado, Chubut, told me that she had once used a public toilet in Buenos Aires and, having no change, had made the mistake of not leaving a tip for the lavatory attendant. "I hope you cleaned up properly, you shitty Bolivian"[2] she heard half-whispered after her as she walked out. "I am not Bolivian", she turned around and stated proudly, "I am Mapuche."

Those living in the cities are perpetually bombarded with images of a better life elsewhere, in the advertising hoardings and posters. For these urban Mapuches the sensation must be that of being neither one thing nor the other, "ni chicha ni limonada" (neither liquor nor lemonade), as they say in Chile, neither able to grab at the freedom that consumerism can buy, on account of their poverty, nor able to dream of a return to what is traditionally - and perhaps erroneously - presented by Mapuche elders as a more noble, idealised, "authentic" Mapuche existence in the communities, due to their lack of knowledge of their own language and roots and the "corruption" of their urban ways. They are truly stuck. José Ancán Jara is scathing about the way some Mapuche organisations have glorified the rural communities to the detriment of the city-dwelling Mapuches:

> "The rural community is seen as the last place where the most important traditional cultural elements of the Mapuche, such as language, religion, etc., reproduce themselves freely. Nevertheless, this fundamentalist view has glossed over the complexities of contemporary Mapuche ethnicity, and even led to the internal discrimination that juxtaposes the "pure" and "authentic", in other words the rural, with the "impure" or awinkado (Europeanised), the urban."[3]

This is the dilemma of urban Mapuches: to be too dark-skinned to succeed in mainstream society's terms, but to be too *awinkado* to be accepted as pure Mapuches. The meaning of the word *winka* in Mapudungun is "thief", but it has come to mean invader or usurper, and, by extension, Spanish or European. *Awinkarse* is therefore to 'turn European', but is used with a sense of becoming 'impure', 'decadent'.

The low self-esteem in which many urban Mapuches hold themselves is the main reason why they have often chosen to conceal their indigenous identity. The main consequence of this was that for a long time the number of urban Mapuches was something of a mystery. As we will see in chapter 12, it was not until the 1992 census in Chile that the government had any real idea of the extent of Mapuche presence in the city (400,000 in Santiago alone).

During the Buenos Aires talk, María Luisa described the lot of the young urban Mapuches as follows: "The land is fertile, but they live very badly. In the city the kids learn to steal, they take drugs. They finish up with a bullet in the head, or in prison, or else in a gang. They are all the children of Mapuches who once lived in the communities." That is only partly true: very many of these children of Mapuches have never lived in the communities; neither have their parents.

Jorge Nahuel is the *werken* of the Co-ordinating Committee of Mapuche Organisations in Neuquén, the largest and oldest Mapuche organisation in Argentina, representing over fifty different communities. Now in his forties, he was brought up in the city, as a Christian, but knows the communities he represents perhaps uniquely well, so is in a good position to comment on the city versus community debate. In the tranquil surroundings of the inner courtyard of the organisation's *Ruka* ('dwelling' in Mapudungun, here it means HQ) in Neuquén, with the only other sound coming from the teenagers playing pool inside, I asked him how they would have to deal with being Mapuches while living in the city:

> "That is the challenge that every Mapuche has to face if they want to take up their identity, and it is a permanent, daily commitment. They face this choice, of saying either: "I want to be Mapuche" or "I want to give up my identity", and as soon as they take up their Mapuche "being", it is a struggle against all those other elements that are colonising them daily. Most of us who have reclaimed our identity, here in the city, are from the city culturally; we have very little to do with rural community life."

– Can the severing of roots be countered?
"We start from the principle that we are not rootless; that we are part of this territory and that this is Mapuche territory. We are not in another people's space; we are inside our own territory. Therefore, with that perspective, we feed on all the community knowledge, practices and thought, because we are permanently in contact with it, while we reclaim our identity here. We are not going to beat our breasts because we were born here. We are part of a reality, which is the permanent expulsion of our brothers and sisters from the communities. Yet at this historical moment, we are reclaiming our identity here, where we are, and we believe we have a fundamental role within the project that we are moving forward as a people."

– Why does the negation of identity occur?
"Because of the racism suffered on a permanent, daily basis. We live in a racist culture, one that has plenty of tools at its disposal. It is experienced in daily life and in a more systematic way in the education of our children: we prepare them, we comb their hair, we 'polish them up' every morning so they can go and be colonised. In school their struggle is a permanent one too, because they are receiving a complete extraneous, colonising culture, while at home they are receiving another type of education. The struggle they have is the one that is going to define how we will project ourselves as a people."

"Most Mapuches today are victims of that racism and that discrimination, and as a consequence they are forced to conceal their identity. Yet though an identity can be concealed, disguised, it can never be destroyed. It is only a matter of generating the conditions to enable it to flourish with its full force. Not as a hidden, protected element that we only take out in moments of intimacy, but as something that can be externalised at any time. This is the goal towards which we are working politically."

So for Jorge Nahuel the goal, the project, is the recovery of Mapuche identity. But in the here and now.

The Golden Age could be now

The forging of this identity does not simply mean looking back, seeking a return to some sort of "Golden Age" of Mapuche society, prior to the arrival of the rapacious, corrupting *winka*. Jorge and others have understood that to reject all aspects of the modern world would be to also misunderstand the lessons of Mapuche history. Even before contact with the Europeans, Mapuche culture developed and changed, and after contact the Mapuche adopted certain introduced elements that soon became indispensable. First and foremost there was the horse, without which life in a Mapuche community would now be unthinkable, but also goats and cattle. Many vegetables that were brought by the Europeans, such as garlic and onion, have become indispensable in the Mapuche vegetable garden. It is a matter of taking the best and leaving the rest in interactions as equals, not of subservience. The *kultrun* and the laptop can both be useful communication tools for the modern Mapuche, as both respond equally usefully to tapping fingers.

As Prof. William Rowe of Birkbeck College put it, in his book Memory and Modernity: Popular Culture in Latin America:

"... the search for purely Indian expression is romantic and anti-historical, and actually leaves the Indians deprived not only of those dimensions of their culture which the Conquest destroyed but also of the European materials and technologies which they appropriated for their own use."[4]

In any event, it still tends to be the older Mapuches who look back, who are convinced that the traditional ways are always best, while it is the young who are most willing to embrace the new, be it digital cameras or rap music. In this re-

Mural in the Ruka in Neuquén with the emblem of the Mapuche Parliament in the shape of a kultrun.

spect Mapuches are no different from any other society. It is young Mapuches who are keenest to learn their 'old' language, Mapudungun.

Recovering Mapudungun

There are an estimated 5,000 to 7,000 spoken languages in the world, with 4,000 to 5,000 of these classed as indigenous. More than 2,500 are in danger of immediate extinction. Mapudungun is not endangered, but it has survived despite being suppressed to varying degrees for over a century. Only now is there an awareness gradually growing among Argentina and Chile's educators that it should be taught in schools. Thankfully, for Mapudungun at least it is not too late.

In Argentina the teaching of Mapudungun is suffering from a problem of supply and demand. Young urban Mapuches are clamouring to learn the language of their ancestors, and there are just not enough people with the skills to teach it. Fresia Mellico, who translated the Universal Declaration of Human Rights into Mapudungun, says she would have to clone herself several times to meet the current demand for classes. As it is, she is constantly on the move to meet her commitments, from Neuquén to Buenos Aires, to Bariloche, and over the border to Temuco.

To compound the problem, there are now many young *winkas* who are sympathetic to the plight of indigenous peoples, and are keen to learn their languages, while perhaps in the past they would have preferred to study English. I asked one Mapudungun student in Buenos Aires, Leonardo Acuña, why he is interested in Mapuche culture. His answer was, I suspect, typical: "I always like to find out about the other history, that of the losers, the excluded, the exploited. I like to study the different views of the world of the different original peoples."

The reason for the huge demand for Mapudungun among young urban Mapuches is that they do not speak their language because their parents do not speak it either. The community, the *lof*, is the transmitter, through the stories of the elders who live there, but primarily through the religious ceremonies, which are the cement that holds the *lof* together. This is not to say that all Mapuches in the communities speak Mapudungun; even there, very often parents have encouraged their children to speak Spanish, feeling it would be socially advantageous to speak it fluently, on account of the perceived stigma attached to having a "Mapuche accent." Nevertheless, if the link with the community is severed, the language more likely to be lost.

Writing down Mapudungun

This section provides a brief summary of the history of Mapudungun as a written language and a snapshot of the language today. Traditionally Mapuche knowledge was not written down, but passed from generation to generation orally in the *lof*; the language was used to convey the knowledge of the skills, whether animal husbandry, silversmithery, weaving or basket making. There is evidence that centuries ago the Mapuche used the *kipu*, the knotted rope also used by the Incas, to record data[5]. The symbols on their textiles and ceramics were also a graphic representation of Mapuche thought, another precious source of knowledge, along with Mapudungun. To quote U.N. environmentalist Klaus Toepfer, "losing a language and its cultural context is like burning a unique reference book of the natural world."[6]

What we know of Mapuche history prior to the conquest often comes from Spanish texts written by military or ecclesiastical historians, who from the standpoint of the "true" religion tended to pre-judge Mapuche culture and religion, deeming them to be false cults and superstitions. It is ironic that a standard written form was not created for the Mapuche language until after their subjugation, and that this was due in large part to *winka* academics, and the proselytising zeal of Christians, rather than to Mapuches themselves.

The first work on Mapudungun was conducted by German linguistician Rodolfo Lenz, whose *Estudios Araucanos* were published in 1895-97. His trail-blazing path was followed by Fray Felix José de Augusta, who published his *Diccionario Araucano* in 1915. Augusta was also German, a priest and physician who worked as a missionary among the Mapuche in the late 19th century.

We owe the seminal work, the autobiography of Pascual Cona, *Kuyfike mapuche yem chumgechi nhi asdmogefel egvn*, to Padre Ernesto Wilhelm de Moesbach, to whom Pascual Cona dictated it in 1929. Moesbach was also a German missionary, working a couple of decades after Alberta.

More recently came the proposal of a unified system for the phonemic transcription of *Mapudungun*, by Adalberto Salas, Robert Croese and Maria Catrileo, in 1986. Croese is a translator of Dutch origin, who conducted his studies of Mapudungun under the auspices of the Summer Institute of Linguists in the eighties, helping to found the Metrenco Church Growth Center south of Temuco.

Some Mapuches, particularly the members of *Aukiñ Wallmapu Ngulam* ("Consejo de Todas las Tierras" - Council of All the Lands) and others on the political left, see Salas, Croese and Catrileo's system, known as "Unified", as an overly academic system, and a *winka* interference and imposition. For this reason they tend to prefer the work by Anselmo Ragileo Lincopil, the "grafemario" (grapheme proposal) for the Mapuche la nguage (known simply as "Ragileo"), also from 1986.

There is little doubt that agreement upon a standard form of written Mapudungun that is acceptable to all would greatly advance its teaching and dissemination. It is very hard to teach a language when there is not even agreement upon the name of that language. Unified tends to use *Mapudungun*, Ragileo prefers *Mapudugun*, but other variations, such as *Mapuzugun, Mapuzungun* and *Mapundungun*, also exist.

To offer a couple of further examples: the word for "head" is spelled *lonko* in Augusta, *longko* in Unified and Ragileo, and *logko* is also found; the word for "big" is *futa* in Unified, *fütha* in Augusta, *fvxa* in Ragileo, and *buta* is also used. The situation is reminiscent of English prior to the printing press.

How many people speak Mapudungun today? The answer is, we don't really know. Once again it is the Summer Institute of Linguists, the translators of the New Testament into Mapudungun, who have been most active in attempting to find out. Ethnologue.com, the website run by SIL International, estimates that today Mapudungun is spoken by approximately 440,000 people, 400,000 in Chile (200,000 active users) and 40,000 in Argentina. These figures are based on Croese's research from the 1980's, so are inaccurate inasmuch as they are certainly out-of-date, but also because to a large extent they ignore those Mapuches living in Chile's cities who have some knowledge of the language, but are unable or unwilling to use it outside the home. For Mapuches Spanish is still very much the language of social interaction in the city, and is used for virtually all written purposes.

Things are changing slowly, but the process of language recovery will be a long one. Mapuche poet Jaime Huenún, from Valdivia, writes his poems in Spanish, and has them translated into Mapudungun by Victor Cifuentes. He explains why this has been necessary:

> "Only 30% or 40% of Mapuches from the south speak Mapudungun (Huenún is a Williche, a southern Mapuche) and many of the poets write in Spanish, because their families have lived for a generation or more in the cities. You must also consider that for a long time it was a considered offensive to speak Mapudungun and stigmatised. The acceptance of this 'exotic' language only began in the early '90s."[7]

The ancient "exotic" Mapudungun language is now being reappropriated by young Mapuches, who are breathing new life into it. Through it they are interested in rediscovering a cultural heritage that in many cases has been lost to them for a generation or more. A lost cultural heritage deemed by some scholars not to exist at all.

Mapuche culture

> *"In the very depths of the sea lived a large snake that was called CAI-CAI. The waters obeyed his orders and one day they began to cover the earth. TEN-TEN, another snake who was just as powerful as the first, who lived at the top of the hills, advised the Mapuche to climb up a hill when the waters began to rise. Many Mapuches did not manage to climb the hill and died, and were turned into fishes. The water rose and rose, the Mapuches put their pitchers on their heads to protect themselves from the rain and sun. They made sacrifices and the waters calmed and those who had survived came down from the hills and populated the land. This is how the Mapuche were born."*[8]

The above is the myth of the creation of the Mapuche people, which has clear affinities with the Old Testament story of Noah's Ark. It has been passed on orally from generation to generation. Such passing on of a body of traditional beliefs is generally regarded as denoting a culture. Yet in his recently published book, "Los

Mapuche en la sociedad chilena actual", Alejandro Saavedra Peláez controversially denies the existence of a Mapuche culture today:

> "From my point of view, and irrespective of whether I like it or not, I consider that in our times a Mapuche culture does not exist beyond the attempts at theoretical reconstruction of what the Mapuche cultures in the past were. [...] The Mapuches of today may be in a position – if they are lucky – to remember bits of their traditional culture, but not to reproduce it."[9]

This view would seem to suggest that if a culture is suppressed and denied for long enough, if its continuity is stifled, then those who inherit it are no longer entitled to reclaim it. Nonetheless, irrespective of whether Professor Saavedra considers they have a culture or not, thousands of Mapuches continue to engage in what they consider to be cultural activities, and they will continue to do so. These activities include their ceremonies, such as the *nguillatún*, their main rogation ceremony, and *Wiñoy Tripantu* to mark the rebirth of the year; they include their traditional crafts, such as silversmithery, carpentry and weaving; they even include their own sports, primarily *palín*, reminiscent of hockey, which is becoming increasingly popular among young Mapuches. Originally the preserve of the communities, they are being recreated in the cities. Against all the odds, Mapuche culture is alive and well, or so this book will attempt to demonstrate. The state of health of Mapuche culture depends to a large extent on the *machi*, the spiritual healer.

The role of the Machi in Mapuche society

Mapuche women play a leading role in preserving and handing down Mapuche culture, not just because the body of knowledge passed on from mother to child through songs and stories prevents the chain from breaking, but also because it is the *machi*, usually a woman, who safeguards the health of the community, because she knows the medicinal properties of plants and interprets the clues the natural elements provide about the wellbeing of the environment. For this reason, the many Mapuche communities that no longer have a *machi* today find it all the more difficult to keep their traditional knowledge alive.

In view of the machi's strong bond with the surrounding nature, it is no surprise that it is often Mapuche women, rather than men, who are in the forefront of environmental struggles; two such women are the Quintreman sisters, the symbols of the resistance against the Ralko Dam project.

María Pichiñán, who is one of the leading members of the *Newen Mapu* women's organisation in Neuquén, told me what she sees as the role of *machis* in

Mapuche society. Their quasi-mystical status clearly emerges from María's words:

> "Here in the *Puel Mapu* we have the *pillankuse*, which is the name we give to the *machi*. The *pillankuse* is the person who carries forward our philosophy of life. She has the responsibility for conducting ceremonies to bind our relationship with the *newen* (the various forces of nature). She can transmit her knowledge through *pewma* (dreams). Right from the time she is in her mother's womb, she has been learning to know every element of nature, such as the *lawen*, the various medicinal plants of the *Wallmapu* (Mapuche world). The *pillankuse* is in charge of all this knowledge, which she continually acquires from her infancy until she dies, because we Mapuche do not have a time for learning and another to stop learning. The *pillankuse* thinks of her community on a daily basis, she has the role of teaching all her people the importance of nature, the diversity of our *Wallmapu*."

The *lonko* is the traditional head of a *lof*, and is generally male; but this figure has become redundant for Mapuches living in the cities. The *machi*, on the other hand, can still be a point of reference for urban Mapuches, especially in Chile's cities, by offering traditional medicinal alternatives to conventional western treatments.

Mapuche women perhaps feel the tension between the desire to live in a traditional way and the demands of modern life more acutely than the men. While most men, even the elderly, will wear western clothing most of the time, even for ceremonial purposes, it is the women who tend to wear traditional dress, the *chamal*, headgear and jewellery, so they are a more exposed, easily identifiable target for racist abuse. The influence of the *machismo* of mainstream Argentine and Chilean society on Mapuche men, as expressed through advertising and the media, also serves to undermine the nature of traditional Mapuche society, often claimed by Mapuches - rightly or wrongly - to be more egalitarian.

In her book "When a flower is reborn", Rosa Isolde Reuque Paillalef offers the view that a particular form of sexism developed in Mapuche society due to the need to fight the Spanish invaders. In order for her to give birth to more children, and so more warriors, a woman would become the wife of her husband's male relative if he died. The implication is that the egalitarian nature of peacetime Mapuche society was thereby lost.

This sexism became worse when combined with "European" sexism:

> "This sexism with a Mapuche label takes on a zealous intensity, it's reflected in the arrogant way men order women around, that superiority of the male before the female, in the fields, at the dances, after a few drinks, at sports events, when there's a visitor in the household."[10]

Add to racism and *machismo* the scourge of alcoholism, to which urban Mapuche men often fall prey, and you have a potent cocktail of problems for Mapuche women. They need to be tenacious if they are to wear their identity as a badge of pride.

One such tenacious woman is Lorena Norín, who lives in Santiago. Daughter of a Mapuche father and *winka* mother, after being made redundant she decided to learn English to improve her job prospects, while not abandoning her roots. She told me how she would like to join the Mapuche project of recovery by becoming a teacher:

> "I am very proud of my race, but unfortunately some Mapuche people try to hide their race because in Chile racism is very severe, so not all Mapuche people feel proud about their race. Well, nowadays it is changing because young people are trying to find out about their roots and they are visiting Mapuche communities. I say that it is a process and I hope that in the future native people will have an important role in society, in Chile and in Latin America. In fact one of my ambitions is to be a teacher, because I know that I would teach how to know and respect native people, and of course my warrior race..."

After this brief introductory overview of the urban Mapuche today, in the next chapter we will begin our chronological account of the history of contacts between the Mapuche and the *winka* by looking at the period when the Mapuche kept the Spanish Empire at bay, the age of the Mapuche's warrior heroes.

Notes

1. Quotation from "Urban Mapuches: reflections on a Modern Reality in Chile" by Jose Ancán Jara (Abya Yala News, volume 10, no. 3, summer 1997).
2. "Boliviana de mierda" - an insult all too common in Buenos Aires.
3. Jose Ancán Jara, op. cit.
4. "Memory and Modernity: Popular Culture in Latin America", William Rowe, Verso, London, 1991, p. 57.
5. This is discussed by Mapuche hierologist Aukanaw, in "La Grafia del Idioma Mapuche" (http://www.geocities.com/aukanawel/obras/cienciasecreta/grafia/grafia.html#1)
6. From a speech by Klaus Toepfer, executive director of UNEP (United Nations Environment Programme), ENS Nairobi, Kenya, 8 February 2001.
7. Interviewed in El Mercurio, article entitled "Poesía mapuche pensada en español", 15 January 2004.
8. Translated from José Bengoa, "Historia del Pueblo Mapuche", 2nd edition. Santiago: Ediciones Sur, 1987.
9. "Los Mapuche en la sociedad chilena actual", Alejandro Saavedra Peláez, LOM, Santiago, 2002, p. 208.
10. "When a flower is reborn. The life and times of a Mapuche Feminist", by Rosa Isolde Reuque Paillalef, Duke University Press, 2002, p. 236.

NO MAN'S LAND: FIRST ENCOUNTERS BETWEEN THE ORIGINAL PEOPLES AND THE EUROPEANS

Chapter two begins the trilogy of chapters dealing with the history of the Mapuche prior to their subjugation by the Chilean and Argentine states in the late 19th century. The chapter focuses on the time prior to the two states' independence from Spain.

The Spanish bringing the gifts of Christianity and forced labour to the New World first encountered the Mapuche in the early 16th century; what they found was a developing agricultural society - a people called *Reche* at that time - that was well able to defend itself. Thanks to the bravery and skills of leaders such as Lautaro and Caupolicán, the Spaniards were unable to conquer them, so, nearly a hundred years later, they found themselves forced to be party to what was to be the first of many treaties and *parlamentos* over the next century and a half.

The period between the late 18th and 19th centuries was in many ways the "golden age" of Mapuche society; they had tamed the horse, and had become successful traders of livestock and crafters of silver. It was in this period that their presence in Argentine Patagonia became consolidated, as they merged with the Tehuelche, in a process known as Araucanisation.

The diverse geographical areas that made up the *Wallmapu* were inhabited by Mapuche groupings with equally diverse ways of living in relation to the land, whether coast, mountain, lake or plain. The differences and similarities are explained in this chapter. Finally, as a foretaste of what was to come, the chapter ends with a brief consideration of the first of what were to be Europeans' boundless imaginings for Patagonia, the giants and monsters, and the arrival there of the first European dreamers and schemers.

The *Wallmapu* - Terra nullius

The Mapuche's land is the *Wallmapu*, with the *Puel Mapu* in the east, the *Gulu Mapu* in the west, *Willi Mapu* in the south and *Piku Mapu* in the north. The

Mapuche have never seen themselves as divided by the supposedly "natural" barrier of the Andes.

For Europeans the *Wallmapu* was the "new" world. Discovered by Europeans, conjured into existence on the very moment that their eyes first observed it. Their selective vision identified the land, but did not register the people. They saw no one there, only a land ripe for the taking: a *terra nullius*.

Literally meaning "nobody's land" in Latin, *terra nullius* is a fiction employed by the colonial powers. Webster's defines it as a "territory not annexed by any nation"; if you do not consider the original inhabitants of a land to be a nation, then you are free to annex it for yourself. In Australia the concept was used by the British for their land settlement policies: the colonisers did acknowledge the presence of indigenous peoples, but justified their land acquisition by saying that the Aborigines were too primitive to be actual owners, and that they had no readily identifiable hierarchy that the British Government could recognise or negotiate with. Until Norman Barnett Tindale published his map of Aboriginal group boundaries at the time of European contact in 1974, after 50 years working on it, the popular view was that Aboriginal groups roamed across the landscape, with no fixed territories.

In South America too, the subjugation of the indigenous populations of the new world was legally authorised, by what Erica Irene Daes, rapporteur of the United Nations Working Group on Indigenous Populations, has referred to as "doctrines of dispossession."[1]

Two such doctrines were the Papal Bulls, *Romanus Pontifex*, of 8 January 1455, and *Inter Caetera*, of 3 May 1493. The former declared war against the whole of the non-Christian world, giving *carte blanche* to colonisation, exploitation, and slavery. However, it was in the latter bull that Christian dominion over the new world was officially established. It stated that: "the Christian religion be exalted and everywhere increased and spread, that the health of souls be cared for and that barbarous nations be overthrown and brought to the faith." Just months after Columbus' 'discovery', Pope Alexander VI, Rodrigo Borgia of the infamous intriguing family, had given the new world to Spain on a plate, by declaring all the land west of the 40° longitude to be Spanish possessions, with Portugal taking the lands to the east (in fact mostly ocean). The booty - the 'empty' land of South America - had been divided up before any European even set foot on it.

The *Puel Willi Mapu* - Patagonia - was anything but an empty land when Fernão de Magalhães (Ferdinand Magellan) became the first European to come ashore there in 1520. Indeed, it is estimated that there has been a human presence in the vast region for at least 12,000 years; the concrete evidence of this are cave paintings, such as the famous *Cueva de las Manos* (Cave of the Hands), negative hand prints and representations of hunting scenes, in Alto Río Pinturas, in today's province of Santa Cruz. Richly diverse cultures had coexisted there for centuries, as they had west of the Andes.

The Mapuche pre-Contact

At the time of the arrival of the Europeans in the area today known as Chile – *Gulu Mapu* in Mapudungun - Mapuche culture extended its influence between the Río Aconcagua (north of today's Valparaíso) in the north and the Island of Chiloé in the south.

At that time the Mapuche were known as *Reche* (which in Mapudungun means "pure/authentic people"), or at least this was the name that the Jesuit missionary, Luis de Valdivia, identified as being used by them in 1606. Guillaume Boccara[2] postulates an "ethnogenesis" of the Mapuche in around the 17th century. For simplicity's sake, I will stick to using the name Mapuche, rather than choose an arbitrary point to change from Reche to Mapuche.

It has been estimated that the Mapuche population at the time of the European arrival was at least half a million, which would mean a population density of approximately one person per square kilometre. The Mapuche had technical knowledge of methods of agriculture, fishing and hunting, fruit gathering, and had tools for these purposes. The areas of concentration of the population were directly related to the type of natural resources available there.

The area of Arauco and the eastern side of the Cordillera de Nahuelbuta seem to have been the most densely populated, mainly because they benefited from an abundance of natural resources, permitting a higher population than a pre-agrarian economic system could normally feed. The sea, the source of fish, molluscs and edible seaweed, was close at hand; the rivers and lakes provided fish and aquatic birds; the nearby Andes allowed one of the staple Mapuche foods, the pine-nut of the *pewen* (araucaria), to be collected.

For hunting, there was also an abundance of guanacos, pudú and huemul deer. The puma was hunted with domesticated dogs (*kiltros*), and traps (*wachi*) were also set to catch animals and birds.

The Mapuche were in a state of proto-agrarian development, meaning that they were aware of the small-scale reproduction of certain vegetable species, but had not developed full-blown agriculture as such. The system they used, known as *roce* (slash-and-burn), consisted in the clearing of a piece of woodland, generally by burning, to sow seeds there.

In the valleys of north and central Chile, agriculture proper began to develop under the influence of Inca domination. The Mapuches of the south did not know of these methods yet, though they did incorporate the use of *wa* (maize) and *kinwa* (quinoa), which came from Peru. Their basic foods were potatoes and pallares beans, which they cultivated in the wood clearings mentioned above. The *pewen* nut was used to make the flour that was the basis of the Mapuche diet; the *pewen* tree grows at an altitude of over 600 metres above sea level.

The breeding of *wekes* (llamas) and *chiliwekes* (guanacos), a smaller relative of the alpaca and vicuña, was widely practised, but on a subsistence level, for personal consumption. Their wool was much appreciated for use in preparation of textiles, which were traded with the Incas to the north. Later, with the arrival of cattle, pigs and sheep, brought by the Spanish, major changes were to take place to the Mapuche economy and to all aspects of their lives.

First Encounters in the *Gulu Mapu*

In the 15th century, the inhabitants of what is now northern Chile fell under the influence of the Inca Empire. These invaders also tried to conquer central and southern Chile, but the troops of Topa Inca Yupanqui, the 10th Inca emperor, never succeeded in crossing the River Maule.

The fierce, indomitable character of the Mapuche led to their being referred to by the Incas with the contemptuous Quechua term "Auca", meaning barbarians. Some scholars maintain that it is from this term that "Araucanos", the preferred term of the Spanish for the Mapuche, derives.

In 1536-7, Diego de Almagro the Spanish conquistador also pushed south as far as the Maule River, but returned to Peru empty-handed.

In January 1540 Pedro de Valdivia began his march south with his troops through the Atacama Desert, following Almagro's route, and founded Santiago in 1541. In 1544 the Pikunche, the indigenous inhabitants of the area north of the River Maule, were brought definitively under the control of the Spaniards.

On 11 February 1546 sixty well-armed cavalrymen left Santiago with a large contingent of indigenous auxiliaries. A few weeks later, in Quilacura, the Spanish armies and the Mapuche faced each other for the first time, with the Mapuche holding firm and Valdivia being forced to flee with his men under cover of night.

Four years later, Valdivia continued his march south to the Bío-Bío river, where he founded Concepción, and moved further south. The hour of invasion had come; the Mapuche would need a special champion.

Lautaro and Caupolicán

It was becoming clear to the *lonkos* that gathered to discuss events that they were dealing with an invasion of conquest, and the grim prospect of forced labour in the mines and fields as a consequence. Thankfully, the perfect antidote to this fate had been found with the emergence as *toki* (military leader) of Lautaro (*Leftraru* in Mapudungun), a brilliant horserider and military tactician, who had been taken prisoner by Valdivia and subsequently become his servant.

When first confronted with the Spanish on horseback, Mapuches had feared that rider and horse were one indestructible entity, like a centaur, but Lautaro's knowledge acquired with the Spanish helped demystify the enemy. He taught his warriors to ride, and to use what were essentially guerrilla tactics, such as sudden unexpected attacks on isolated forts, and luring the Spanish forces away from the forts in order to attack them.

In December 1553, Lautaro and his warriors attacked and destroyed the fort of Tucapel, near what today is the town of Cañete. Valdivia rushed to defend the fort, but his army was devastated, and he was forced to flee. He was caught by Lautaro and subjected to summary Mapuche justice, accused of "wishing to enslave us and to populate the land with peoples from other worlds, and to take possession of all of them"[3]. Legend has it that he was killed by being forced to drink molten gold, the element he most sought, in a kind of Dantesque *contrapasso*[4].

Lautaro was killed by the Spanish at the Battle of Mataquito in 1557, along with 600 of his warriors. The lance of battle dropped by him was taken up by Caupolicán, who had fought with him at Tucapel. Caupolicán (*Queupolicán* in Mapudungun) triumphed in the battle of Villagrán, but suffered three disastrous defeats at the hands of the forces of Don García Hurtado de Mendoza, losing more than 6,000 men. He fled to the mountains near Cañete, where he was captured by the Spaniards and gruesomely executed by impalement in 1558.

That very year saw the arrival in Chile of the first Spaniard who had come to praise the Mapuche: Alonso de Ercilla y Zuñiga, the writer of the epic poem "La Araucana." Indeed, is mainly thanks to Ercilla y Zuñiga's poem that Lautaro and Caupolicán, the work's subjects, have enjoyed such heroic status in Chile. Here is just a taste of the lavish praise that Ercilla y Zuñiga heaped upon the two great *tokis*, his description of Caupolicán from Canto II:

"Varón de autoridad, grave y severo,
amigo de guardar todo derecho,
áspero y riguroso, justiciero."

"A man of authority, serious and stern,
a friend to be kept, wholly upright,
rough and tough, just."

And of Lautaro from Canto III:

"Industrioso, sabio, presto,
de gran consejo, término y cordura,
manso de condición y hermoso gesto,
ni grande ni pequeño de estatura."

"Industrious, wise, quick,
a good counsellor, good with words and prudent,
meek of condition and beautiful of gesture,
neither big nor small of stature."

The Torture of Galvarino

The third great Mapuche hero was Galvarino, a *lonko* who was taken prisoner by the troops of Governor Hurtado de Mendoza at the battle of Lagunillas in 1557.

Pour encourager les autres[5], Hurtado de Mendoza had his captive's hands chopped off. Mapuche legend has it that, after the hatchet had chopped his left hand off, he proffered his right for the same thing to be done to it, after which he demanded to be given the *coup de grace*. As he was not killed, he ran off swearing vengeance.

At the time the Mapuches' knowledge of cauterisation techniques must have been good, because Galvarino was to do battle with the Spaniards again, this time with lances lashed to the stumps of his arms, before eventually being recaptured and hanged.

Galvarino's story has served perhaps more than any other to perpetuate the Mapuches' reputation for courage and tenacity. Yet there was one enemy against whom courage was not enough. It was in this period that the most effective killer introduced by the *winkas*, contagious disease, first broke out. It is calculated that typhus (*chavalongo* in Mapudungun) killed 30 per cent of the indigenous population, something like three hundred thousand people. In 1563, five years later, smallpox appeared, and claimed approximately 100,000 victims[6]. These "plagues" mainly affected the Pikunches and Mapuches north of the Bío-Bío, who had had more contact with the Spaniards.

The war raged on, with battles and massacres, with the balance of success sliding one way and then the other, with the establishing and sacking of forts, towns and gold mines, the destruction of *rukas* and fleeing of Mapuches into the mountains out of reach of the invaders.

The 16th century came to a close with a great victory for the Mapuche led by *toki* Pelentaro (*Pelentraru*), at the Battle of Curalaba, which forced the evacuation of the towns the Spaniards had established south of the Bío-Bío up to that point. According to the Mapuche's own historians[7], *toki* Pelentaro was - like Lautaro - a great leader and military strategist, and under his command the Mapuche infantery (*namuntulinko*) made important logistical and technical advances, with significant use in particular of units of *waikilaf* (lancers) and *lekay* (boleadora throwers). The Spanish had become aware that an enemy that cannot be defeated must be negotiated with.

Treaties between equals

On 6 January 1641, 91 years after the war had started, Spaniards and Mapuches met under the flag of truce for the first time to make the Treaty of Kilín. In the agreement the Spaniards were forced to recognise the River Bío-Bío as the frontier and the independence of Mapuche territory; they agreed to depopulate the territory, with the exception of the Fort of Arauco, in return for which the Mapuches undertook not to cross the frontier, to allow the missionaries to preach in their territory and to return their prisoners.

Perhaps unsurprisingly, the peace did not hold. Over the summers that followed, incursions were repeatedly organised into the interior of Araucanía, either as punitive expeditions to catch some group of Mapuches for some supposed outrage, or else to take captives to be sold as slaves in Santiago or in the north of the country.

The period that followed the peace of Kilín was still war by any other name. During the 18th century the hostilities were punctuated by a large number of *parlamentos* (agreements, literally 'parleys') between the Mapuche leaders and the representatives of the Spanish Crown, most notably in Tapihue in 1774, and in Negrete - the location on the banks of the Bío-Bío that was most favoured by both parties - in 1726, 1771 and 1793, the latter held with Governor Ambrosio O'Higgins of Los Angeles, *Libertador* Bernardo's father. Negrete was also the venue for the final *parlamento*, in 1803, just 7 years before Chilean independence. The years that followed were a boom time for the Mapuche.

The tradition of the Mapuche horseman

If we can speak of a golden age of Mapuche civilisation, then the "short century"[8] between 1793 and 1881 is that age.

Since the time of the arrival of the Spanish, Mapuche society had changed profoundly, and evolved from a pre-agrarian society to that of the 19th century, with a very highly developed mercantile economy, with Mapuche groups trading with each other from region to region and with the *winkas*. The comparative peace that followed the Negrete Treaty of 1793 enabled the population to increase and more hands to be put to economically useful work.

Horticultural work was generally carried out by the women of the community, on small cultivated plots, usually close to the family dwelling. There peppers, parsley, coriander, cabbage, beans, corn and pumpkins might typically be grown. The Mapuche were the first to cultivate *Fragaria chiloensis*, the Chilean strawberry, which was taken to France and "married" to the North American *Fragaria virginiana* in the early 18th century, thus creating the fruit we know and love today[9].

The economy had changed from one based on hunting and fishing to one based on horses, cattle and sheep. This was the age of the Mapuche no longer as hunter-gatherer, but as the skilled keeper of livestock often depicted in Chilean and Argentine school history books, proud astride a lively steed bedecked in silver livery.

The horses present in the Southern Cone in the 19th century were necessarily all descended from those brought over by the Spanish. It has been calculated that the twelve horses abandoned by the first settlers of Buenos Aires in 1541 could have increased to 100,000 by 1580[10]. By the time the Mapuche routed the Spanish army in 1598 at the Battle of Curalaba, they already had more horses in their possession than those of the whole Spanish army in the region. They learnt to breed and train them, and became highly skilled horsemen and women.

In the same way, sheep and cattle came to completely replace llamas and guanacos as the Mapuches' livestock. Whereas guanacos had been bred for community consumption, the new herds were used for trade with the *winka*, bringing about a significant change in Mapuche society. Indeed, the word *kullíñ* in Mapudungun means both livestock and currency, in much the same way as *pecunia* came to in Latin (from *pecus*, cattle). Animals were exchanged for various types of merchandise, clothing, trinkets, sugar, *mate* and, less auspiciously, alcohol.

A more positive consequence of trade with the *winka* was the increasing access this provided to silver, which not only afforded them a new currency of exchange, but was also used by the skilful artisans, the *retrafes*, who melted it down to transform it into magnificent jewellery to adorn bodies and horse harnesses. Increased trade east of the Andes meant that the Mapuche drew the attention of the Europeans there.

The Araucanisation Issue

Those who claim that Argentine Patagonia was essentially an empty land, and so ripe for settlement, set great store by the idea that the Mapuche were not the original occupiers of the land they inhabit. This view has it that the indigenous people who populated the land were culturally feeble, and did not deserve to survive autonomously, so were overrun and suffered a process of transculturation, first by the Mapuche and then by Europeans. The introduction of Mapuche culture in Argentina is known as araucanisation, but the word must be handled with care, as its use is very rarely neutral. When Argentine historian Rodolfo Casamiquela, one of the key espousers of the araucanisation theory, was giving at talk at the Universidad Fasta in Bariloche in July 2005, he was heckled by young members of the Limay Mapuche community. A press release handed out by the Limay community read: "the reactionary approach whereby "Mapuche equals Chilean and Tehuelche equals Argentinian" is absolutely inappropriate, as it does not consider that both peoples exist prior to the States cited respectively. Non tendentious researchers sustain and demonstrate the coexistence of both and other ethnic groups east of the Andes for various centuries." In his own statement, Casamiquela replied defiantly: "They tell me I'm racist; if racist means saying that the Mapuches come from Chile, then I am racist"[11].

The alternative view, that the Mapuche had inhabited both sides of the Andes prior to the Spanish conquests, is expressed by Chilean historian Carlos Ruiz Rodríguez:

"The Mapuche nation or people had a simultaneous development on both sides, so the links observed starting from the 17th century are only the part visible to *criollo*[12] eyes of a much earlier phenomenon. [...]. A late 'araucanisation', in which the Mapuche appear by invading neighbouring peoples, not only would not explain the ancient and sometimes close contacts between the cultures of the east and west of the southern Andes, but also would not enable us to understand why a people different from the Mapuche would act in alliance with them from the first decades of anti-Spanish resistance: the Puelches supported the lowlanders (*Lelfunche*) and the uplanders (*Wenteche*), the inhabitants of the Andean foothills (a region called *Inapire Mapu*), and because of this Martín Ruiz de Gamboa founded San Bartolomé de Gamboa on the ancient site of Chillán, a foundation that is not explained by the need to establish a settlement between Santiago and Concepción and reinforce the north-south axis, but to contain the communities that were arriving from the east."[13]

Casamiquela refuses to accept this theory, instead insisting that "there was no Mapuche [in Argentina] in 1865 and they arrived in 1890."[14]

Though there had been movements across the Andes by Mapuches in pre-contact times, and debate exists as to how sporadic and intermittent these movements had been, from the mid-17th century onwards they undoubtedly became more regular.

Travelling to the *Puel Mapu* was very much a rite of passage for young Mapuches. After they had made such a journey, they were afforded new status in the community: they were now men. On the traveller's return, a ceremony known as *nampulkán* was held by their family and friends in their honour.

Warring with the Spanish also had the effect of prompting many Mapuches to seek a safer place to live. The Mapuche considered the east to be the main cardinal point, the direction from which all life arises; their sacred dance, the *choike purrún*, is also known as the *puel purrún*, the dance of the east. What better place to seek a better life? According to Argentine anthropologist Carlos Martínez Sarasola:

"Traditions had it that where the Sun rises, beyond the enormous mountains, there was an enchanted place of pines, snows and lakes. And beyond this, the plain, which they thought to be almost infinite. That beautiful place was the current province of Neuquén, in Argentina, perhaps the place most used by the Mapuche to cross the mountains, on account of its ideal geographical conditions, with a large number of mountain passes. Thus the Mapuche came across the Pewenche, with whom they made their first contacts."[15]

The tendency to travel east more regularly prompted the Mapuche to replace the *ruka*, their traditional dwelling made of wood and straw, with the *toldo*, a tent made of hides stretched over wooden poles. These were much more mobile than the *ruka*, enabling groups to move with their herds to find better pasture land. The villages composed of these *toldos* became known as *tolderías*. The routes over the Andes between the Pacific and the Pampas were known as *rastrilladas* (from the word "rastrillar", meaning to drag or rake), as they were formed through the frequent passage of these *toldos*, dragged by the Mapuches' horses. These *rastrilladas* were originally very narrow, as the travellers walked in single file, to avoid the thorny bushes that abounded there.

The Mapuche *toldo* was akin to the teepee of the U.S. Plains Indians, with whom the former share other aspects of their culture and development. The latter too benefited from the introduction of Spanish horses, the use of which spread northwards from New Mexico. Horses revolutionised the Plains Indians' bison hunting techniques, in the same way as they did for the Mapuche-Tehuelches with their respective animals[16].

The Mapuche originally established themselves in the Andean foothills on the Argentine side (Neuquén, Río Negro), and later spread inland, across the Pampas as far as the province of Buenos Aires. The Tehuelche, the inhabitants of the plains of the Pampa and Patagonia, were the next to come into contact with them and under their influence.

Now those who ventured over the Andes were presented with a situation where traditional skills needed to be re-acquired and supplemented. Contact and exchange with the Tehuelche, a people of nomadic hunters, no doubt served to hone the Mapuches' traditional hunting skills. They began to use the *boleadora*, a stone covered in leather and attached to a length of rope, which is thrown and, if well aimed, wraps around the prey's legs, bringing it down. Its use is believed to date back 10,000 years in Patagonia, but it became far more effective when on horseback, now giving the hunters a significant advantage over their prey.

One of the reasons why Mapuches had journeyed east of the Andes was in search of salt. There were salt mines in the mountain range, controlled by the Pewenche, and the Salinas Grandes, huge salt flats, in the middle of the Pampa. *Werkens* were often sent in advance to pre-announce a salt-collection expedition, and to request safe passage. So important was the control of salt supplies, that in 1834 the great *toki* Kalfukurá settled there, the event that is generally considered to have sealed the definitive hegemony of the Mapuche over the Tehuelche. In the next section we will look at the various ethnic groupings east and west of the Andes that made up the Mapuche in the 19th century.

Unity in diversity: a Mapuche ethnography

Over the course of a few generations, the Mapuche and the Tehuelche merged to become one culture; but within that culture there was still considerable diversity.

In this section we look at the different regional and cultural groups that made up the People of the Land.

The area where the various groups of the *Gulu Mapu* lived, with the exception of the Pikunche, is that now covered by the seven Chilean regions of Arauco, Bío-Bío, Malleco, Cautín, Valdivia, Osorno and Chiloé[17].

The Pikunche, the people of the north, lived south of Copiapó, and were the first to suffer the effects of the European invasion, being forced to work in mines and under the system of *encomiendas*, the labour and tribute demanded by the Spanish *conquistadores* from indigenous communities.

The Lafkenche, the people of the shore, were the inhabitants of the coast, of Arauco, Malleco and Cautín. Their staple diet was fish and seafood, and they used a trawl-fishing technique employing vegetable fibres, and also harpoons and tridents. The women collected varieties of seaweed to cook. The men took advantage of the low tide to catch sea urchins, mussels and crabs.

This area around Arauco where the Lafkenche lived was the main theatre for the war between the Mapuche and the Spanish, which meant that much of the population gradually migrated to safer areas of the interior of the *Gulu Mapu*. The permanent presence of forts on the coast meant that the pacified Mapuches of the area established fluid contacts with the *winkas*. Many were displaced from the land during the 19th century, to make way for the huge estates that were being formed, associated with coal extraction.

The Wenteche, the uplanders, lived in the area between the Río Malleco and Temuco. The area they inhabited was densely populated, since their stock reproduced very easily in the high plain areas of the Andean foothills.

The Nagche or Lelfunche, the lowlanders, were the largest Mapuche grouping of the late 18th and 19th centuries. They occupied the plains and rolling foothills sloping down from the Cordillera de Nahuelbuta to the central valley (Traiguén, Lumaco, Los Sauces and Purén on one side and the area of Chol Chol and the current town of Galvarino on the southern side), which were fertile terrains well suited to agriculture and animal breeding.

The high degree of mobility of the different Mapuche groupings enabled considerable exchange between groups that inhabited different ecological niches. The Lelfunche, for example, visited the coast seeking marine products, which the coastal Mapuches exchanged with them for cereals.

The Pewenche, the people of the araucaria, lived on the east of the Andes, between the snow-capped mountains of Chillán to the north and the ridges and crevasses of Lonquimay and Bío-Bío to the south. Their staple diet was the nuts of the araucaria, the monkey-puzzle tree, which they gathered to eat raw, boiled or toasted and also to make flour. Each community had its own araucaria wood for supplies. They also used the nuts in trade with the groups on the Pampa. They did not have a solely vegetarian diet, but also hunted guanaco and huemul deer, and fished.

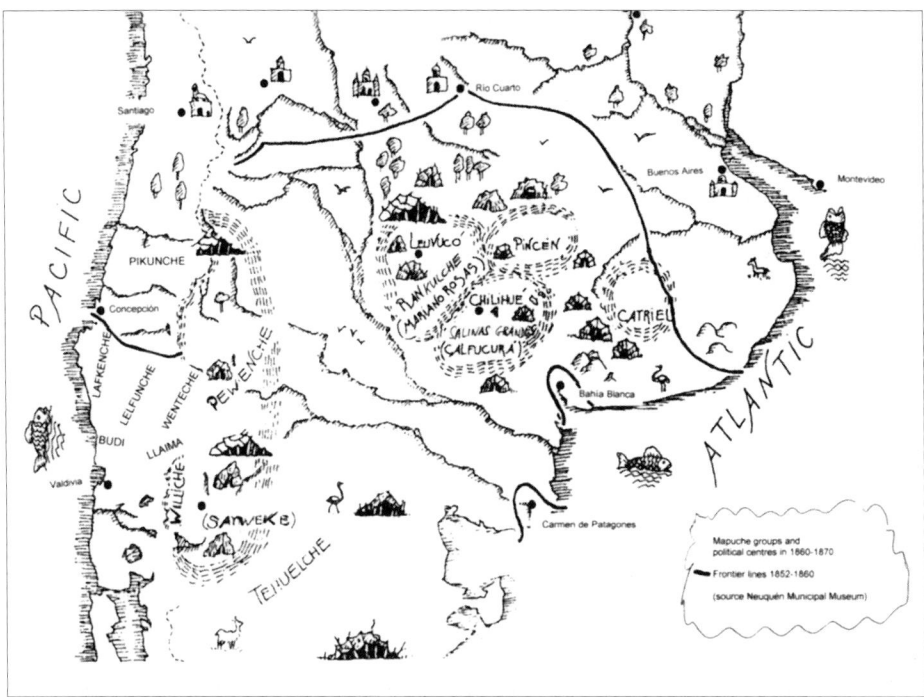

Map of Mapuche groupings in the mid-19th century

First they came under the influence of the Northern Tehuelche, in a process that Casamiquela calls tehuelchisation (as opposed to araucanisation), and subsequently that of the Mapuche, whose language they adopted. With the arrival of the Spanish, the introduction of cattle and sheep became an increasingly important part of their economy, as they controlled the Andean mountain passes through to Chile. Jesuit missionary Diego Rosales, who visited the region in 1653, said of them: "All those who go for salt ask them for permission and give them some payment."[18]

The people of the Llaima, from whom the great *toki* Kalfukurá came, also lived in the Andean foothills, and are considered by some to have been Pewenches, although the general consensus is that they were a separate grouping. They were famed as warriors, and ate the *pewen* nut and horse meat, as did the Pewenche. The Mapuches of the valleys tended to consider them backward and warlike.

In the *Gulu Mapu*, the territory of the Williche, the people of the south, reached as far as the island of Chiloé; in the *Puel Mapu* they inhabited the southern region of the current provinces of Neuquén and Río Negro, in what is now the Nahuel Huapi National Park, and the surrounding areas.

Other groupings from the southern part of the *Gulu Mapu* were the Mapuches of Lake Budi. Their greatest chronicler was *Lonko* Pascual Coña, who gives us a major insight into the life of his people through the book that he dictated to Father Ernesto Wilhelm de Moesbach. For example, from this description of the sowing of maize we can see that the whole community participated in both the work and the rewards:

> "The head of a household ploughs his land to sow maize. He second-ploughs it well, because maize does not grow on land that is not well worked. He also makes *chicha* (corn beer) and makes ready everything needed. He then dispatches one of his youngsters as a messenger and tells him: "Go, ask the members of my group to work; tell them that your master sends you to let them know; tell them all to come, the women too, to help me mark the land for sowing."[19]

The Mapuches of the Budi came under the influence of the Spanish more than most other groups, apart from the Lafkenche; this was principally because of their proximity to the forts of Valdivia and Toltén, and the consequent military and missionary activity.

Another grouping were the Boroans, renowned for their bravery and ferocity, particularly because the Spanish attempts to construct a fort in this area were repeatedly foiled. They were traders in blankets, and regularly travelled to the *Puel Mapu* and the north of the *Gulu Mapu* to trade. This meant that they were more racially mixed than other Mapuches.

East of the Andes, in the *Puel Mapu*, lived the Puelche, the people of the east; they lived on the Atlantic coast and their communities were also scattered over the provinces of Buenos Aires, Río Negro and Chubut. They adopted the horse and lived off the *ñandú* (rhea) and the wild cattle of the Pampa. They were gradually absorbed by the Mapuche migrations.

With the passage of time the Mamulche, the wood people, came to populate the *Mamull Mapu*, what is today the Pampa. The political capital of the Mamulche was in Leuvucó, now in the Province of La Pampa; this was the confluence of age-old trade and migration routes in various directions. Their territory bordered that of the Pewenche to the west and the Tehuelche to the south, with whom they established close relations through trade in livestock, salt, tools and clothing, and also through military pacts.

The Mamulche were in turn made up of a number of other groupings, including the Rankulche (the people of the *rankul*, a type of reed) - generally called the *Ranqueles* by the *winka* -, the Chaziche (people of salt), the *Manzaneros* or people of the apple (*geyu*). Apple trees had probably originally been planted in the area by the Jesuits, after 1670, when the first Jesuit mission was established in Nahuel Huapi by Padre Nicolás Mascardi.

The Tehuelche developed as a people in what is currently Argentine Patagonia, from the Río Colorado to the south of the Province of Santa Cruz. Further south of the Tehuelche were the Yahgans, Alacalufs and the Selknam (Ona).

The Tehuelches' main prey was the guanaco and the rhea. After the arrival of the Spanish, they adopted the horse for hunting, and made highly effective use of the *boleadora* to that end; prior to that they had hunted on foot and primarily used bow and arrow. They ate horsemeat and used horsehides to cover their tents.

Hunting on horseback was mainly a male preserve, while the women hunted smaller animals on foot, such as foxes, maras and *quirquinchos* (armadillos). Hunting was their main source of sustenance, but they also gathered edible roots and seeds to make flour for *tostadas* and pancakes.

The Gununa'kena and Mecharnúekenk, the Northern Tehuelche, lived north of the River Chubut and in the Río Negro and Pampa regions. What distinguished the Northern from the Southern Tehuelche was their different languages, as there was no stable frontier between them. It was mainly the Northern Tehuelche that absorbed the arrival of the Mapuche from across the Andes, and with it their culture.

The Aonikenk, the Southern Tehuelche, lived in the region approximately between the Strait of Magellan and the River Chubut. They were composed of bands made up of several dozen families. These bands had chiefs, and each had a territory over which they migrated seasonally, with summer and winter settlements; the main function of the chiefs was to order the direction of the migrations and the hunting strategy, determined by the movements of the fauna. In summer they stayed closer to the mountains and by its lakes and in the winter close to the coast, migrating following the course of Patagonia's rivers.

To summarise, the Mapuche-Tehuelche were a people composed of a number of different peoples, occupying different ecological niches – seashore, mountain, plain – which conditioned the way they lived. This patchwork quilt of peoples far too complex to be understood by the first European to land in Patagonia, who saw the different as freaks, or else did not see them at all.

Giants and monsters, dreamers and schemers

In contrast with the *Gulu Mapu*, where a belligerent coexistence between Mapuche and *winka* lasted for centuries, the vast space of Patagonia had been completely autonomous from white society and its centres of population since Magellan's expedition disembarked on the coast in 1520. For three centuries the sovereignty of the Spanish crown and the *criollo* authorities over Patagonia amounted to no more than formal aspirations or isolated military enclaves.

Absence of real knowledge of the region meant that free rein could be given to fantasy, and the Tehuelche, seen rarely and from afar, became giants in the fertile imaginations of European sailors. From Atlas to Goliath, giants abound in the biblical and Graeco-Roman traditions, so European travellers had been brought up on them and were well prepared to encounter them. There was also a widely held belief that that the further from the equator you were, the taller you grew. People of supposedly perfect height lived in temperate lands, pygmies lived close to the equator, and giants far from it.

Returning home weary and half-starved from their journeys to the Americas, the sailors soon regaled their amazement-hungry audiences with tales of monsters. Antonio Pigafetta, who was Magellan's chronicler for his voyages in the 1520s, wrote of an encounter with a race of giants, whom - according to Pigafetta - Magellan referred to as "Patagons", hence the name Patagonia.[20]

Pigafetta gives this account of an encounter with a giant while travelling along the east coast, heading towards what would become known as the Straits of Magellan:

"One day, when no one was expecting it, we saw a giant, completely naked, by the sea. He jumped and danced and, singing, spread sand and dust over his head... He was so tall that the tallest among us reached only to his waist."[21]

The sailors attempted to bring the "Patagon", as they called him, back with them to Europe, but he died on the journey, as indeed did Magellan.

Other explorers reported sightings of and encounters with Patagonian giants: explorers such as Sir Francis Drake in 1577 and Pedro Sarmiento de Gamboa in 1580.

This was still the state of affairs as late as the mid-18th century. In 1766, the "Dolphin", a ship commanded by Commodore John Byron, grandfather of the poet, returned to port in London after circumnavigating the globe. Rumours leaked from the crew that they had encountered a tribe of nine-foot giants in Patagonia.

However, by the mid-19th century, interest in giants was gradually transforming into an interest in monsters. The dinosaur fever that gripped children in the 1990s, thanks to Spielberg, was also around in London in 1845, thanks to paleontologist Richard Owen, Darwin's scientific adversary. There was great excitement over the exhibition of the fossils of the mylodon, glyptodon and megatherium identified by Owen, and many Europeans were more interested by the monsters found under the ground than the people on it. English travel writer Bruce Chatwin was first prompted to visit Patagonia on account of his curiosity about the piece of brontosaurus in the cabinet in his grandmother's dining room.

In short, Patagonia was a blank canvas. Ever since it first revealed itself to the European gaze, many have chosen to project their nightmares, such as giants, cannibals and monsters, onto it; and also their dreams.

In our times Jean Baudrillard, the French social theorist, has been drawn to the desertic nature of Patagonia, because, as he puts it "I want to find nothingness. Nothingness is also a place..."[22]. Over a hundred years earlier the writer and ornithologist W.H. Hudson trod the same path before Baudrillard. In his book "Idle Days in Patagonia", first published in 1893[23], he relates in great detail his spiritual interaction with the Patagonian landscape:

> "[...] It has a look of antiquity, of desolation, of eternal peace, of a desert that has been a desert from old and will continue to be a desert for ever; and we know that *its only inhabitants are a few wandering savages* who live by hunting as their progenitors have done for thousands of years. Again, in the fertile savannahs and pampas *there may appear no signs of human occupancy*, but the traveller knows that eventually the advance tide of humanity will come [...]." [my italics]

The Mapuche-Tehuelche – like Australia's Aborigines – had no cities, so their presence in Patagonia was not considered by Europeans to be either permanent or significant.

With time on their hands and money in their pockets, travellers in the Victorian age set out in search of what Edmund Burke, erstwhile guru of today's Conservatives, referred to as "the passion caused by the great and sublime in nature."[24] The first of such travellers, the Columbus of the second wave, was German explorer Alexander von Humboldt (1769-1859). Prior to Humboldt, the Spanish colonies were practically only accessible to Spanish officials and the Roman Catholic mission, but he was to pave the way for the legions of sensitive souls that were to follow. He was greatly respected by Charles Darwin and Goethe, and met both Simon Bolivar and Thomas Jefferson.

Humboldt was followed by waves of tourists of the pen and brush. It would take a tome to discuss in depth all the books that were published on travels in Patagonia in the 19th century. Suffice it to say that many are still in print today, and on sale in the bookshops of Buenos Aires, offering a vision of Patagonia by Europeans and for Europeans, their positions on the shelves virtually unthreatened by the presence of books by the inhabitants of the region at the time of these explorations, with only Pascual Coña occasionally challenging their domination of the shelf space.[25]

Along with the respectable, the disreputable also came to colonise the empty land. As in the USA in the same period, where the figure of the fur trader selling alcohol to the Indians has moved into the more sordid mythology of the Wild West, in the *Mapu* too the people who sought out the Mapuche for trading purposes were often no angels. Indeed, those taking liquor and wine to trade with them were often wanted for crimes by the Spanish authorities, and often more intent on swindling or robbing them than doing fair business with them.

After the American War of Independence, the British Government needed a new location to transport convicts as a deterrent, and to have them out of sight and out of mind; they opted for Australia. At around the same time, in 1779, the first Spanish settlement in Patagonia, Nuestra Señora del Carmen (now Carmen de Patagones), was founded. Like the British, it was common practice in the early 19th century for the Buenos Aires authorities to deport common criminals and political dissidents; they were sent to Carmen, where they would serve out their sentences working as farm labourers, after which they were released.

So it was that both Patagonia and Australia were initially colonised by those specially selected by the best judges in their respective lands.

We will see in the next chapter that in the early years of independence a fragile coexistence still prevailed between the Europeans and the region's Original Peoples, and it would take time yet for the new nations to see the full potential for exploration and exploitation of the Mapuches' land.

Notes

1   In her preliminary working paper presented to the UN Commission on Human Rights, on "Indigenous People and their Relationship to the Land" (20 June 1997).
2   "Etnogénesis mapuche: resistencia y restructuración entre los indígenas del centro-sur de Chile (siglos XVI-XVIII)", Guillaume Boccara, Hispanic American Historical Review 79.3, 1999.
3   From Padre Diego Rosales' "Historia de Chile", cited in "Historia del Pueblo Mapuche" by Jose Bengoa (Ediciones Sur, Chile, 1987).
4   The rigorous correspondence between the crime and the punishment, as in the "Inferno" in Dante's Divine Comedy.
5   "In this country it is good to kill an admiral from time to time, to encourage the others." - Voltaire (from Candide).
6   For a more detailed treatment of these epidemics, see "Viruela y Fray Chaparro", by Dr Pedro Martínez Sanz, Pontificia Universidad Católica de Chile, Ars Medica, vol. 10, no. 10.
7   Carlos Contreras Painemal, Jorge Calbucura and Reynaldo Mariqueo, "Héroes y mártires mapuche" (http://www.mapuexpress.net/biblioteca/heroes-mapuche.html).
8   I have borrowed the concept of the "short century" from Eric Hobsbawm who, in his book "Age of Extremes", considers the "short century" from 1914-1991.
9   G.M. Darrow, "The Strawberry: History, Breeding and Physiology", chapter 4, PGDIC 1999.
10 The statistic is from "Argentina" by James R. Scobie, p. 65, Oxford University Press, New York, 1964.
11 Reported in Azkintuwe, 3 August 2005.
12 "Criollo" means those of Spanish extraction that were born in Latin America.
13 Carlos Ruiz Rodríguez, "Migraciones y contactos entre los pueblos originarios de Chile y Argentina en el período prehispánico y entre los siglos XVI y XVII", cited by Adrián Moyano, "Pequeño paso hacia una historiografía mapuche", Bariloche, 2000.
14 Quoted in *Periódico El Chubut*, Sunday 2 October 2005.
15 Quoted from "Mapuches, lágrimas de la luna", an article published online by the Fundación Desde América (www,.desdeamerica.org.ar). Note that Sarasola is reluctant to explicitly contradict Casamiquela's thesis.
16 Other interesting parallels were drawn between the cultures of the Sioux in particular - the quintessential "red Indian" of popular culture - and the Mapuche, by Aukanaw, the great Mapuche expert on cultural and religious customs. He points out the similarities between the Sioux smoke lodge (*inipi*) and the Mapuche *truftrufn*, and between the Sioux sacred pipe (*can'nun pa*) and the Mapuche pipe, the *kitra,* in his notes on Frithjof Schuon's introduction to the book "The Sacred Pipe" by Hehaka Sapa (Black Elk) (the book and the introduction, but not Aukanaw's notes, are published by the University of Oklahoma Press, 1953).

17 Bengoa discusses the groupings in this section extensively in his "Historia del Pueblo Mapuche", cit.
18 Quoted on a caption for an exhibit in the Municipal Museum of Neuquén.
19 Lonko Pascual Coña, "Testimonio de un cacique mapuche", Pehuén Editores, 2000, p. 148.
20 Some doubt exists as to the origin of the name Patagon. Although it is popularly believed that the name derives from the Spanish for "big feet", it is more likely that it comes from a character in the Spanish chivalric tale Primaleón, popular at the time of Magellan's voyage. The Patagon in Primaleón was a member of a race of flesh-eating giants, so implicit in the name Patagon may have been the suggestion that the Tehuelche were even cannibals.
21 Pigafetta, 1519, quoted in Peillard 1964: 100-5. This quote in turn is taken from "The Patagonian Giants" by Jean-Paul Duvials, in "Patagonia", British Museum Press, 1997.
22 Cited from an interview with journalist Mario Markic, by Esteban Ierardo, in the online magazine Temakel (www.temakel.com).
23 Hudson, W.H. "Idle Days in Patagonia", New York, E.P. Dutton & Co., 1917, p. 221. First published 1893.
24 "On the Sublime", Edmund Burke, ed. J.T. Bolton 58.
25 Here is just a sample: "Narrative of a Journey Across the Cordilleras of the Andes" by Robert Proctor (1825), "Rough Notes Taken During Some Rapid Journeys Across the Pampas and Among the Andes" by Francis Bond Head (1826) and later "Across Patagonia" by Lady Florence Dixie (1880) and "Climbing the Andes" by Clemente Onelli (1904).

RELUCTANT COMPATRIOTS:
THE MAPUCHE AND THE NEW STATES

The period considered in chapter three covers the few decades immediately following Chilean and Argentine Independence, when the countries' southern frontiers - and the Mapuches who lived beyond them - were largely ignored by the new national governments. Forts were established more out of a concern for defence than as a prelude to attack. The military men, Rodríguez and Quiroga, Bulnes and Rosas, did slowly turn their attention to the region, but strategically, to maintain the precarious balance of power. This was a fascinating period that saw the presence in the *Wallmapu* of powerful, charismatic leaders, such as Rosas and Kalfukurá, men of science, such as Darwin and "Perito" Moreno, convicts and bandits, and – perhaps strangest of all – Orélie-Antoine de Tounens, the King of Araucania and Patagonia.

"Our Compatriots the Indians"[1]: pawns in the Independence game?

When Napoleon invaded the Iberian Peninsula in 1808, this sounded the death knell of Spain's overseas empire. Within months, independence movements were forming all over Spanish Latin America, and in less than ten years virtually the whole region had broken up into independent states.

In Chile a provisional government was established in Santiago in 1810. In Argentina - then the Viceroyalty of La Plata - an open *Cabildo* was set up in Buenos Aires to administer the territory pending the restoration of Ferdinand VII. Ferdinand was indeed restored in 1814, enabling Spain to attempt to reassert its authority over the region; but Ferdinand proved disastrous as king.

Following defeat by the Spanish royalists at Rancagua in October 1814, the Chilean patriots' leader Bernardo O'Higgins escaped to Argentina and, with the military leadership of José de San Martin, then returned to defeat the Spaniards at Chacabuco in 1817. O'Higgins was proclaimed head of state, and independence was formally announced one year later on February 12.

On 9 July 1816, an assembly was held in San Miguel de Tucumán, in the north of today's Argentina, declaring the country independent under the name of the

United Provinces of Río de la Plata. Intense fighting followed until the royalists were defeated, but they remained a threat from their base in Peru until it was liberated by Simón Bolivar in 1824. In the years that followed, Buenos Aires lost Paraguay, Bolivia and Uruguay. What remained, today's Argentina, was frequently disunited until 1860. The main cause of this disunity was the schism between the "unitarios" and the "federales", the former who favoured a strong central government, who tended to be the *porteños* of Buenos Aires, and the latter the supporters of a confederation of provinces.

How did all this affect the Mapuche? While the Southern Cone's *criollo* intellectuals and military men were fired by the patriotic ideal, the indigenous people of the region tended to respond pragmatically to the changing circumstances, forging alliances with the forces that were deployed against each other according to their own perceived interests. The new nations were extraneous to them, other people's business, until they came to impinge directly upon them. Tehuelches and Rankulches had famously united to support the city of Buenos Aires against the British invasions in 1806, and offered to again in 1807, seeing the English invaders as a greater threat than the *Cabildo*[2]. In the so-called *Guerra a Muerte* (War to the Death) that took place between 1818 and 1824, when the Chilean patriotic forces pursued the remaining royalists following the latter's defeat at the Battle of Maipú, Mapuches were present on both sides; while some sided with the patriots, optimistic that a new regime could not be worse than the old one, many correctly understood that their land was threatened more by the expansionist drive of the *criollos* than by the Spaniards, whose expansion had been stabilised centuries before, so saw their struggle for independence best served by allying with the Spanish. To quote a testimony of Mapuche oral history: "Everyone said 'the king is best; he has a lot of land. The Chileans are poor; they steal yours'."[3]

The founding fathers of the new nations had no doubt that the indigenous peoples were included as an integral part of these nations. They also wished to stress that theirs were new nations composed of the combined attributes of two noble races, different from the Spanish: "From the fusion of the ancient American race with Spanish blood emerged the characteristic type in which are found the energies of a soldier, the tenacity of the farmer, and the dreams of a poet."[4] In the new Chile, in particular, the heroism of Lautaro, Caupolicán and Galvarino could be commandeered for the patriotic cause. It was no coincidence that the rather secretive group of patriots, including San Martín, who planned American independence against the Spanish, decided to call itself the "Logia Lautaro", identifying itself with the great *toki*.

Bernardo O'Higgins granted the Mapuche Chilean citizenship, and famously stated: "I consider Pewenches, Puelches and Patagones just as much our fellow countrymen as the others."[5] San Martín was of the same view; in his General Order of 27 July 1819 to inspire his forces, he declared:

"Companions of the Army of the Andes: We have to conduct the war as best we can (...) when the clothing runs out, we will dress in the garments that our wives make, and if not we will walk naked like our compatriots the Indians. We are free, and the rest is of no importance... Companions, let us swear not to put down our weapons until we see the country entirely free, or die with them as men of courage."

Although San Martín's understanding of the vestments of indigenous peoples was somewhat shaky, his inclusive intentions were clear. He too shared Bolivar's dream of a united continent, the *Patria Grande*. With his Crossing of the Andes in 1817 to liberate Chile, he was also symbolically denying the validity of the mountain chain as a frontier. As we have seen, the Mapuche also saw it as no obstacle. The River Bío-Bío, on the other hand, turned out to be a more impregnable natural barrier than the Andes.

Chile's wild southern frontier

The area south of the river Bío-Bío was known to the Spanish in colonial times as *La Frontera*, the border between the Spanish possession and the Mapuche nation, as recognised by the Treaty of Kilín of 1641. From this date, for more than two centuries, the Bío-Bío was respected as a geographical frontier and the lands to the south of it as territory of the Mapuche people in full exercise of its right to self-determination. Though Mapuches like to see the Spaniards' inability to conquer them and signing of treaties as an indication of their military power, it was probably also the case that the Spanish Empire was already overstretched, and Chile was not sufficiently important in the scheme of things to justify a full-scale invasion south of the Bío-Bío.[6]

Today there are Mapuche activists who see the recognition of this frontier by the Spanish as the cornerstone of their aspirations as a people, the importance of which must not be underestimated, as it demonstrates an acknowledgement by another sovereign power of their existence as a people and of the integrity of their frontiers. This is stated forcibly by Reynaldo Mariqueo and Jorge Calbucura:

"This fact, unparalleled in the history of the Indigenous Peoples of South America, was the result of the failure of the Spanish Crown to subjugate the Mapuche Nation militarily. The signing of this treaty, in accordance with international norms and procedures, together with the other 28 treaties signed over two centuries of diplomatic relations, gave the Mapuche Nation a privileged position in the history of the Indigenous Peoples of South America as the first and only indigenous nation in the continent whose sovereignty and autonomy were legally recognised."[7]

Yet the Treaty of Kilín and the 28 others were effectively torn up by the founding fathers of the new nations and their patriotic progeny, who saw the extension of its frontiers as maximum goal of a nation. O'Higgins considered the Mapuche and the country's other indigenous peoples to be sheltered under the Chilean "umbrella", no longer autonomous, but part of the unitarian project. The creation of the new Chilean nation meant that, while on one hand the Mapuche were now free agents who could move about the republic, on the other the lands south of the Bío-Bío were up for grabs.

Initially, however, in the early years of independent Chile, the southern frontier was more or less abandoned, forgotten by central government. This is how José Bengoa, Chilean historian and writer of the seminal work "Historia del pueblo mapuche", describes the frontier in the early part of the 19th century:

> "The situation of the frontier was rather ill-defined, politically and socially. There the authority, property, origin and social status of people were all rather unclear. It was an unstable area, where laws did not arrive with the same force with which they were issued. The "central country" [around Santiago] looked to the north, which provided it with rich minerals, and left the "country of the south" alone, to its own problems. Until mid-century, the question of Arauco was put on the back-burner."[8]

In the area of the Bío-Bío there were around 700 soldiers, poorly armed and with no uniforms, split between a number of forts, such as Los Angeles, Nacimiento, Angol, Negrete, Mulchén, Arauco and Concepción. The frontier administration used powerful local Mapuche leaders to maintain peace and order in the region. Many of these learnt Spanish, began to dress like Chileans, and even adopted the Christian religion, or at least were not violently opposed to it.

One aspect of Christian teaching that they did not readily adopt was the requirement of monogamy. It was the *lonkos* themselves who indulged in polygamy; irrespective of other attractions it may have had for them, they saw it as too strategically important for them to abandon, as it enabled them to forge alliances by taking the daughters of other *lonkos* as their wives, as well as giving them many more children than would otherwise be possible, and consequently more warriors to fight the Spanish and then the Chileans. European women were also taken captive as wives. There were also many cases of convicts and adventurers who ventured into Mapuche territory and became "mapuchised", joining communities and adopting their customs and language.

In short, the Mapuche of the *Gulu Mapu* were very permeable to external influence - and the traffic was two-way - as for the time being they still had political independence, and no fear of disappearance. In the *Puel Mapu*, if anything, they could feel even more invulnerable, at least for the time being.

Outposts of Argentine Civilisation

East of the Andes, the Spanish had shown little interest in colonising the area of the Pampa and Patagonia, which were off the beaten track, namely the silver route to and from Potosí. Forts were established south and west of Buenos Aires to meet defensive requirements, to protect this route from incursions, rather than with a view to expansion. The following is an account of the decision to found one such fort, at Salto de Arrecifes, 200 km due west of Buenos Aires. It is taken from the official website of the town of Salto:

> "In August 1737 Pampas Indians robbed farms, committed other offences and killed Christian people in the place called "El Salto del Arrecifes." Immediately Captain Don Juan de San Martín began the first onslaught against the Indians and, completing the mission of leaving "guards" where it seemed convenient, at the end of 1737 he established "The Advanced Guard of the Salto."[9]

Though it was garrisoned, "more than political and military, the frontier was a cultural one"[10], marking the division between two ways of life. The problem for those who wish to understand the Mapuche way of life from their own perspective is that, while there are many accounts of the situation from the point-of-view of the new settlers, soldiers and politicians, very little has been handed down to posterity of what the 'troublesome other', the Mapuche, thought. Young Mapuche historian, Anahí Meli, who lives in Bahía Blanca, has often commented to me about her frustration at having to arrive at an understanding of the views and motivations of her people in this period through the biased filter of *winka* accounts. This arduous task of peeling off others' layers to expose their own history is yet another strand of the process of recovery that is taking place among Mapuches today.

In the early 19th century the only enclave of the Argentine state south of today's Province of Buenos Aires was Carmen de Patagones, which was founded in 1779 by Don Francisco de Viedma y Narváez, who named it Nuestra Señora del Carmen. The town was virtually isolated, as contacts by sea with Buenos Aires and Montevideo were infrequent. The colony was only able to survive thanks to friendly relations with the local indigenous population.

With the coming of independence, an awareness began to develop of the area as an economic resource. So Carmen de Patagones started to prosper, thanks to the abundant salt to be found near the town, which was becoming increasingly essential for the burgeoning *saladeros* (meat-salting plants) of Buenos Aires to meet the demand for Argentine beef.

The Salinas Grandes (Great Salt Lakes) are located in the east of what is today the province of La Pampa, on its border with the province of Buenos Aires. Ever since their "discovery" in 1770, annual expeditions to the deposits had been organised by the colonisers to stock up the port of Carmen with salt. Permission had to be sought from the *lonkos* of the zone, in exchange for gifts, to enter and collect the salt supplies.[11]

In 1810 Colonel Pedro Andrés García was sent on a reconnaissance mission to the Salinas. The purpose was to seek alliances with friendly indigenous leaders to enable the new government to put the frontier on a more peaceful footing, in order to foster the populating of the region. The indigenous communities found this military man to be a fair and honest interlocutor; the mission was tense, the atmosphere often threatening, but thanks to the intervention of *lonkos* who were well-disposed to García, such as Victoriano and Kintelén, he was able to return to Buenos Aires not only with the much-needed salt, but also with precious topographical and cultural information. This was the first wedge of penetration into indigenous territory.

Subsequently Victoriano and Kintelén made visits to Buenos Aires to discuss the establishing of towns in the Salinas area, providing these were not accompanied by the militarisation and intimidation represented by forts. In 1815 plans were made for a *parlamento* to be held between representatives of the communities and government. It never took place.

The government was keen to promote the expansion of livestock farming south of the Río Salado, in indigenous territory. In 1815 Francisco Ramos Mejía - a firm believer in integration and harmonious co-operation - was one of those to receive land in the area, in his case in the vicinity of the Laguna Kaquel Huincul, near to today's town of Maipú.

Ramos Mejía's antagonist was Brigadier General Martín Rodríguez, nicknamed variously by the local population as the "Grand Captain" and *gnuru* (the fox), the latter on account of his reputation for treachery. In 1823 he founded the Fuerte de la Independencia (today's Tandil), as a strategic point in the advance on indigenous land. According to the website of the town of Tandil, his mission was:

> "to defeat and drive off the infidels, after their recent depredations, and to conquer these rich territories for the Christian and defend them with the founding of a fort in the zone of Tandil."[12]

On 7 March 1820, at Ramos Mejía's ranch, Miraflores, a prominent group of Tehuelches and Rankulches, including *lonko* Lincón, signed a treaty of "reciprocal fraternity and security" with Martín Rodríguez. Soon afterwards "the fox" had Ramos Mejía, his family and the indigenous families that lived on his land taken prisoner and sent to Buenos Aires, accusing them of planning hostilities against the province. Rodríguez was punishing them for the actions of *lonko* Pablo Gaylquin de Boroa, who in turn had attacked Salto as a reprisal against Rodríguez' persecutions and castigations of "infidels."

In this time of intrigue, betrayal and shifting alliances, a fragile status quo was maintained; this worked as follows: friendly lonkos were supposed to participate in the military forces, notify the government of any tribes arriving from tierra adentro[13] and from Chile and obtain information on their movements and behaviour. In exchange, the indigenous settlements were permitted to remain in certain territories and to receive livestock and provisions, such as tobacco, bread, cards, liquor, cotton towels, sugar and mate. These alliances were not permanent, rather proving to be fraught with conflict, since relations were not based on equality, but rather on an increasing dependence upon criollo products.

Serving to further confuse this complex system of clientage were figures such as *Pichi-Rey* (Little King) Carrera, a dissident general from Chile, who had been exiled by O'Higgins and was attempting to put together a force to dispute power with him again. In Argentina he became involved in the conflict between Buenos Aires and various bands of Mapuches, Tehuelches and Pewenches, organising and participating in *malones* (raids). Another notorious bandit was José Luis Molina, a foreman from Miraflores ranch, who, among other dubious exploits, led the destruction and plundering of the new settlement of Dolores.

In 1828 a large military force moved south from Tandil, by land and by sea, to establish the fort that was to become the town of Bahía Blanca. The encroachment upon the Mapuche's land was now moving on apace. An encroachment presided over and facilitated by Juan Manuel de Rosas.

Rosas and the "defensive" desert campaign of 1833-34

It is said that a prophet is without honour in his own land. Rosas (1793-1877) is without honour mainly because he made the mistake of leaving his own land - he spent the latter years of his life in Southampton and died there, where he is buried - so enabling his enemies to write the "official history" that fills Argentina's school history books in his absence, and represent him in unflattering terms. In Bahía Blanca a street in the city centre that was formerly called Rosas is now known as Patagones; this is highly unusual, the reverse of the normal course of events whereby generals push indigenous names off the maps.

A pragmatic and astute politician and manipulator of men, Rosas governed the Province of Buenos Aires from 1829 to 1832. He resigned in 1832 to embark upon the Desert Campaign and was replaced by Juán Ramón Balcarce, who unsurprisingly took advantage of his absence to plot against him. Many history books that consider the period are so preoccupied with what was happening back in Buenos Aires that they too relegate the campaign that was so devastating for the indigenous peoples of the *tierra adentro* to a footnote, if that.

Such books usually claim that Rosas' reasons for conducting the campaign were that the malones were halting settlement and progress in the region. In fact Rosas' motivations were decidedly more complex. He calculated that by keeping the best soldiers from Buenos Aires with him, he would be able to thwart any pretensions to challenge him with arms; by staying away and aloof from the political struggle, he would be able to avoid expending energy without glory, and also to incite discord from afar, so that only his name would be unsullied; and, last but not least, he would have large quantities of lands in which to install his friends, to extend cattle raising and enhance his own prestige.[14]

So it was that in early 1833 Rosas embarked upon his desert expedition. The enterprise was commanded by Juan Facundo Quiroga, chosen by Rosas because at that time, thanks to his military exploits, he was more popular than Rosas himself. Quiroga was to be known by the grand title of General Director of the War against the Barbarians. The expedition was composed of three divisions: the left division, led by Rosas himself, with General Angel Pacheco as his second-in-command; the central division, which was initially led by Quiroga, who was succeeded by General Ruiz Huidobro, as he had to remain in San Juan due to poor health; and the right division, commanded by Brigadier General José Felix Aldao. All apart from Rosas had belonged to the regiment commanded by General San Martín.

Rosas began his march from Bahía Blanca on 22 March with 2000 men and by mid-May had reached the Río Colorado. As well as soldiers, the expedition also included land surveyors, who were the first to make maps of the area, astronomers, artists, physicians and naturalists.

The central division battled against the Rankulche, whom they defeated at Las Acollaradas, south of San Luis, but they were then forced to retreat due to a shortage of supplies. After initial successes, the right column, active in the Andes region, also had to withdraw.

Rosas led the only successful division. He divided his troops into various columns to cross the desert in various directions. Leading one of these, General Angel Pachecho went along the Río Negro as far as the island of Choele-Choel, where he attacked the villages of *lonko* Loncoy and destroyed the group led by Payllarén. He then continued operations along the Río Negro, arriving as far as the confluence of the rivers Limay and Neuquén.

The statistics of the campaign vary depending on whose account you believe: between 3,000 and 10,000 indigenous people killed, between 1,000 and 4,000 taken prisoner, and between 1,000 and 4,000 captives set free.

Charles Darwin, who had written admiringly of Rosas, when describing the scenes of massacre of those he calls "wild Indians", writes insightful and prophetic words about the present and future of Argentina's Plains Indians:

"Every one here is fully convinced that this is the most just war, because it is against barbarians. Who would believe in this age that such atrocities could be committed in a Christian civilised society? The children of the Indians are saved, to be sold or given away as servants [...].I think there will not, in another half-century, be a wild Indian northward of the Río Negro. The warfare is too bloody to last; the Christians killing every Indians, and the Indians doing the same by the Christians."[15]

On 25 May 1834 - a date chosen for its historic resonance, as 25 May 1810 is Argentine Independence Day - Rosas addressed his troops on the bank of the River Naposta, declaring that: "The beautiful regions from the Andes to Magellanes are open for our children."

Far from a great conquering advance, the results of the campaign, considering the high cost in terms of indigenous lives, were very modest. To quote Alfredo Terzaga, Rosas' biographer: "Anyone who today looks dispassionately at the details of this campaign cannot fail to notice the contrast between the extraordinary magnitude of the effort and the paucity of the results achieved."[16]

Though its success was trumpeted, it would appear that the campaign's only achievement - apart from the furtherance of Rosas' political ambitions - was to gain a period of tranquillity for the settlers in the Province of Buenos Aires. In contrast, the invasion of Mapuche territory west of the Andes was an altogether quieter affair.

Bulnes and the United Army conspiracy

Despite Rosas' patriotic rhetoric, Argentina's nationalist historians have certainly been perturbed by the fact that Rosas seems to have been in league, at least tacitly, with Chilean General Manuel Bulnes, who was to become president of Chile in 1841.

The *Ejército Unido* (United Army) was the name given to the joint Argentine-Chilean army of liberation led by General San Martín that won the Battle of Maipú against the royalists in 1818; this unity was marked by the symbolic embrace between O'Higgins and San Martín. When Mapuche historians look at the events of the 1830s, it seems clear to them that the United Army had not been disbanded, but was still active against the Mapuche. Here is the uncompromising account of events from issue 2 of the magazine *Werken Kuruf* (messenger of the wind), published in Neuquén in 2000:

"In 1833, three columns of the "United Army", commanded by Chilean General Manuel Bulnes in the Andes, Juan Manuel de Rosas in the centre and Facundo Quiroga on the coast, entered Mapuche territory, killing 6,000 men, women and children from the communities who lived there and taking 4,000 Mapuches prisoner, leaving forts along the way."

So the editors of *Werken Kuruf* have not doubt that Manuel Bulnes participated in Rosas' campaign. Alfredo Terzaga, on the other hand, states that he did not, but was within a hair's breadth of doing so.[17] In any event, if we accept that Bulnes was conducting a similar and parallel campaign in the same period as Rosas, then whether they were acting in concert is a moot point, but an academic one as far as the Mapuche are concerned.

In contrast with Rosas' "glorious" campaign, the occupation of Araucanía took place with the historical equivalent of a press blackout. Since Lautaro and Caupolicán were seen as the heroic fathers of the Chilean nation, to attack their people might be seen as a form a patricide. José Bengoa explains the dilemma:

"The killing of Indians that was implicit in the advance of the Chilean army beyond the Bío-Bío came up against the myth of our nationality. It was like killing an ancestor. Araucanian blood, the origin of our libertarian character, was being spilled by the sons of these Caupolicáns. The ideology was simple and efficient: to deny the existence of the fact."[18]

It is within this context that most historical accounts of the post-independence period in Chile consider the Mapuche only in terms of their support for renegades, such as Vicente Benavides and the Pincheira brothers, who had fled south following the Civil War of 1829, and were attacking and robbing at will under the pretext of maintaining Spanish sovereignty in the region. The wisdom of the backing of these dubious figures by some Mapuches is certainly questionable, and was presumably a vain attempt to maintain the status quo that Spanish sovereignty represented; it was certainly costly for them, as their support for marauders provided justification for them to be "dealt with."

The Civil War between the conservative Joaquín Prieto and the liberal Ramón Freire saw the former victorious. Prieto commissioned Bulnes to hunt down the Pincheira brothers. They were fighting in the mountains around Chillán, apparently with the support of some of the Pewenches of the area. Bulnes' army ventured into the mountains and surprised the Pincheiras' camp near Lake Epulafquén, killing them.

A compelling argument can be offered in support of the thesis that Bulnes and Rosas were indeed acting in concert to destroy the Mapuche: Epulafquén is located in Argentina, in the province of Neuquén. Why would Rosas allow a Chilean General to violate Argentine territory, if it did not suit his own purpose? In his capacity for *realpolitik*, Rosas was only rivalled by the great Mapuche leader Kalfukurá.

Kalfukurá: lord of the salt flats

Another of Rosas' controversial allies was Mapuche *toki* Kalfukurá, who, according to Sarasola, was "the most powerful *cacique* (indigenous leader) in Argentine history."[19] In around 1818 many groups of Boroans came to settle in the Salinas Grandes area. They too had been involved in supporting the Pincheiras in various skirmishes, but separated from them to move to the Salinas.

They settled near the laguna of Masallé, west of the Salinas Grandes; their leader was Mariano Rondeau. One morning in 1834 two hundred or so Mapuches arrived from across the Andes to trade, which was not unusual. Their leader was Kalfukurá ("Blue Stone" in English), and they came from the Llaima, or possibly from Collico. The unsuspecting Boroans were taken by surprise and massacred, and Rondeau was killed. So it was that Kalfukurá established his power base in the Salinas Grandes, the beginning of a domination of the Pampas that was to continue for 40 years, first by Kalfukurá and then by his descendants.[20]

Kalfukurá created an indigenous confederation, by persuasion or force, unifying dozens of caciques and their tribes and making his capital in the strategic centre of salt extraction. He was so bold and astute that the Mapuche oral tradition sometimes even credits him with magical powers.

It is unclear whether Rosas had made a pact with Kalfukurá or with the Boroans, but if we look at the question pragmatically, it would seem to have suited Rosas' interests to have a strong figure such as Kalfukurá in the Pampas for the sake of stability, as the increased tranquillity that this engendered would benefit the populations and large farms of the "frontier."

However, as we will see in the next chapter, stability and tranquillity would be insufficient for the expansionism overseen by the leaders that were to follow Rosas. In the meantime, men of vision were already being drawn to Patagonia.

The arrival of scientists and sovereigns

First came the explorers, then the soldiers, then the artist-adventurers and scientists, all to the "empty", beckoning land of the Wallmapu. In 1836 Charles Darwin was with the crew of "The Beagle", meeting Rosas and Patagon Tehuelches, on his way to the Galapagos and his contemplations on the origins of species.

In 1873 Francisco P. Moreno – the scientist explorer so famous he had a glacier, the Perito Moreno, named after him - began his journeys of study to Patagonia, sponsored by the Sociedad Científica Argentina and the Government of the Province of Buenos Aires. Moreno's curiosity about the geography of the region was also prompted by his desire to have specific information available for discussions over the frontier boundary with Chile: his was not a pure scientific interest, but one with a patriotic flavour. On the Chilean side, Guillermo Cox was conducting similar research at the same time, travelling from Puerto Montt, through the Las Lagunas route, as far as Nahuel Huapi and Limay in Argentina.

In 1881 Luis Piedrabuena embarked upon a journey on board the corvette "Cabo de Hornos" to reconnoitre the coasts of Patagonia and Tierra del Fuego, and to perform hydrographic, zoological and botanical studies.

The measurement of territories and the stocktaking of species was carried forward by adventurous, inquiring minds, but it also undoubtedly contributed to an unarrestable process: the consolidation of ownership.

We cannot close a chapter on the turmoil of mid-19th-century Patagonia without mentioning the man who would be king.

Many, including Bruce Chatwin, have given accounts of this "curious and semi-comic episode" in the history of the Mapuche[21], an abridged version of which goes as follows:

Orélie-Antoine de Tounens was born in 1825 in the Dordogne in France. He had read of the Araucanians in Ercilla's "La Araucana", and something in that book struck a chord in the recesses of his mind, making him resolve, bizarrely, to be their king.

He travelled to South America, arriving in the area south of the Bío-Bío on 28 December 1861, and was received by one of the leading Mapuche *caciques* in the region, *toki* Kilapán.

Some say that there is supposed to have been an ancient Mapuche legend that the end of wars and the risk of slavery would coincide with the appearance of a bearded white man. Another version has it that, on his deathbed, Kilapán's father, Mañin, had prophesied that a king would soon arrive to govern the Nation.

At any rate, 100 *lonkos* were convened to a ceremony. They met in a clearing, surrounded by dozens of horsemen galloping and shouting in a *troya* (ritual high-speed horse-ride) in honour of the Frenchman.

The candidate to the Crown pronounced a fiery speech, in which he promised that he would prevent Chile from occupying the line south of the Bío-Bío and would maintain their independence. Those present at the assembly listened approvingly. After which - incredibly - Tounens was indeed proclaimed King Aurelio Antoine I of Araucanía and Patagonia.

In 1862 he was kidnapped by Chilean soldiers, declared a madman, and deported to France. From there he made several attempts to reclaim his throne; in 1870 he even declared war on the Chilean state, returning to France to seek support. He died in 1878, in Tourtoirac.

Interestingly, an heir to the throne still exists. His name is Prince Philip of Araucanía and Patagonia, an elderly, rather portly French gentleman (real name Philippe Boiry), who is said to have purchased the title. He has visited Argentina and Chile, but has tended to be greeted with hostility or ridicule by the local media and the cold shoulder by most of the Mapuche organisations. The Prince is supported by some Mapuche organisations in Europe, such as Mapuche International Link, of Bristol, who see his figure as instrumental in their attempt to have the treaties signed between the Spanish throne and the Mapuche recognised. The section on the King on the a MIL website states: "within the process of historical consolidation of the independence of the Mapuche nation, the most prominent authorities of the Mapuche people (*Tokis, Lonkos, Machis*) along with the lawyer Orelie Antoine, of French origin - naturalized Mapuche - formed the Kingdom of Araucania and Patagonia in 1860. In this way the Mapuches reaffirmed - to the world - their right to self-determination and the validity of the frontier established with Spain in the treaty of Killen in 1641."[22]

Boiry himself says indigenous rights should be recognised, but stops short of demanding Mapuche independence: "Chile should recognise the rights of the autochthonous minorities, as established by the United Nations. It is not a matter of asking for independence; that is ridiculous. But it would be very good if they could be given a cultural autonomy, as Spain does with Catalonia and the Basque Country."[23]

The episode of the King of Araucania and Patagonia may appear somewhat comic, but its repercussions were deadly serious. According to the Chilean indigenous organisation Coordinadora Indigenista (CONACIN), "the experience sounded the alert for the Chilean state."[24] It is their view that the activities of King Aurelio unduly drew the Chilean government's attention towards the region, meaning the army would be sent to deal with the matter as soon as they were available. José Bengoa, on the other hand, is of the opinion that the episode probably made little difference, as burgeoning capitalism in Europe needed land and resources, so the region would have become too tempting to resist sooner or later.

One thing is certain, the time of uneasy coexistence between an independent Mapuche territory and the Chilean and Argentine states was well and truly over, and would not return. In just two decades after Aurelio Antoine I reigned over the Kingdom of Araucanía and Patagonia, scientists would be the only human forms moving about the Patagonian landscape and the names they gave to it would have "overwritten the indigenous toponymies and thus wiped from the map even the memories of difference."[25] The next generation of politicians and their acolytes would soon be representing the last free Mapuches as "savages", an "indigenous problem" demanding a drastic solution.

Notes

1 The heading is taken from Sarasola's book "Nuestros paisanos los indios", which in turn comes from the San Martín quotation given below.
2 See Sarasola, "Hijos de la Tierra", pp. 89-91.
3 Cited in Bengoa, *op. cit*. p. 141.

4   From the "Guía ilustrada de Nicaragua", cited by Jeffrey L. Gould in his book "To die in this way. Nicaraguan Indians and the Myth of Mestizaje, 1880-1965", Duke University press, 1998, p. 138. Chapter 4 deals with the incorporation of indigenous identity in the new nation of Nicaragua, and has resonance for the whole of Latin America.
5   In a letter to Prieto from 1830, cited in Bengoa, *op. cit*. p. 137.
6   This is the view of Collier and Sater ("A History of Chile", CUP 1996, p. 5).
7   The text of this paragraph is quoted from "The Mapuche Nation" by Reynaldo Mariqueo and Jorge Calbucura, 2/9/2002, Mapuche Documentation Centre.
8   *Op. cit*. p. 152.
9   Translated from the website if the town of Salto: saltonline.com.ar.
10 Sarasola, "Hijos de la Tierra", p. 81.
11 See Sarasola, "Nuestros paisanos los indios", pp. 160-163.
12 www.tandil.com/cuidad/leyendas/malon.htm.
13 "Tierra adentro" (literally "inland") was the expression used at the time, along with the "desert", to describe the Pampas and Patagonia.
14 This according to Enrique Barba, "Unitarismo", p. 102, cited in Germán Ibáñez, "Juan Manuel de Rosas y el nacionalismo de los ganaderos bonarienses."
15 Darwin, "The Voyage of the Beagle", Chapter V. Available online at http://www.literature.org/authors/darwin-charles/the-voyage-of-the-beagle/chapter-05.html.
16 Alfredo Terzaga, "Historia de Roca", Vol. II, publ. by A. Peña Lillo, Bs. As., 1976, p. 162.
17 *Idem*.
18 Bengoa, *op. cit*, p. 149.
19 Sarasola, *op. cit*., p. 110.
20 For a re-evaluation of the figure of Kalfukurá, see "Noticia de Calfucura", by José Miguel Varas, Rocinante no. 29, March 2001.
21 As it is referred to by Simon Collier and William Sater in their "History of Chile", Cambridge University Press, 1996, p. 96.
22 http://www.mapuche-nation.org/.
23 Interviewed for Azkintuwe, 5 September 2005.
24 Available in Spanish on http://mapuche.info.scorpionshops.com.
25 Jens Andermann, Birkbeck College, "Argentine Literature and the 'Conquest of the Desert'" (www.bbk.ac.uk/ibamuseum/texts/Andermann02.htm).

SAVAGES AND STATECRAFT:
PREPARATION AND EXECUTION OF THE PACIFICATION OF ARAUCANIA AND THE CONQUEST OF THE DESERT

This chapter narrates the final years of the Mapuche as a free people, the period leading up to and including the cataclysm for them that has come to be known as the Pacification of Araucania in Chile and the Conquest of the Desert in Argentina; a cataclysm painted by the two states as progress. The chapter is framed with considerations on Patagonia's museums, which provide a self-serving version of the history of the region.

The 1850s saw internecine strife between the nations' military and political leaders, as their differing visions for their countries came into conflict. Politicians such as Alberdi and Sarmiento saw European settlement as the route to civilisation. However, the desire to populate the southern frontiers led to an increase in *malones* (raids) and violent reprisals. The Mapuche were therefore increasingly seen as a hindrance, due in no small part to their representation as "savages" in the writings of Echeverría and the paintings of Blanes and Rugendas. While men of science such as Moreno and Domeyko saw assimilation of the nations' original peoples as the solution to the "indigenous problem", the likes of Popper and MacLennan gleefully set about the task of wiping them out.

The plan to conquer the Mapuche, left incomplete by Rosas and Alsina in Argentina and by Bulnes in Chile, was finally executed by Roca and Saavedra. The Mapuche's final stand, the *Futa Malón*, was doomed to fail, and they were defeated.

Manufacturing the Past

There are a large number of historical museums in Patagonia, as most of the towns of any size have one. Though the grandeur of the buildings and the quality of the exhibits may vary - the one in Viedma small, grubby, and with one solitary, forlorn member of staff, while the one across the river in Carmen de Patagones, capacious and pristine clean - they all seem to follow the same basic pattern, or rather, the same route-map through time. First come the arts and crafts of pre-contact indigenous cultures, such as weapons, ceramics and textiles; then artefacts of the arrival of the military, such as models of forts, uniforms and Remington rifles; these are followed by photos and maps denoting the coming of the railways and the telegraph; finally come the memorabilia from the sitting-rooms of civilisation, clothing, furniture, gramophones. The subtext is clear: the rifle and the railway brushed aside the presence of the natives to make way for civilisation.

Originally privately financed, by the wealthy or the church, museums came to prominence as public institutions in the middle of the 19th century, the period that concerns us here. According to Prof. Graeme Davison, an expert of the history of museums in Australia, "it is mainly nations that found, fund, foster and sometimes fetter museums"[1], because they are seen as advancing national aspirations and expressing a national sense of identity and character.

The Museum of Natural Sciences of La Plata is visited annually by a million people, and is perhaps the world's most prestigious Spanish-speaking museum of natural sciences. It was founded in 1884 by Perito Francisco Pascasio Moreno, and its imposing classical columns make it clear to the visitor who coyly climbs its steps that it is important, stately and monumental.

The exhibition rooms of the museum may be well-lit and neatly ordered, as they represent the "official history", but perhaps there are also certain other rooms that are always kept locked, so that their stench and clutter cannot escape; they are the dark, sordid negative history of statecraft, and it is to those rooms that we will attempt to gain access in this chapter.

The Age of Violence

The 1850s were times of violent upheaval in Chile and Argentina. In Chile, 1851 was the year of the revolution against the government of Manuel Montt, in which Mapuches participated, along with frontier troops and civil militias, against the authoritarianism and centralising tendencies of Santiago; they were defeated at Loncomilla by Montt's army, led by Manuel Bulnes, now ex-president. In 1859 a second revolution took place against Montt, and again Mapuches sided with the revolutionaries: the Wenteche, the uplanders, supported the regionalists of Concepción. The revolution again failed in the south, and many insurrectionists fled to the Southern frontier.[2]

2 February 1852 was the date of the Battle of Caseros in Argentina, in which the Grand Army of rebel General Urquiza fought against Rosas; apparently the Mapuche of the Pampa were split in their loyalties, with Rankulche in the "Grand

Army" and Chaziche among Rosas' troops.[3] The former were victorious, and the defeated Rosas went into exile in England.

Rosas' exile marked the end of the fragile equilibrium he had established, and gave carte blanche for the Argentine state to expand southward and westward. A convenient pretext would assist this expansion process, and malones provided this.

Malones, landscapes and the mythology of nationhood

National histories are often constructed backwards from the present, using key signposts from the past as supports. Latter-day leaders and opinion formers can look back over a sea of potentially famous faces and a morass of potentially memorable dates and select those best suited to their view. So we have the history of civilisation in Britain beginning with the arrival of the Romans in 45 BC, with the previously existing cultures summarily dismissed as barbarism.

The intellectuals of the new nations of the Americas were able to see the gaining of their respective independences as another year zero, undermining the significance of all that existed before that time. Clashes of cultures had the "superior" culture coming up against the "inferior", inevitably to defeat it.

The *malones* were the raids that Mapuches made on the large farms that were spreading across the Pampa in the early 19th century, to steal livestock and take prisoners, often to be taken to Chile for sale or exchange. The increased presence of settlers meant more raids, so the farmers demanded more protection, so causing the militarisation of the area to increase, exacerbating the situation in a literally vicious circle. During the course of the 19th century the *malones* came to represent the quintessence of the barbarity of the "savage", in contrast with all that was civilised about European culture.

Esteban Echeverría was the founder of the literary and intellectual group known as the Generation of 1837. His epic poem La Cautiva (The Captive Woman) is considered to exemplify the Argentinian nationalist aspirations of the time. It is also an archetypal text of the Latin American form of Romanticism, which avoids European Romanticism's idealisation of nature and sees the natural world as an obstacle to the "civilising" projects of the new Latin American states.

"La Cautiva", the story of a white woman kidnapped by "savages", was written by Echevrría in 1837, and was instrumental in creating the image of the "savage" that has endured and still dogs Argentina's indigenous peoples to this day. Here are two representative verses, with my translation:

¿Dónde va? ¿De dónde viene?	Where does he go? From where does he come?
¿De qué gozo proviene?	From what does his pleasure arise?
¿Por qué grita, corre, vuela,	Why does he yell, run, fly,
clavando al bruto la espuela,	thrusting his spurs in the brute,
sin mirar alrededor?	without looking around?
¡Ved que las puntas ufanas	See that the boastful tips
de sus lanzas, por despojos,	of their lances bear as spoils
llevan cabezas humanas,	human heads,
cuyos inflamados ojos	whose inflamed eyes
respiran aún furor!	still breathe rage!
Así el bárbaro hace ultraje	Thus the barbarian insults
al indomable coraje	the indomitable spirit
que abatió su alevosía;	that demolished his treachery;
y su rencor todavía	and his rancour still
mira, con torpe placer,	gazes, with vile pleasure,
las cabezas que cortaron	at the heads cut
sus inhumanos cuchillos,	by his inhuman knives,
exclamando: - "Ya pagaron	exclaiming: "Now the Christian's
del cristiano los caudillos	caudillos have paid our power
el feudo a nuestro poder"	their dues for the land."

In this extract, Echeverría uses many of the common devices of degradation, such as the apparent pointlessness and bestiality of the "savages'" actions and the use of the singular to describe the enemy, as in "Charlie" used by G.I.s in Vietnam and "Gerry" by the Allies in WW2. Note also how strangely inappropriate the words put in the "savage's" mouth are, such as the *criollo* term *caudillos* and the European *feudo*.

The process of nation-building in 19th-century Argentina went hand-in-hand with the fomenting of immigration and settlement. Juan Alberdi, also of the Generation of 1837, condensed their reform philosophy in the phrase that formed the underlying spirit of the Argentine Constitution of 1853 - *gobernar es poblar* (to govern is to populate). Alberdi's view was that "the deserts without roads, their unexplored rivers, their unpopulated coasts, are the great enemy of this country, the vast territory is the cause of disorder and backwardness, rendering impossible the centralisation of government and generating anarchy ...."[4] For Alberdi the task of defeating the enemy desert could only be accomplished by populating it with immigrants.

The main instigator of the revulsion of Argentina's intellectuals at the uncivilised "savage" was Domingo Faustino Sarmiento, the great educator, the grandfather of the nation, and another member of the Generation of 1837, whose statues stand proud in so many main squares of Argentina's towns.

Due to his political activities and his outspokenness, Sarmiento was forced into exile during Rosas' presidency. He spent much of that time in Chile, in fact, where his writings were published in Chilean newspaper *El Progreso*; this means that he was in a unique position of influence over the views of both countries' élites with respect to the "indigenous question." Born in San Juan, Sarmiento's admiration for Northern European countries was only exceeded by that for the United States.

Considerably influenced by the works of Alexis de Tocqueville, among others, Sarmiento saw the future of his country as a battle between civilisation - enlightened European culture - and barbarism - represented by indigenous culture.

Sarmiento saw the environment as having a key influence on society, and so viewed the product of the desert - *el vacío* (literally "emptiness") - as barbarism. Though Sarmiento did not know the Pampa at all, he believed the effect of this environment could be countered by culture and education. So there was at least hope for the barbarian, soldier hero Facundo Quiroga, the subject of his famous tome, "Facundo."

While Sarmiento believed the barbarian could be saved, "savages" were beyond salvation. He contrasted his own view with that of Ercilla, the author of "La Araucana", declaring his repugnance for the "savage", in this famous quote:

> "... Above all, we would like to remove the savages from all American social questions, as for them we feel, without being able to remedy it, an unconquerable loathing, and for us Colocolo, Lautaro and Caupolicán, despite the civilised and noble robes in which Ercilla clothed them, are no more than disgusting Indians, whom we would have had hanged..."[5]

Just as Echeverría's poetry was not above politics, the visual arts of the nineteenth century were also not neutral. The landscape paintings by the U.S. artists of the time have been accredited with shaping the vision of the West that Hollywood was to adopt a century later[6]; the depictions of a vast panorama of mountains against the sky, forming a backdrop to dwarf human activity, were the wide screen format of their day. The many artists who painted the landscapes of Argentina and Chile in the 19th century were likewise the interpreters of the new vision of these lands, their canvas to paint myths on. In a sense this constituted a second "discovery", a form of marketing of the country for the purposes of colonisation in the new world of the "age of capital."[7] The patriotic task of these artists was to make the landscape attractive yet its inhabitants repellent.

Many of the painters were influenced by the European schools, transposing their styles to the new world. In *Un alto en el campo* (A Stop in the Countryside), for example, by Argentine Prilidiano Pueyrredón, who had studied at the École Polytechnique in Paris, it is a civilised Pampa that is represented, in a neo-classical style, the resting characters expressing grace, gentility and beauty. Likewise, the work of Juan Manuel Blanes - who was trained at the Accademia in Florence - with his representations of resting, contemplative gauchos against a classical backdrop, offers a tranquil Pampa to the viewer. The work of Eduardo Sivori, who also trained in Paris, is of a similar ilk. These are reassuring, inviting images of a calm, temperate world, remarkably similar to Europe, offering no threat to the potential immigrant.

Quite a different perception is gained from the work of Alexander Von Humboldt's friend Moritz Rugendas, the German who travelled and painted the length of Latin America. Rugendas had had dealings with the Mapuche in the area of *La Frontera*, in Chile, and became fascinated by the idea of representing them in his work. Perhaps fired by an enthusiasm for phrenology, a pseudo-scientific theory imported from Europe whereby the shape of the skull is indicative of mental faculties, briefly in vogue among Latin American intellectuals, Rugendas executed scores of sketches of heads of Mapuche men and women.

He was even more taken by the idea of the *Cautiva*, drawn to the subject with a mixture of fascination and revulsion. Blanes, mentioned above, also painted the *Cautiva*, and Angel Della Valle, some of whose work is of the serene variety described above, also produced similar works, such as *La vuelta del malón* (Return from the Raid) from 1892.

In the paintings of the *Cautiva* by Rugendas and Della Valle, the faces of the captive heroines are looking up to the heavens, with beatified expressions reminiscent of Catholic saints, belying the terror of their situations.

Symbolically, the stealing away - and presumably the rape - of the white woman may be seen as a violation of the body of the state. The identification between body and nation is not new to psychology, and the maintaining of the integrity of both somehow ennobled the national project. On a more socio-political level, there may also have been a concern for the 'genetic pool' of the new nation. In her book "Gender & Nation", Nira Yuval-Davis discusses how 'superior' races were fearful of 'contamination' when wishing to increase their populations:

> "In settler societies […] the call has been to 'populate or perish'. A certain critical mass of people was seen as crucial for the viability of the nation building process there. Although immigration was encouraged as a quick way to achieve this goal, measures were originally take to keep 'undesirable elements out'."[8]

The *Cautiva* poem and paintings were therefore a form of political manifesto/pamphlet warning against the dangers of miscegenation - the mixing of races - in the formation of the new state, which was to be wholly European.

Della Valle's *Malón* and Rugendas' Romantic depictions, inspired by Echeverría's poem, were entertainments for the salons of the rich that served to propagate the negative, threatening image of the Mapuche. While the readers and viewers were shocked, righteously angered and possibly even titillated by these works, it cannot be said that they were informed by them. In contrast, in recent years there have been a number of works published or republished about the frontier and life as a captive of the Indians, in response to the current interest in Argentina in the history of the region from the point of view of the other. In his 1877 work *Una excursión a los indios ranqueles* (An Excursion among the Ranquele Indians), Lucio V. Mansilla tells that the Rankulche's prisoners of war, of both sexes, were expected to wash, cook, cut wood, tame horses and look after livestock. In 1999 two volumes were published of the memoirs of Santiago Avendaño, compiled by Father Meinrado Hux.[9] According to Avendaño, many captives were adopted by families as domestic servants, clothed and fed and treated like their own children. English aristocrat George Chaworth Musters also writes affectionately of living with the Tehuelche in his book At Home with the Patagonians, published in London in 1870 and republished in Spanish as *Vida entre los Patagones* in Buenos Aires in 1997. At the time, however, such sympathetic representations of the Mapuche did not fit the template for the new nation. Fear of the 'other' was also rife in Chile, and there too this fear was expressed through its literature.

Chile: Central Valley, central values

In the colonial period, Chile was smaller than Uruguay, and only occupied the Central Valley, the area from Santiago to the Bío-Bío. There a certain cultural and racial homogeneity existed - Spanish and *mestizo* - as most of the indigenous peoples of the region had been wiped out. There developed a stable, structured society, which is symbolically represented by the house (*casa*), of Spanish aristocrats and their *mestizo* servants, all catholic. The idea of such a house is a recurring one in Chilean literature, from José Donoso's *Casa de Campo* (Country House) to *Casa Grande* (Big House) by Luis Orrego Luco, to Isabel Allende's *Casa de los Espíritus* (House of the Spirits). Outside this house, savages are beating their drums and shouting out their war cries.[10] So, according to Chilean historian Mario Góngora del Campo, this small state of Chile came to symbolically represent the future nation of Chile. The savages, the indigenous people, lay outside the walls of the house, the frontier. To the north were the "indigenous" countries, Peru and Bolivia, and to the south was the space of barbarism, Araucanía and beyond. The last quarter of the 19th century was the period of the expansion of the community of the Central Valley, in which the other areas had to be brought into civilisation, and into the Chilean nation, which were synonymous, in a process of civilisation and chileanisation (*chilenización*).

Domeyko, the assimilationists and the "Araucanian problem"

In the grand tradition of San Martín and O'Higgins, some intellectuals in Chile saw assimilation as the best way of dealing with the nation's indigenous peoples; Ignacio Domeyko was one of those who were of the view that the so-called Araucanians could and should be incorporated into the Chilean state, thus linking the present nation with a "heroic" indigenous past. His view was due in no small part to the epic poem "La Araucana" by Alonso de Ercilla, the work that provided the stimulus for him to visit the region to explore and engage the "natives", as it had done for other travellers, such as Orélie-Antoine de Tounens.

Physicist and minerologist Ignacio Domeyko arrived in Chile in 1838, invited by the government to establish a mining school in the northern town of Coquimbo. In 1844 he was commissioned to conduct a geological survey in the south. Early the next year he spent three months in the land of the "Araucanians", and he subsequently wrote down his experiences among the Mapuche in two books, *Mis Viajes* (My Travels) and *Araucanía i sus habitants* (Araucanía and its Inhabitants).

In the decades that followed independence, the Chilean government struggled to find a solution to what it termed the "Araucanian problem." In 1823, Interior Minister Mariano Egaña devised the idea of negotiating with the Mapuche to advance the frontier and build a line of forts inside their territory, in order to colonise the land above the line. This plan was put on hold, due first to the pursuit of the remaining royalist factions, and then to Chile's war with Peru and Bolivia in 1836. After 1840, despite government inactivity, settlement, much of it illegal, continued south of the Bío-Bío.

By 1845 there was open talk among Chilean intellectuals of military conquest of Araucanía, as the idea of a semi-autonomous indigenous territory within the republic was unbearable to them. The fertile land was to be settled, also to boost Chile's economic development. Bringing matters to a head, the many German-speaking settlers in the region were complaining of increasing raids on their settlements; *malones* were an issue here too. The militarists in Congress, led by Senator José Diego Benavente of Concepción, went so far as to propose a campaign to remove all Araucanians from the south and forcibly resettle them in Copiapó, in the Atacama desert.[11]

Domeyko soon realised that the processes under way in the region were complex, and were more detrimental to the Mapuche than to the settlers:

"I observed from the road ... the manner by which the most civilised speculators had established themselves in this part of Araucanía; instead of being populated, the country was undergoing depopulation. Because no sooner had a Chilean illegally bought or usurped some land from the Indians, than he expelled the poorest Indians. After tearing down their huts, the settler fenced in the land and placed 200 or 300 cattle there, to live there throughout the year."[12]

Domeyko saw frontier life as a general descent into savagery, laziness and alcoholism, and the region as a haven for criminals. Though he was clearly sympathetic to the Mapuche and exercised his mind to the task of improving their lot, Domeyko was far from considering them his equals; his was the paternalism that was typical both of many of the missionaries that had preceded him in the region and of many politicians to come. As Domeyko's biographer Pablo-Raúl Arreola describes:

> "[...] he still believed that they, like most Indians, lacked something that hindered their full potential as human beings. Like the great Christian apologists before him - Bartolomé de Las Casas and Vasco de Quiroga - Domeyko considered the Indian mind that of a child, fully capable but lacking in reason. Domeyko thought that a rigorous infusion of Christianity, complemented by instruction in the practical arts, would help the Mapuche rise above their current state. A renewed missionary effort, he later argued, was the solution."[13]

Missions had already gained a strong foothold in Araucanía, with the active encouragement of the Chilean government. In 1838 they had invited Italian Franciscans to establish missions among Mapuches living along the southern frontier near Valdivia and Nueva Imperial. In 1848 President Bulnes brought over Italian and German Capuchins, on the basis of a contract signed between his government and the Vatican, to conduct missionary work in the area between the rivers Cautín and Toltén, and the Franciscans were moved further north, in the south only retaining their mission in Chiloé.

Though its indigenous origins have not been glorified as much as those of, say, Mexico - perhaps due to the lack of a Chilean Diego Rivera - it is interesting that it has been possible to incorporate the heroes of the Mapuche resistance against the Spaniards, such as Lautaro, Caupolicán and Galvarino, into the composite Chilean identity. Chileans, generally speaking, are proud of the brave heritage of Mapuche resistance, and have adopted it as their own, with images of strong, heroic Caupolicán and Lautaro often to be found in places such as Chilean children's books. In Chile's *winka* population it is perfectly possible for pride in their mythified Indian ancestors to coexist with disgust at the real Indians of today.

In contrast, a similar glorification process has never occurred with the great indigenous leaders in Argentina, such as Kalfukurá. Argentina has notoriously always considered itself a bastion of Europeanness on the South American continent, so there is no place for the indigenous peoples in the Argentine national identity.

This does not mean that they were not studied. As the conquest of land and knowledge went hand in hand, scientists were dispatched to inventory the Patagonian "desert." Scientists such as the disciple of Alexander Von Homboldt, the French naturalist Alcide D'Orbigny, who visited the region a few years before Darwin. During 1829, in the area around Carmen de Patagones, D'Orbigny met, studied and conversed with Mapuches and Tehuelches, documenting his findings in *El hombre americano* (The American Man), published in 1839. He concluded that these indigenous peoples possessed what he called their own "national character", meaning that they were "immutable and rebellious against civilisation."[14] Yet the Europeans' ways of bringing civilisation were questionable, to say the least.

The Main Square in Bahía Blanca: European Lessons in Civilisation

The statue of Bernardino Rivadavia stands proudly in the main square of Bahía Blanca, gazing down benignly over the city. Briefly President of Argentina in the 1820's, Rivadavia planned to induce industrious European peasants to migrate to Argentina, to turn the Pampa into a tapestry of small holdings.

Bartolomé Mitre, later also to become President, was Minister of War for the Government of Buenos Aires from 1853-1859. Mitre was another europhile, but more enamoured of their swords than their ploughshares, as he idealised European military power, capacities and virtues. It was his idea to bring over Italian combatants, fresh from their own independence struggles, to assist Argentine state expansion.

The 600-man Italian Agricultural Military Legion was founded in 1855, with the purpose of founding a colony - Nueva Roma - near Bahía Blanca. Commanded by Colonel Silvino Olivieri, this colony was an experimental attempt to develop the fortress into something more permanent and constructive, forming a centre for population and a basis for the creation of livelihoods.

On 19 May 1859 the then small town of Bahía Blanca was attacked by a large force led by the now elderly Kalfukurá's son Namunkurá and other prominent *caciques*. The attack was repelled by the local garrison, thanks to the assistance of the Italian Legion.

Bahía Blanca local historian Dr Julia Rossignol de Girón describes the scene the next day:

> "The population observed a column of smoke that was not coming from fires from the houses. It was the bodies of the defeated, in an infernal, dantesque pyre.
>
> The square of the cruel slaughter is today the main square of the city, with its rosebeds, its trees from different countries, its children's playground, its pensioners whiling away their days playing cards, the craft fair and the attentive gaze of Bernardino Rivadavia, from his statue in its privileged position.
>
> Nobody remembers them."[15]

Shocking though it may have been, the slaughter in Bahía Blanca was but a small skirmish in a long war of attrition.

1820-1876: First blood on the Pampa

Argentinians often remember the Conquest of the Desert as having taken place in two campaigns: the first, ultimately unsuccessful one by Rosas, and the second by Roca, which freed up the Pampa and Patagonia for European settlement. Before we look at Roca's campaign, first it is necessary to mention that between 1820 and 1884 there were in fact no less than 21 campaigns conducted south of Buenos Aires; this according to the Argentine Army itself, whose authority we have no reason to doubt in this case.[16] It would seem that for two-thirds of a century the Buenos Aires government could think of nothing else but their Indian problem.

General Martin Rodríguez conducted three different campaigns, in December 1820-January 1821, in March 1823 and in January 1824, followed by a campaign by Colonel Federico Rauch during the Summer of 1826-27.

Four campaigns were conducted south of Mendoza against the Pincheira brothers between 1828 and 1832, the first and last led by General José Félix Aldao. It was Aldao, along with Ruiz Huidobro, who accompanied Rosas on his famous campaign of 1833-34.

There were six further campaigns between 1855 and 1872, directed primarily against the Rankulche and *toki* Kalfukurá, of which the Bahía Blanca slaughter was a part.

Although these campaigns met with varying degrees of success, their intention was clear: the extermination of the "other." To consider the aims and consequences of each campaign in detail would merit a book in itself; suffice it to say that the level of internecine conflict between the indigenous groupings also played its part, as it had done in the past. At the Battle of San Carlos in 1872, for example, the forces of Kalfukurá were defeated by General Rivas, assisted by a large number of warriors commanded by *lonko* Cipriano Catriel, who is said to have ordered those who would not fight against their "brothers" to be shot. Kalfukurá's defeat and flight seem to have buoyed up the government in Buenos Aires, as did his death in 1873. His son Namunkurá took up the fight against the *winkas*.

1876 saw the adopting of a radically different approach.

Walls have often been used to keep enemies out, from Roman Hadrian's Wall to the controversial Israeli wall in the West Bank. In contrast, when Adolfo Alsina, Argentine President Nicolas Avellaneda's Minister of War, had a fortification constructed, its main function was in fact to keep livestock in. The project was financed by the Banco de la Provincia, who provided the credit to the government for the works to be executed.

It was a ditch along the frontier, three and a half yards wide by two yards deep. The project dated back to 1869, but only began to be implemented in 1876, with the digging of about 120 miles, with 82 outposts and five forts dotted along it. The plan was to cover the nearly 500 miles between Bahía Blanca and the south of Córdoba.

In early 1876 a concerted indigenous offensive took place under the command of Juan José Catriel (Cipriano's brother), Namunkurá and Renke Kurá, with 1,000 Mapuches brought over from Chile. They took 200,000 head of cattle and four thousand horses, which were probably taken to Valdivia to be sold. Two months later the government troops, using Remington rifles, were able to defeat them at the battle of Paragüil. It was then that Alsina decided to build a defensive system that, if it could not prevent the *malones*, would at least stop them escaping with the booty.

It seems it was built too late, as after their defeat at Paragüil the indigenous forces were irreversibly debilitated. In any event, Alsina died in December 1877, and was replaced by General Julio Roca, whose approach was far more proactive than that of his predecessor, offering a final solution to the indigenous problem.

Roca's intention was to dust off Rosas' old idea and take possession of the route to and from Chile by means of an expedition to reach the confluence of the Limay and Neuquén rivers.

1878-1884: The wild boar hunt

Both Alsina and Roca had been in agreement that it was indispensable to occupy Neuquén militarily, to prevent the region from being annexed by Chile. After Roca had assumed power, on 4 October 1878 Law 947 was sanctioned, which ratified a campaign against those whom Roca defined as "barbarians, savages and bandits" in his speech to the Congress. Roca had famously said of his adversaries: "With the Indians you must proceed like the Europeans do when they hunt wild boar; you must not take pity on them."[17]

During 1878 Roca sent numerous columns of the army to reconnoitre and prepare the terrain for the campaign to follow. These columns were led by Colonel Nicolás Levalle, Major Camilo García, Lieutenant Colonel Teodoro García, Lieutenant Colonel Lorenzo Vintter, Colonel Conrado E. Villegas, Colonel Rudecindo Roca, Sergeant Major Germán Sosa, Colonel Eduardo Racedo, Lieutenant Colonel Rufino Ortega and Lieutenant Colonel Benito Herrero.

The campaign proper began in April 1879. Roca commanded 6 divisions with 6,000 troops, deploying his forces in a fan-like manner over 1,700 kilometres, from Buenos Aires to Mendoza, on the frontier line. Faced with the advancing army, the caciques of the Pampa - with the exception of Namunkurá - did not stand their ground. Some fell back to the Andes and others surrendered.

The first stage of the campaign was relatively easy, until Namunkurá engaged with Roca's forces at the confluence of the Limay and the Neuquén, but was defeated. Namunkurá took refuge in Chimpay and then in Aluminé, organising the resistance, but in early 1881 the troops commanded by Villegas - by this stage Roca was President - received orders to occupy The Triangle, the name given to the province of Neuquén. It was there that the true confrontation occurred, with the bloodiest battles taking place.

Roca informed the Congress of the Nation that at the end of the first phase of the campaign 14,172 Indians were reduced, prisoners or dead.

1882-1885, the second phrase, saw what by this stage were mopping-up operations, the campaign of the Andes by General Villegas and the campaigns by General Vintter, Lieutenant Colonel Lino Oris de Roa and Major Miguel Vidal in Patagonia.

The second phase culminated in 1885, with the military occupation of Neuquén. On 24 March 1884 Namunkurá surrendered to the army with 331 of his men. In the same period the governor of Patagonia, General Vintter, ordered the final attack against Sayweke and Inakayal. Inakayal and Foyel were defeated, losing 30 men and both being taken prisoner.[18]

Sayweke, isolated and demoralised, surrendered on 1 January 1885 with 700 warriors at fort Junín de los Andes. When the second phase had concluded, the territory of today's province of Neuquén and further south, as far as Santa Cruz, were under the control of the national government.

As Sarasola puts it:

"Everything was over. The torment of having to bear a merciless and incessant persecution had reached an end. The great Sayweke, the last of the unyielding, tired, hungry, stiff with cold, infinitely sad in his defeat, is the symbol of the drama of the Indians resisting the conqueror of the "desert." That desert that for thousands of years the Indians had attended to, filling it with life."[19]

Mapuche historian Pablo Mariman Quemenado puts it more succinctly and dramatically: "So it was that life finished and surviving began."[20] Meanwhile in Chile, Colonel Cornelio Saavedra, an old frontier hand, who had been intendant of Arauco from 1857, was planning his own final solution to the indigenous problem.

Saavedra's plan for "pacification"

Though the first stage of the colonisation of the land south of the Bío-Bío had already begun, with the spontaneous occupation of uncultivated land by independent settlers, in 1861, as a Deputy in the Chilean Parliament in the government of José Joaquín Pérez, Saavedra formalised this process by presenting his plan for the "Pacification of Araucania."

Like Sarmiento, Saavedra looked with admiration at the North American experience of the period, and devised his plan along the same lines as that followed there. The colonial method for the settlement of indigenous territory had been for the settlers to open up the frontier, and the state followed. José Bengoa explains how the new US model followed by Saavedra differed:

> "The state took responsibility for the process, since it was the sole purchaser of land. Firstly, the army advanced, conquering the occupants of the territory, establishing fortified frontier lines and bringing the indigenous peoples under control and concentrating them in reservations. Then the state and private capital, when this was available, installed the infrastructure, especially the railways. After the army came the train. Pacifying the territory, and with the railways under construction, the state then proceeded to auction the land, and the immigrants arrived. Inasmuch as there were peace and communications, European immigration could be attracted, in the form of respectable families, not bands of soldiers of fortune. Starting from these three elements, it was possible to form towns and cities and foment progress."[21]

Despite some opposition to Saavedra's plan, it was approved, and as a result he was named the Army's Commander in Chief of Operations in the territory of Araucanía and charged with its pacification.

Over the next two decades, presented as a succession of occupations and foundings of towns, the process of moving the frontier southward appears inexorable: the advance from the Bío-Bío to the Malleco and the founding of Angol in 1862, from there incursions were carried out to break the Mapuche's economic base, burning sown fields, stealing livestock, interrupting trade, abducting women and children. In 1870 the advance to the banks of the river Toltén to Lumaco, in 1878 the occupation of the banks of the River Traiguén.

In 1879 the process was temporarily stalled by the War of the Pacific (1879-84), breaking the synchronism with the Conquest of the Desert. The army of the frontier was moved to the north to occupy Antofagasta to defend Chile's nitrate mines. After they had annexed slices of Peruvian and Bolivian territory, the attention of the army again returned to the Mapuche territory.

Futa Malón: The Great Uprising

By this time the Mapuche had clearly understood that their entire way of life was at stake, and so made a concerted effort to repel the enemy, in a war of national liberation, in what is known as the *Futa Malón* (the great uprising) of November 1881.[22]

The forts of Lumaco, Toltén, Nueva Imperial, Tirúa, Galvarino and Temuco were attacked, a last-ditch attempt to prevent the inevitable.

To commemorate the *Futa Malón*, 121 years later the Mapuche activist group Kolektivo Lientur prepared a document, part of which states the following:

"It is said that peoples are great and their cultures last over time to the extent that they are able to take the sky by storm, to perform incredible epic feats. From that 5th day of November 1881, the Mapuches, commanded by the *lonkos* Esteban Romero (Truf-Truf), Melivilu (Makewe), Epul (Tromén), Lienan (Temuco), Marileo Kolipi (Purén), Epuleo (Victoria), Millapán and Necul Painemal (Chol-Chol), Ñanco (Tirúa), Painecur (Toltén), Neculman (Lonquimay) and Namunkurá (puelche), along with other military chiefs, spilled their blood on the battlefields of the *Wallmapu*, attempting to perform the almost impossible: to stop the advance of the Chilean military forces and to avoid the loss of independence of our people.

Our brothers perhaps knew they could not win and that most of them would die in that uprising. Yet they organised and fought, making it clear that the yielding of Mapuche independence had to be paid for with their lives, since the previous sacrifice of so many *tokis* and warriors against the Spaniards could not be in vain."[23]

Despite their unquestionable courage, obeying a cultural imperative to fight to the last man, they were mainly fighting with lances and *boleadoras* against a veteran army using repeater rifles.

In 1881 Temuco was founded, consolidating the line of the Cautín and the general uprising was crushed. The campaign culminated in 1883 with the founding of Villarica, taking the last bastion of resistance. Bengoa sums up the importance of the founding of Villarica:

"The founding of Villarica marked the end of independent Mapuche life. The towns filled with settlers, land was divided up and the indigenous peoples were herded away on reservations; the railway pushed onwards, changing the territory forever. So it was that four centuries of Mapuche resistance, undoubtedly an extraordinary page in the history of peoples, had come to an end."[24]

Postscript to a conquest: nation-builders or grave-robbers?

In January 2003 Jorge Nahuel and other representatives of the Co-ordinating Committee of Mapuche Organisations of Neuquén were in negotiations with the Argentine National Parks Authority to try to reach an agreement over ratification of the presence of Mapuche communities in national parks, such as Parque Lanín. Jorge told me that one of the most intractable issues was how to represent the figure of Perito Moreno in relation to the National Parks. The Park Authority views him as the father of the national parks system, whereas the Mapuche view him as a robber of Mapuche land.

Moreno was not just a robber of land. Inakayal and Foyel were two *lonkos* whose communities were located in the area of Tecka, in the south-west of what is today's Chubut. In October 1884 they were taken prisoner during negotiations with a military commander who had stationed a fort on their land. Their homes were destroyed and they and their families were force-marched to the El Tigre prison in Buenos Aires, while their land was sold by the government to the British Tecka Land Company.

A year and a half after Inakayal and Foyel's capture, Moreno was given permission to provide accommodation for them and their families. Inakayal died in the museum on 24 September 1888. Instead of being buried, his bones, brain, scalp and death mask joined the museum collection. His skeleton remained on display in the Museum's Anthropological Galleries until 1940, when it went into storage. In one of the dark rooms that I mentioned at the beginning of this chapter.

On 19 April 1994, the Day of the Indian in Argentina, the urn containing Inakayal's bones was returned to Tecka, to be covered by stones in a *chenke* (tomb), with his descendants present at the ceremony. An archaeologist from the Museum of La Plata accompanied the urn on its journey, and formally apologised to Inakayal's descendants on behalf of the institution.

Rankulche *lonko* Panguitruz Nuru, son of Painé Nuru, was imprisoned as a child and handed over to Juan Manuel de Rosas, who made him his godson and baptised him Mariano Rosas. After years of captivity, he escaped to the base of his community at Leuvocó, where he led his people until his death. A few years later, when the forces of the Third Desert Expeditionary Division invaded Rankulche territory. Panguitruz' tomb was desecrated, and by order of the leader of the expedition, his skull was taken and sent to Estanislao Zeballos, who donated it to the Museum of Natural Sciences in La Plata, where it was displayed for 123 years.

Zeballos defended such actions in these terms: "Barbarism is cursed and in the desert not even the remains of their dead will be left."[25] The defeat of the Mapuche was intended to be total, including the destruction of their religiosity. As a finishing touch to the conquest of their land, their cemeteries were subjected to profanation, all in the name of Christianity.

On 28 August 2000, to much celebration, the body of Panguitruz Nuru was finally returned to his people in Leuvucó.

Visiting Viedma Museum in 2001, I was able to see the mummified body of a Tehuelche in the foetal position, accompanied by the description: "Burial of Tehuelche of Idevi. The individual was placed in a curled up position wrapped in hide." In recent years the Mapuche organisations of Viedma and Carmen de Patagones have protested against such exhibits, even carrying out raids to reappropriate their sacred items and cultural artefacts. I spoke to the curator if the Museum of Carmen de Patagones after one such raid, and she told me the artefacts that the Mapuches took from the museum were in fact reproductions of Tehuelche weapons, such as *boleadoras*, and not the real thing. "They had to be recovered by the police", she said.

Burke and Hare were notorious grave-robbers, who paid for their crimes, but the robbing of Mapuche graves to fill Argentina's museums was commonplace, and the crime unpunished. The Mapuche were allowed no dignity, even in death. There is an old Mapuche saying:

> "An Indian who profanes a white man's tomb is put in prison;
> a white man who profanes an Indian's tomb gains a doctorate."

For the sake of balance, we should not present Moreno as simply a grave-robber an apologist for conquest. He was conducting his scientific research at the very time that the subjects of his studies were being slaughtered, and his reaction to this appears troubled and contradictory:

> "I am certain that on that occasion the sacrifice of thousands of lives could have been avoided; of course many more Indians than Christians lost their lives. During that struggle useless slaughters took place of human beings that, believing themselves to be the owners of the land, defended it from the invading civilisation."[26]

Moreno was clearly shocked and saddened by the killing. Juan Bautista Alberdi, on the other hand, was triumphalist:

> "Today under independence, the native does not appear or constitute a world in our political and civil society. We, who call ourselves American, are none other than Europeans born in America. The native does us justice: he calls us Spanish to this day. I do not know of a distinguished person in our societies who has a Pewenche or Araucanian surname. The language we speak is from Europe... The savage is conquered: in America he has neither domain nor dominion. We, Europeans of race and civilisation, are the owners of America... "[27]

Other Europeans had even fewer scruples. In the 1880s the Rumanian Julius Popper and his band of Yugoslavian and Austrian soldier-peons amused themselves by hunting the Selk'nam, having themselves photographed with their killed "prey." The following decade Scottish ranch manager Alexander MacLennan, known as the *Chancho Colorado* (Red Pig), paid what he called "good money" - pounds sterling - in exchange for the ears, testicles and breasts of the Selk'nam.

However aberrant such behaviour may have been the fact remained that the self-proclaimed civilisers had won. In the next chapter we will see how the Mapuches' lives would change when reduced to living under the yoke of the Chilean and Argentine states.

Notes

1. From the paper delivered at the Museums Australia National Conference 2002, in Adelaide.
2. See Bengoa, *op. cit.*, ch. 5 and Collier and Sater, *op. cit.*, ch. 4.
3. According to journalist and historian Adrián Moyano, who has studied the period.
4. Darwin, "The Voyage of the Beagle", Ch. V.
5. Cited in "Neuquén: 75 Años de Capitalidad", Editorial Sur Argentino, Neuquén, 1979.
6. Specifically the so-called Hudson River Valley School, see article in *The Guardian* of 27/12/2001, "Artists set scene for Hollywood Westerns."
7. As the period from 1848-1875 is called by Eric Hobsbawm in his book of the same name.
8. "Gender & Nation", Nira Yuval-Davis, Sage Publications, 1997, p. 29.
9. "Memorias del ex cautivo Santiago Avendaño", P. Meinrado Hux, 2 volumes, El Elefante Blanco, Buenos Aires, 1999/2001.
10. The concept of the house as microcosm, influenced by the works of Mario Góngora, was outlined by José Bengoa in a talk delivered at the Cambridge University Centre for Latin American Studies on 5th May 2003.
11. The formal project was proposed in 1853. "Sesiones del congreso nacional; Cámara de Senadores: 24 August 1853, pp. 201-204."
12. Cited by Pablo-Raúl Arreola in "Of Conquest and Civilization: Ignacio Domeyko and his Works on the Araucanian Indians in Chile" (www.iacd.oas.org).
13. Pablo-Raúl Arreola, *op. cit.*
14. Cited in "La Patagonia como innovación: imagines científicas y concreciones políticas, 1779-1879" by Pedro Navarro Floria, CONICET, Argentina, Scripta Nova issue 69, 1 August 2000.
15. Cited from Dr. Girón's article "Bahía Blanca: La cuidad. Aspectos históricos. El último malón", in the online cultural magazine "El Muro." (www.elmurocultural.com).
16. The list is compiled from information on the Argentine Army's website, www.ejercito.mil.ar/ejercito/historia/desierto.asp.
17. This quote from Roca is cited in "Los conflictos territoriales de los pueblos indígenas en la Patagonia", by Dr Darío Duch (http://www.pueblosindigenas.org/tierras.htm).
18. For a more in-depth discussion of the Conquest of the Desert, see Sarasola, "Hijos de la Tierra", chapter five.
19. Sarasola, *op. cit.*, p. 147.
20. Pablo Mariman Quemenado, "Elementos de Historia Mapuche", article available on the websites of the Rehue Foundation (www.xs4all.nl/~rehue/) and the Ñuke Mapu Documentation Centre (mapuche.info.scorpionshops.com/). Pablo Mariman is professor of history at the Institute of Indigenous Studies of the Universidad de la Frontera.
21. Bengoa, *op. cit.*, pp. 172-3.
22. For more in-depth analysis of the Futa Malón, see Bengoa, *op. cit.* Chapter 9, and for the buold-up to the Pacification, ch. 6-8.
23. www.nodo50.org/kolectivolientur/.
24. Bengoa, *op. cit.*, p. 325.
25. Cited in Vezub, *op. cit.*
26. Cited in "Viajeros de la Patagonia: Francisco Moreno", on the website www.temakel.com.
27. Quote from "Juan Bautista Alberdi. El redactor de la ley." In "Selección de textos de Oscar Terán", Universidad Nacional de Quilmes, 1996, pp 122 and 57-58. Cited in "Naciones indígenas (Análisis Histórico y constitucional de los casos de Argentina y Chile)" by Sonia Fernández, University of Comahue, Neuquén. Alberdi was in fact writing in 1852, before the Conquest.

REDUCTION AND REPRESSION

PART TWO

LAND FOR SALE:
POPULATING MAPUCHE LAND AFTER THE CONQUEST

The victory over the Mapuche was marked by a commemorative painting by Blanes and photos by Antonio Pozzo, Moreno and Encina, the former highly idealised, showing Roca as glorious victor dominating the Patagonian landscape, the latter, using a newer, more truthful medium, inevitably showing a more ambiguous reality, a more dubious victory.

Chapter five is the first of four in the central part of the book, covering the period from the defeat of the Mapuche up to recent times, a long century of changing relations and unfulfilled aspirations. This chapter looks at the aftermath of the capitulation of the Mapuche. In Argentina, forced abandonment of land and imprisonment, with those eventually able to return finding their land now in others' hands. In Chile, poverty, and a new life in severely circumscribed areas, the *reducciones*, Chile's reservations.

The newly "acquired" land enabled the region's economy to develop fast, as railway and telegraph lines and barbed wire fences traversed the land, and as the communication routes and property boundaries on the new dominions were mapped for the first time. The instigators, financiers and perpetrators of the military campaign now became its beneficiaries. Powerful landowners and their organisations began to dominate the region, as immigrants arrived in waves from all over the world.

Directing history: paintings and photos of conquest

When Roca chose the historically resonant date of 25 May (1879) to occupy the Río Negro, it is no surprise to find that this event was also represented on an artwork, an oil painting by the artist Juan Manuel Blanes entitled "The military occupation of the Río Negro by the National Army on 25 May 1879." The fact that Roca made great efforts to ensure that the march reached the banks of the Río Negro for 25 May fuelled the suspicions of his rivals, who interpreted the campaign as a highly theatrical, only moderately risky operation.

Cacique Villamain poses with his womenfolk after being defeated, December 1882.
Photo: Carlos Encina and Edgardo Moreno

The artwork was commissioned by the national government, on the tenth anniversary of the event, as a homage to Roca. The General himself discussed the arrangement of the figures, the uniforms, horses and harnesses with the artist; the work also brought together the main figures of the campaign, such as Villegas, Racedo, Uriburu and Levalle, who in reality were never actually in the same place at the same time during the campaign. Roca stands in the middle, flanked by his generals; with the presence in the scene of the priest Espinosa, a *Cautiva* and her son, a handful of subjugated Indians, plus representatives of the artillery, infantry and navy, who played little or no part in the campaign, and even some scientists, the painting is a kind of martial version of the nativity, with the whole of the new world of the Pampa represented symbolically and in microcosm. The original painting hangs in the National Historical Museum of Buenos Aires, yet, more significantly perhaps, a copy was ordered by the Governor of Río Negro to be placed in Viedma Airport, to greet all the visitors to the area who pass through.

The Conquest of the Desert marked a new technological stage of warfare, as it was accompanied by photographers. Italian Antonio Pozzo shadowed Roca's 6,000 men, creating the "first graphic report to be realised in Argentine territory"[1], copies of which appear in many of Argentina's museums. Three years later, Pozzo's camera was followed by those of Edgardo Moreno and Carlos Encina, in the campaign of 1882. The two photographers' official assignment was to perform mensuration and topographic survey work, but with the 190 volumes of photos that they filled, they clearly went beyond this strict remit. They were to create a sort of visual inventory of the new riches and acquisitions of the nation.

In his valuable book on the photos, *Indios y Soldados* (Indians and Soldiers)[2], Julio Vezub provides the subtext for 38 representative photos from this collection, explaining in detail how the photos are self-subverting, in the sense that they actually reveal elements that are quite the opposite of the intentions, if not of the photographers themselves, certainly of the Argentine government that commissioned them.

The Indian caciques and their sons were often snapped dressed in uniform, and often looking smarter than the slovenly soldiers. From Rosas' time it was customary to give gifts of uniforms to friendly *caciques*. In contrast with Rosas, who had an understanding of the ethnographic subtleties of the inhabitants of the Pampa and Patagonia, Roca saw the enemy as homogeneous and foreign, *el indio*, as did Echeverría before him. Yet the photos reveal a heterogeneous world - the Pampas and Patagonia were populated with Rankulches, Chaziches, Tehuelches, Pewenches, Boroans and Manzaneros – each with their own distinctive forms of dress, behaviour and custom.

The photos of the soldiers' families' huts, which copied the models of the indigenous *toldos*, revealed that many of the soldiers' wives were Indian and black. Despite the supposed horror of civil society at the Mapuche's practice of taking white *cautivas*, the photos show that the soldiers were also not averse to capturing Indian women and taking them as their wives.

Most powerfully of all, a photo of the soldiers in their quarters reveals an item taking pride of place on a table - a skull. This was clearly a trophy, rather than an exhibit, as these were not scientists but soldiers. This begs the question: who the civilisers and who the barbarians?

The photos reveal that this was not a desert, but a place of abundance and prosperity; as traders, hunters and livestock farmers the Mapuche and the Rankulche were doing well, and the land was prospering. The invasion was against a relatively prosperous society, then; yet the official version was of westward progress[3] filling a void of abandonment. If anything, abandonment followed the campaign, rather than preceding it. Revisiting the region ten years later, Perito Moreno found the following situation:

> "The wide valley of the Collón-Curá is less populated today than twenty years ago, when the Indians of Molfinqueupu had their villages there, but it is to be hoped that its current owners will not leave such a beautiful piece of land in such abandonment. Fort Sharples is in ruins, uninhabited, having completed its mission. [...] I must confess, I expected to find more progress in these places."[4]

While the land lay abandoned, its former stewards were rotting in prisons or forced labour camps. The lucky ones were herded into reservations, such as Cushamen, which was formed from remnants of the Mapuche and was led by *lonko*

Nahuelquir, who had collaborated with the army, acting as their local guide. Those who had fought and been defeated had been force-marched to Buenos Aires and then on to various points the length and breadth of the country, from where most never returned. The Isla Martín García, in the Río de la Plata, was the place of confinement where many captured Mapuches spent the last days of their lives, to be wiped out by hard labour, privation and epidemics. It was there that many were also introduced to Christianity. Judging by this account, the prison chaplain Padre Birot took to the task with some glee:

> "We carried out something like two hundred and forty baptisms of infidels (sick, children, old people). 56 of these neophytes have already died and others will certainly die too. We continue to teach, baptise, and occasionally, to bury. The baptisms have reached 386. The Thieves of Paradise are now up to 81. These Indians die as they have lived. On the Pampa they took livestock, here in a few days they steal heaven."[5]

Pincén was one of the last great *caciques* of the Pampa, an ally of Namunkurá; he was pursued, captured and imprisoned by Roca's troops in 1879. While I was visiting Martín García, which boasts such illustrious political prisoners as Yrigoyen, Perón and Frondizi, I asked the guide whether Pincén, who was incarcerated there with his family, was considered a political prisoner. "No" – she replied – "he was a common delinquent."

The Reductions

According to Pablo Mariman Quemenado[6], the consequences of their defeat were catastrophic for the Mapuche. Most of their livestock was pillaged, to be shared out between officers and troops, with the rest being auctioned off.

Both sides of the Andes, their territory was expropriated, supported by legislation that declared that all land not directly occupied by Mapuches belonged to the state. In Argentina much of this quickly passed into private hands, so when the few *lonkos* who managed to return from their internal exiles came to reclaim their land, they found it in the possession of "soldiers, pioneers, gringos, priests, traders and speculators."[7] The few communities that were left were banished to the most inhospitable areas; in other words, to those no one else wanted.

One such community was the *Lof* Prane, who had been part of the large group of Mapuche-Tehuelche communities under the command of *toki* Valentín Sayweke that inhabited the area in the north east of the province of Chubut. Ana Prane, who is the great granddaughter of the *lonko* of the Prane at the time of the Conquest, and now lives in a small flat in Esquel, told me of her ancestors' vicissitudes:

"The Prane community ended up here in these valleys in around eighteen ninety, ninety-five, after the Conquest of the Desert, when the *lonkos* were all imprisoned and taken away into captivity, in Choele Choel, in the province of Neuquén. After a long period of captivity, they left Choele Choel, and travelled south, and came to populate the Nahuel Pan."

They found the land they had lived on in the valley was now occupied by the Welsh settlers who had arrived in the meantime, so they made their new home further up in the mountains, in the area called Nahuelpan, along with eight other communities.

In Chile the years immediately following defeat were equally traumatic, ones of major change, with the *konas* [warriors] of before who were fortunate enough to be left having to become *campesinos*, subsistence farmers. Bengoa describes the period as "years of fear, of epidemics, of hunger, of the loss of an identity and the reformulation of a new culture as an ethnic minority within Chilean rural society."[8] Groups of hungry Mapuches would hang around the forts for long periods hoping to be fed by the soldiers, as they were unable to make any kind of living themselves.

The army considered the Mapuche leadership structure important and did not wish to dismantle it, but the settlers, tradesmen and industrialists interested in occupying their land wished them to be quickly and completely dispersed, while the state officials were intent on what could be called a middle position, that of integration of the Mapuches into Chilean society.

There was agreement between all sectors that it was necessary to "reduce" the Mapuches in order to divide up their land. It was finally decided that they would be split into small communities, each under the leadership of a *lonko*. These communities were granted *titulos de merced* (land entitlements) in the name of the *lonko*. This was the model that was to endure from the turn of the 20th century to the present day. The communities had to eke out a living on a reduced space for production and reproduction, with poor, small-scale and subsistence as the key words to describe them.[9]

The State took possession of a territory of around 90,000 square kilometres, which was decreed *propiedad fiscal* (state property). On the basis of legal principles formulated in 1813, the Comisión Radicadora de Indígenas (Indigenous Settlement Commission) was created. This commission was responsible for confining the surviving Mapuche population on reservations. First used in the USA in 1786, reservations were created in Chile in 1860 under the Indigenous Reservation Laws. Over the course of 35 years (1884-1919) some 80,000 Mapuches were confined in around 3,000 *reducciones*. During this same period of time, more than nine million hectares were awarded to foreign and Chilean settlers.

So the 19th century ended with the Mapuche definitively conquered. Such humiliation – that of being held in limbo, in reserve, as the word "reservation" implies – had profound and lasting effects for the Mapuche people. Chilean official history has tried to explain this humiliation through reference to some intrinsic flaw in the Mapuches, as a blunt affirmation such as "we needed their land" was somehow discomfiting. This flaw has been identified by the eminent Chilean historian, Sergio Villalobos, of the University of Chile. He believes the Mapuche are entirely responsible for the dire condition in which they found and find themselves:

> "People always think of a terrible domination, with plundering and violence, but they never bear in mind that the Araucanians were active protagonists in their own domination. [...] They needed iron, liquor and wine; they only had poor quality chicha, made of maize or strawberries; they were interested in mirrors, trinkets, decorations, clothes and goods. [...] They themselves sold their lands for a few carafes of liquor... the Araucanian was always accessible to that domination [...]."[10]

In "The Open Veins of Latin America", Eduardo Galeano famously said that Europeans gained the natural riches of Latin America in exchange for mirrors and trinkets. According to Villalobos, the Mapuche have nothing to complain of with such an exchange, as they got not only what they deserved, but what they wanted. Meanwhile, the railway lines moved slowly but inexorably across Patagonia, "like the fingers of a hand", in the memorable image used by Eduardo Galeano[11], drawing the wealth of the country to Buenos Aires and away to Europe.

Plotting the new Argentina: trains, telegraphs and barbed wire

Carmen de Patagones and Viedma were the bases of operations during the Campaign of the Desert. Carmen de Patagones was originally called "Fuerte de Nuestra Señora del Carmen de Patagones" ("Fort of Our Lady of Carmen de Patagones"). After the Campaign the forts were destroyed, to emphasise that there was no longer any need for them. Colonel Lorenzo Vintter, the founder of the town of General Roca, when asked whether to call the place a fort or a town, supposedly said to the secretary of his garrison: "'fort' is synonymous with power, with domination, with conquest. We have not come to dominate, but to civilise. Just put 'town'."[12]

In 1827 Carmen de Patagones was the only enclave of the Argentine state in Patagonia, with no more than 800 inhabitants. Yet by the end of the century new towns were breaking out like measles all over the formerly immaculate face of the "desert." Such towns, built on the sites of the forts, loudly and proudly declaim the history of their foundation on the many websites available for the casual tourist to stumble upon.

The train arrived in Bahía Blanca in 1884, when the Campaign was in full swing. By the end of the century, the railway line from Bahía Blanca had arrived at the confluence of the rivers Neuquén and Limay, following in the wake of the slaughter. The railway was built by the Argentine Southern Rail Company, at the request of the government, due to what was referred to – by the Neuquén Municipal Museum – as the "alarming possibility of armed conflict with Chile." The two countries, who had conspired to eliminate or subjugate the Mapuche, were nevertheless still rivals in the great land grab speeded up by the Iron Horse.

In 1922 the train reached Carmen de Patagones. By 1934 it had reached Bariloche, and – thanks to a bridge – had connected the area south of Viedma with the capital.

Just as the railway provided the means to take the raw materials away, and the telegraph to organise this, so barbed wire provided the means to keep the livestock in. After the Conquest of the Desert, the demand for this simple device for demarcating territory increased exponentially. Though most of the railway lines have now gone, supplanted by the lorry and the coach, the use of barbed wire has still not gone out of fashion. It is the enduring reminder of the carve-up of the *Mapu* after the Conquest of the Desert.

Conquest went hand-in-hand with map-making. In Argentina, the consolidation of the state was also accompanied by its mapping. Thanks to Europeans such as Woodbine Parish, John Arrowsmith, Martin de Moussy and Carl Ritter, the physical detail of Argentina was committed to paper and centralised governmental control.

Likewise the towns. Only decades earlier the Pampas and Patagonia had been home to *tolderías*, the loose communities of indigenous peoples, extended family groups, with *lonkos*, but without rigid hierarchical structures. Now the grid was spreading out unarrestably from Buenos Aires. The Spanish *cuadrícula*, or grid, the model used all over the Spanish-speaking world, with its system of streets and blocks laid out with regular precision, with the central plaza as its focal point, surrounded by an imposing Catholic church, government offices, residences of the wealthy and businesses. Entrepreneurs and financiers had pride of place in the new towns, as befitted those who had encouraged and financed their creation.

"To the victors the spoils" or "who pays the piper"

It is interesting to note that in 1882, in the middle of the Pacification, the first bank was opened in Araucanía by José Bunster. According to Chilean journalist Aníbal Barrera, author of "El Grito Mapuche", it was Bunster who instigated the conquest and occupation of the Mapuche's land, by proposing a concerted effort by the Chilean and Argentine states to defeat them, a suggestion that was accepted by Saavedra and Roca.[13] As a result of the conquest, Bunster ended up the owner of 25,000 hectares of land and with time one of the main usurpers of land in the whole of the Province of Malleco. The Chilean children's encyclopaedia, Icarito, claims that Bunster was "one of the founders of agriculture in *La Frontera* and the model of an agricultural entrepreneur in the south."[14]

East of the Andes, those who financed the Conquest of the Desert were obviously also first in line when it came to profiting from its results. While many soldiers were awarded large tracts of land in payment for having participated in the campaign, other large areas went to its financiers.

That British companies were among the main beneficiaries of the exploitation of these "new" land resources is beyond doubt. The large estates that were being established so rapidly were necessary for a state that was consolidating its relationship of dependency with the imperial power of the age – Britain – and Europe, where meat, grain and wool, among other products, were needed. Railways and the telegraph were the indispensable tools for facilitating this process.

Eric Hobsbawm refers to Argentina, Chile and Uruguay as "honorary dominions."[15] British holdings in Latin America doubled between 1860 and 1880 to 20%, thanks largely to the development of Argentina.

The Argentine government contracted its first loan with the Baring Brothers bank in 1824. This famous bank continued to be the main lender to the Argentine government until 1890, when it collapsed, through its inability to call in its loans. This financial catastrophe cost the then Argentine President Juárez Celman his job. Did Barings finance the Campaign of the Desert? Suffice it to say that in 1887 Roca travelled to Europe, and was feted at a grand banquet in London by the bank; in their view he must have been doing something right.

In Durlston Castle, near Swanage, stands The Great Globe. This folly, built of Portland stone by John Mowlem at his yard in Greenwich, weighs 40 tons, and is nearly 4 metres high. It was built in order to provide the local people of Swanage with instruction on the geography of the world at that time, which, incidentally, was 1887, the year when Roca was received with honours by London's banking community, and two years after the conclusion of his genocidal desert campaign.

The Globe provides a snapshot of the British worldview of the time. It shows no national political borders, only geographical features, oceans and landmasses, rivers and mountains. The various nation states are identified by their names, the size of their lettering denoting their relative importance in the British Empire, and their complete absence denoting their lack of it.

In South America, the words "Argentine Republic" are written over the Southern Cone. Chile does not appear at all, but is represented by Valparaíso, in lettering the same size as that of Uruguay and Paraguay. Why the prominence given to Valparaíso? Before the completion of the Panama Canal in 1914 reduced its importance, it was South America's most significant Pacific port and a major naval base for the British Empire. From Valparaíso, through its protected companies, the British Empire managed the navigation of its fleet towards Australia and India.

British commercial interests in Chile have a long history, dating back to Francis Drake's sacking of Valparaíso in 1578. Bernardo O'Higgins himself attended school in Richmond, Surrey between 1795 and 1798. In 1818 Admiral Lord Cochrane was appointed Commander-in-Chief of the Chilean fleet, which included three former British ships, two of which were renamed Lautaro and Galvarino, paying lip service to the country's indigenous past through the names of two of its heroes.

In Argentina a strategic alliance was formed during the course of the 19th century between the *estancieros* (the owners of the large estates) and British capital, for the exploitation of the country's land-based riches. During his period of influence, Rosas had been the main spokesman for the interests of this *estanciero* class.

In July 1866, a meeting was held at the house of the Martínez de Hoz family in Chapadmalal, near Mar del Plata, and the Sociedad Rural Argentina was founded. The name Martínez de Hoz may be familiar as that of the economy minister responsible for hyperinflation during the Videla dictatorship of the seventies, in fact it is a major Argentine dynasty. There were four Britons present among the 13 at this meeting in Chapadmalal, one of whom was George Temperley, a major landowner and board member of several large British companies; an area in the south of Greater Buenos Aires and a railway station bear his name today. The Sociedad Rural functioned something like a modern lobbying organisation, to ensure that land sold by the state was at moderate prices and with easy payment terms. The motto of the Sociedad Rural was "to cultivate the soil is to serve the mother country." We might ask which one.

At the very time when the US government was giving a hundred million acres of land free to the US railroads, British capitalists were forming companies in Argentina for the joint purpose of running the railways and exploiting the land. Such companies were the Central Argentina Land Company, formed in 1863, which was a subsidiary of the Grand Central Argentine Railway. The company was founded by North American William Wheelwright, who also had considerable mining and shipping interests in Chile. In 1872 the British government complained to its Argentine counterpart when the company's property in Bahía Blanca was attacked by a *malón*. They clamoured for something to be done, and it certainly was, courtesy of General Argentino Roca.

Another company to be formed was the Southern Rail Company, along with its subsidiary the Argentine Southern Land Company. It was the latter that acquired 900,000 hectares of land in the area of the Cordillera in Chubut after the Conquest of the Desert. This is the very land that was sold to Benetton in the 1990s, land over which Benetton is still in conflict with Mapuche communities. The land came into the hands of the Argentine Southern Land Company under the terms of the so-called Avellaneda Law, which had the purpose of dividing up farmland to encourage the European colonisation of Patagonia; in 1891 the requirement to colonise the land was annulled, and the British capital company acquired the land for large-scale livestock breeding.

The Argentine Fruit Distributors (formed in 1928), based in the Alto Valle of Río Negro, was another subsidiary of the Southern Rail Company. It laid the track, acquired thousands of hectares around it, founded a colony, tested different varieties of fruit to identify the best for growing, introduced the newest technologies and methods and established packing plants by the railways, all in order to transport the fruit abroad. The towns of Cinco Saltos, Cipolletti, Allen, J.J. Gómez and Regina all grew up around railway stations as a result of the fruit packing activities.

La Trochita railway line between Ingeniero Jacobacci and Esquel, which has recently been re-opened as a tourist resource, played an important role in the development of the region. All the materials and goods arrived along this route, and it was from its stations that the wool and hides produced and livestock bred in the Valle 16 de Octobre, the area of Western Chubut settled by the Welsh after the Mapuche-Tehuelche had been removed, and the products of the farms of the Argentine Southern Land Company, all departed for the north. There was also other - human - traffic in the opposite direction.

Nations of immigrants

The new towns needed to be filled, and it was immigrants who were to do the filling. Any talk of immigration today will soon come round to the problems caused by migrants. Driven by hope or fear, whether asylum seekers in the UK, boat people off the coasts of Southern Italy or Miami, wetbacks crossing the Rio Grande, or Paraguayans and Bolivians in Buenos Aires, "they" are very often perceived as the undeserving poor trying to take advantage of the benefits of "our" superior yet tolerant societies. Yet a hundred years ago things were quite different, with immigrants seen as the solution for the development of both Argentina and Chile. As Bengoa has said, "it was thought that migration would bring development and industry, in a word, progress."[16]

As we have seen, Sarmiento and Alberdi were among the architects of this policy in Argentina, which took concrete shape in February 1825, when Bernardo Rivadavia, later to become President, was Secretary of Foreign Affairs. With his Treaty of Friendship, Commerce and Navigation, immigrants were granted certain civil rights, such as the right to practise their own religions and exemption from military service, and an official commission was formed to promote immigration. With this it was hoped to "attract a vanguard of legions of hard-working northern Europeans to help build the country."[17]

In the peak period of European overseas migration, 1821-1932, six countries absorbed 90 per cent of the total migrants; Argentina was second after the USA, with a total of 6,405,000.[18] Disappointingly for Sarmiento and Alberdi, who were so keen to bring White Anglo-Saxon Protestant immigrants to Argentina, with their sense of duty and order and their work ethic, those who actually came were predominantly southern Europeans, mainly from Italy and Spain, each accounting for over 2 million immigrants in that period. Many of these were transient, the so-called *golondrinas* (swallows), who crossed the Atlantic to work the Southern Hemisphere harvest season and then return home.

Many immigrants stopped when they reached Buenos Aires and the other major cities, but the Italians, mostly from Southern Italy, and Spanish from Galicia, with their farming and growing traditions, were the ones who tended to spread further afield, with many settling in the valley of the Río Negro, for example, dedicating themselves to fruit and vegetable cultivation. Many Basques also came to the region of La Pampa and Patagonia. Germans and Swiss tended to settle in the area of Bariloche - founded in 1902 - while the Scots preferred Santa Cruz, and the Welsh Chubut, as mentioned above. The immigrants often became smallholders, sharecroppers and tenant farmers, as their initial goal of becoming landowners was ultimately frustrated. Although some sons of immigrants, such as Carlos Pellegrini, came to achieve political office, for most it was virtually impossible to break through the glass ceiling to join the *criollo* elite.

When discussing immigrants in Argentina and their effect on the Mapuche, we cannot fail to mention the Syrian and Lebanese communities, who soon joined forces to form a single community due to common language and interests. Today there are estimated to be over a million and a half residents of Argentina of Syrio-Lebanese origin,[19] whose ancestors migrated in various periods, beginning in 1861, as a result of the turmoil due to the insurrection against the Ottoman domination. The main wave of Syrio-Lebanese immigration to Argentina was between 1900 and 1930. Such high profile politicians as ex-President Carlos Menem, son of Syrian immigrants, and maverick Colonel Mohamed Alí Seineldin, come from Argentina's Syrio-Lebanese community. Ironically, considering their conflict with the Ottomans, they are known in Argentina as *turcos* (Turks). The Mapuches of Chubut have had a number of run-ins with the Syrio-Lebanese traders who have bought land to which the former lay claim, such as Said Bestene and the El Khazen family, who have crossed swords with the Futa Huau and the Vuelta del Río communities respectively.

Immigrants to Chile during the colonial period were Spanish, of course, mainly from Castille and Andalucía. In the 18th century they were joined by large numbers of Basques, forming what would become the dominant Spanish-Basque elite during the formation of the Republic.

In the mid-19th century, the Chilean government organised the colonisation of the Lakes Region (now the 10th Region) with German settlers, concentrated around the city of Puerto Montt. By 1912 the consolidation of the city and the development of the region were ensured by the arrival of the railway link with Santiago. Incidentally, this is due west of Bariloche on the Argentine side, were Germans also settled; on both sides, they imposed the architectural style of their country of origin on the buildings of their host country.

Once the Mapuche "problem" had been resolved, the way was open for an influx of Germans, Swiss, French and Italians into the 9th Region. The example of the Swiss Luchsinger family is typical. They arrived in Chile in 1883, within the framework of the colonisation policy instigated by the government of Domingo Santa María. The head of the family, Adán Luchsinger – grandfather of Jorge, the landowner who takes such a dim view of the Mapuche (cf. chapters 10 and 11) - was given 62 hectares by the Chilean state, along with a pair of oxen, a cow, seeds and wood. They had been approached in Switzerland and encouraged to migrate by the Chilean Colonisation Agency, and eventually disembarked in Talcahuano.[20]

Chile also had its share of Canton Chinese, Russian Jews, Syrians and Lebanese, who tended to concentrate on commercial activities and remain in the major cities. Further south, the city of Punta Arenas became home to Croatians, Germans and English, as well as Spanish, marking the end of a way of life for the Selk'nam and Ona peoples, who are now only a memory.

The lauded landowner and the unsung worker

In Argentina, those who made fortunes from the toils of their workers on their vast estates often acquired heroic, even mythical status. One example of the landowner as hero was José Menéndez.

Menéndez and his son-in-law Moritz Braun, who were initially rivals, later joined forces to establish an "empire of *estancias*, coal-mines, freezers, department stores, merchant ships and a salvage department."[21] The Braun and Menéndez families founded "La Anónima" company, whose supermarkets and hypermarkets dominate the skylines of many of Patagonia's cities and towns today.

"The King of Patagonia", as he was known, was the patriarch of the Braun-Menéndez dynasty, wielding considerable economic and political power in Argentina and Chile. He was despotic in his relations with his labourers, most of whom were Mapuches, Williches from the island of Chiloé. In June 1943 an issue of *Argentina Austral* was published to commemorate the centenary of his birth; most of the magazine is a eulogy to Menéndez (and his devoted wife):

"José Menéndez [...] was not seduced by the glitter of gold. Easy gain not achieved with the employment of intelligence seemed to him to be a vain conquest. He arrived when a frightening solitude still reigned over the immense Patagonian desert [...]. It was there, with the sole sound purpose of devoting himself to the breeding of livestock, and such was his will and faith to triumph, that he wanted to take his young wife with him. And she followed him blindly, yet knowing that she was abandoning the comfort and pleasures of the big city forever, to dedicate herself with willing devotion not only to the duties of wife and mother, but also to the works of charity from which many people in Punta Arenas were to benefit. [...] José Menéndez, with an iron will, with a prodigious broadness of vision, with an extraordinary spirit of sacrifice, who was an example for the other pioneers, after long years of bitter struggle and innominable toils, succeeded in giving Patagonia *an order, a wealth, a civilisation*, a fecund promise of secure future."[22] [my italics]

Then, as today, wealth-creation was seen by many to be a virtue, even if the wealth was being created for the benefit of the creator. Yet the real heroes of Patagonia are not the entrepreneurs, but those workers whose hard lives have left their signs in the lines of their faces in their old age, if indeed they reach old age. One such hero is Mapuche Marcelo Ñiripil, born in 1900 in Chenqueniyeu, near Bariloche. Now blind, in his time Marcelo both saw and took part in the major transformations that the *Mapu* has undergone. Like his father, he worked for the Southern Land Company:

"My father was a foreman for the British; he took the sheep to the *estancia's* various slaughterhouses. I was twelve years old when I began working as a stableboy; I had to round up the tame horses at sunset."[23]

Later he worked on the railways:

"In 1939, when La Trochita railway was already reaching the River Chubut, near to El Maitén, I worked laying the tracks. I was foreman of a work gang; the wagons brought 400 rails and *quebracho* tree posts, and I divided them up between the *peones* (labourers). I worked that way until the line reached Esquel."[24]

In a generation, the same time that it took for the quebracho trees to disappear from the Chaco, the sons and grandsons of the former lords of these fertile plains had become the serfs of the new lords, the entrepreneurs. No small number of such entrepreneurs have come from Chubut's Welsh community, who are particularly adept at creating myths to show themselves in a positive light.

The Welsh in Patagonia: peaceful coexistence a myth or reality?

The festival of thanksgiving is used in the USA to consolidate the myth of a peaceful coexistence between the pilgrims and the local indigenous people. In much the same way, in Chubut in Patagonia the notion is propagated of peaceful coexistence between the Tehuelche and the Welsh who colonised the region in the mid-19th century.

"The Monument to the Tehuelche Indian" is a statue sculpted by Luis Perlotti that stands in Puerto Madryn, on the east coast of Chubut. He gazes out to sea from on high, seemingly awaiting the arrival of his new brothers. Every year in Puerto Madryn, on 28 July, re-enactments are held of the coming together of two cultures; these celebrations take place with the participation of a few compliant Mapuche-Tehuelches, while the indigenous organisations boycott the event, pouring disdain on what they consider the Uncle Tom attitude of their compatriots.

Here is a description of the 135th anniversary re-enactment in 2000:

> "Yesterday, the Welsh remembered the 135th anniversary of the landing with a recreation of that "meeting of two worlds" that brought the Tehuelches who inhabited the area together with the settlers for the first time. So it was that Nalicys Jones – descendent of the Welsh pioneers who landed in Patagonia – disembarked from a wooden boat in the same place where her ancestors had done so 135 years ago. Waiting on the beach for her was Rosa Chiquichano, from a long line of Tehuelche blood. Face to face, with their feet in the water, they recreated the same embrace that had united their ancestors."[25]

In the mid-19th century, the Argentine government was worried about Chile's intentions regarding the area that is today's Chubut – the obstacle of the region's inhabitants would soon be removed - so it declared its willingness to grant 100 square miles for the establishment of a Welsh colony, *Y Wladfa*.

As a result, in late May 1865 a group of nearly 200 Welshmen and women, seeking a new country to practise their faith without persecution, left the port of Liverpool in a ship called the Mimosa. It arrived at what is now Puerto Madryn on 27 July, 1865, landing its passengers the next day. Initially times were extremely hard, and they risked starvation, but were helped by the Tehuelche, who taught them how to hunt guanaco and rhea, and exchanged meat for bread with them. The towns of Trelew and Gaiman developed around the sites where chapels were built. The settlements eventually began to thrive as Trelew expanded as a port and railway terminal.

On the western side of the Chubut flatlands, the town of Trevelín was also founded, as an offshoot of the Madryn colony. The name means "mill town" in Welsh, and it was indeed the site of the first flour mill in the region. It was established founded following a trek across Chubut in 1883 by John D. Evans, Richard Davies, John Hughes and John Parry, in search of gold. The story goes that during the journey they were attacked, in the so-called Valley of the Martyrs, by the men of *lonko* Foyel, with only Evans managing to escape alive, thanks to the prodigious strength and stamina of his brave horse Malacara ("Ugly Face"), so-called because of a scar on its head. The descendents of the original Welsh colonisers claim that this was the only case of violence between the Welsh and the indigenous peoples. My doubts about this assertion arise from the fact that this seems to fall within the usual good Indian/bad Indian discourse that the Mapuche-Tehuelche refuse to accept, whereby the Tehuelche were Argentine and good and the Mapuche (Foyel) were invaders and bad. In any event, it must not be forgotten that this attack took place in the middle of the chaos and destruction that was the Campaign of the Desert.

In 1902, following border skirmishes between Argentina and Chile, the British Crown was called upon to arbitrate. On 30 April of that year, at school no. 18 in Trevelín, a meeting was held of the Border Commission, headed by Sir Thomas Holditch, the King's Surveyor General of India, designated by King Edward VII, with Argentina and Chile represented by Francisco P. Moreno and Dr José Manuel Balmaceda respectively. Both the Welsh and the Mapuche-Tehuelche communities living in the area declared that they wished to remain part of Argentina. The communities concerned were the 9 *lofs* of the Nahuelpan, including the Lof Prane, who had been driven from the valley by the arrival of the Welsh. The arbitrator decided that the land in question was Argentine, thanks to the key contribution of the declaration by the Mapuche-Tehuelches. At no time were they asked if they would prefer to remain Mapuche-Tehuelches rather than Argentinians.

A more recent visitor from Wales to Patagonia is Dafydd Iwan, the Welsh nationalist singer songwriter, now president and leader of Plaid Cymru, who was there in 1999/2000. He wrote a very sensitive article on his experiences and reactions for the magazine of the Welsh worldwide, *Ninnau*, from which I reproduce the following:

"Vernon Hughes takes us to meet a family of native Indians who live a long, long way out on the plain. We receive a warm welcome, and we are given the rare honour of seeing them perform a ceremony asking their God for rain, and for his help to allow them to live their lives, and to speak the language of their forbears on their traditional territory. I feel humbled by their simple sincerity, and try to tell them that we in Wales are engaged in a similar battle to keep alive our language and culture in the land of our fathers. We exchange songs and gifts, and depart, knowing that we have experienced something very rare – sombre and uplifting at the same time."[26]

Dafydd Iwan's empathy for the struggling community he visited is admirable, and his interest in visiting it in the first place is - sadly – all too unusual. His own experience as a recipient of discrimination as a Welshman helped provide him with the necessary insight into the Mapuche-Tehuelche point of view.

In the last hundred years, attempts have been made by the Chilean and Argentine states to improve the plight of their indigenous peoples, but not always with as much insight as shown by Dafydd Iwan, as we will see in the next chapter.

Notes

1. Gesualdo Vicente, "Los que fijaron la imagen del país", in "Todo es Historia", No. 198, November 1983.
2. Julio Vezub, "Indios y Soldados: Las fotografías de Carlos Encina y Edgardo Moreno durante la 'Conquista del Desierto'", el Elefante Blanco, Buenos Aires 2002.
3. This too was a myth; rather than westward from the sea to the Andes, the campaign was primarily southward from Mendoza. The "official" version has a westward drive from Carmen de Patagones.
4. Moreno (1898), cited in Vezub, *op.cit.*, p. 29.
5. Copello, 1944, cited in Vezub, *op. cit.*, p. 94.
6. Quemenado, "Elementos de Historia Mapuche" (http://www.xs4all.nl/~rehue/art/mariman.html).
7. Sarasola, *op. cit.* p. 181.
8. Bengoa, *op. cit.*, p. 329.
9. The Reducciones are explained in more detail in "El proceso legal de abolición de la propiedad colectiva: el caso mapuche", Jorge Calbucura, on the website of the Rehue Foundation (http://www.xs4all.nl/~rehue/art.html).
10. These comments were part of an article by Villalobos that appeared in the "El Mercurio" newspaper on 14/5/00, which aroused angry reactions from Mapuche organisations in the Southern Cone and overseas.
11. Eduardo Galeano uses this expression in the documentary "Stories of Memory and Fire", shown as part of the Rear Window series on Channel 4, produced by Bandung Limited (1992).
12. Sarasola, *op. cit.*, p. 181.
13. Aníbal Barrera, "El Grito Mapuche", publ. by Grijalbo, 1999, p. 26.
14. Icarito.tercera.cl.
15. Eric Hobsbawm, "Industry & Empire", p., 126, Penguin 1999 (1968).
16. Cited in the article "Del Dolor y la Esperanza de un parto" by the Coordinadora Indianista CONACIN, Santiago Warria, March 2001.
17. "La Colonia Olvidada" by Andrew Graham-Yooll, Emecé, Buenos Aires, 2000, p. 172.
18. Arthur P. Whitaker, "Argentina", New Jersey, Prentice Hall Inc., 1964, p. 54.
19. Statistics from the website of the Lebanese Embassy in Argentina (http://www.ellibano.com.ar/files/archivos/emigracion.htm).
20. As reported in Azkintuwe, 21 June 2005.
21. Bruce Chatwin, "In Patagonia", p. 120, Jonathan Cape, London, 1977.
22. "Argentina Austral", issue 144, June 1943. From the article "A shepherd king in Patagonia" by Mirko Ardemagni, p. 113.
23. *Clarín*, 21st December 1998.
24. Idem.
25. From an article by Carlos Guajardo, the Rawson correspondent of Clarín newspaper, 29th July 2000, reproduced on the website www.casaargentina.org.
26. Reproduced by kind permission of publisher Arturo Roberts (www.ninnau.com).

FRATERNALISM OR PATERNALISM: RELATIONS BETWEEN THE PACIFIED MAPUCHE AND THE STATE UNTIL THE COUPS

We saw in the previous chapter that the defeat of the Mapuche paved the way for the populating of their ancestral lands with European immigrants, according to the vision of the modern states that Chile and Argentina were to become. The indigenous people were not completely forgotten, however, and attempts were made to act through legislation and initiatives to change their status and condition, but almost always with a minimum of consultation with the supposed beneficiaries. In this chapter we will look at such attempts before all bets were off with the *coups d'état* in the '70s. We will look at the formation of the first Mapuche organisations in the early 20th century, and their differing approaches in their subsequent dealings with the state. Governments of all hues, from Ibañez' to Allende's in Chile, from Uriburu's to Yrigoyen's in Argentina, have been exercised about land reform and the indigenous issue, but always with paternalism as the watchword. We look at what this means for one community in particular – the *Lof* Prane – in its 50 years of relations with the Argentine state.

The Chilean State and the Mapuche

Why the persistent inability on the part of the state to consult with its indigenous citizens? Perhaps at the root is its refusal to accept that they are peoples, and to treat them as such. Chilean historian Gabriel Salazar, author of "Historia contemporánea de Chile", explains this in the following terms:

> "The state recognises the existence of ethnic groups, but not of indigenous peoples. To talk of peoples would be the equivalent, in its opinion, to recognising the existence of various nations within the same territory, which would undermine the classic vision of a single nation and a single State. In turn, the indigenous organisations consider that they are peoples, on ac-

count of their history, ethnic identity, religion, language and territory. If all peoples have a basic equality of rights, then ethnic groups can legitimately aspire to self-determination."[1]

The self-determination of their indigenous peoples was and continues to be far too worrying a notion for the Chilean and Argentine states to even contemplate.

Let us consider how the Chilean state has dealt with the aspirations of the Mapuche. In the previous chapter we looked at the expropriation of Mapuche land following the military domination by the Chilean state, their confining on reservations, known as *reducciones*, and the *títulos de merced* that were issued to the *lonkos*, the heads of small groupings of Mapuche families.

It is estimated that between 1884 and 1919 around 3,000 of these *títulos de merced* were granted, thus creating the same number of indigenous communities. The lands available to these families were severely reduced with respect to the past, with approximately 78,000 people now being confined to 500,000 hectares, and 40,000 receiving no land allocation at all. The number of communities remained substantially unchanged until the late fifties, with only the number of people living on the communities increasing (by 1959 over 300,000).[2]

Yet while demographic growth meant that more and more community members were requiring their share of the community cake, the size of this cake was being reduced all the time. According to José Bengoa[3], in the first fifty years of the 20th century, almost one third of the land originally granted in *títulos de merced* was usurped by private individuals; in the fifty years from 1927, the colonists and latter-day estate owners had acquired a total of 25% (approximately 131,000 hectares) of the 526,286 initially assigned.

Together with the gradual, clandestine chipping away at Mapuche land by their avaricious neighbours, there has also been a legal process of fragmentation of the land previously awarded to them. In 1927, in the military government of Carlos Ibáñez - who, according to a much-used Chilean school history book, "restored the principle of authority and order" to Chile[4] - a law was enacted, no. 4169, that allowed the voluntary division of community land provided all the heads of households of the community were in agreement on this. Ironically it was a Mapuche politician, Manuel Manquilef, a member of the Liberal Democratic Party, it was he who was the main promoter if this damaging law. From 1927 to 1972, almost 800 communities, about 125,000 hectares, were divided into family units, giving land titles to approximately 13,000 families[5]. This process was taken a stage further under Pinochet, as we will see.

The fragmentation of the communities also had a highly damaging effect on their internal cohesion, drastically reducing the authority of the *lonko* in terms of the community's relations with the outside world. Though the *lonkos* would still be called upon to deliver judgements on internal community matters, they were no longer necessarily the only interlocutors in relations with the state or local authorities. Conversely, the role of the *machis* gained in importance, particularly in their guise as spiritual intermediaries during ceremonial events, which in a sense were the only occasions when a traditional *lof* truly came together and acted as a community. In the early decades of the 20th century, Mapuches necessarily had to become more outward-looking.

Mapuche organisations of integration and resistance

The idealists in Chilean society saw the Chilean nation as the fusion of two great races, with the whole being greater than the sum of its parts, as we saw when discussing the founding fathers in chapter three. The poet Gabriela Mistral, who, along with Pablo Neruda, had been converted to indigenism in Mexico, and who won the Nobel Prize for Literature in 1945, expressed her aspirations for this marvellous synthesis in these words:

> "The blood of Valdivia and Caupolicán,
> mingled in a splendid alliance,
> give the world a race of proud vehemence."[6]

Even the Chilean armed forces were proud of the Mapuche at that time. In 1944, for example, Chilean Army General and future Commander-in-Chief, Indalicio Tellez, published a book on their prodigious capabilities in the arts of warfare, entitled "Una Raza Militar." He no doubt hoped their skills would rub off on him.

Such calls for integration were echoed, or rather foreshadowed, by Mapuches. In 1926 the Mapuche organisation Unión Araucana was formed, with its motto "God, fatherland and progress." This organisation seemed to show an inordinate adulation for the virtues of the dominant culture. According to José Mariman, they "were to make fervent calls to combat polygamy, alcoholism, ignorance, technical disadvantage and in favour of private property."[7] The former were the perceived vices of the "pagan past"[8] of Mapuches, the latter the key virtue of the ethos of the Chilean state.

Though tendencies such as those of the Unión Araucana were in the direction of integration, paradoxically, as encroachment and fragmentation assaulted the integrity of Mapuche communities, and as governments - particularly military governments - sought ways to integrate the Mapuche into mainstream Chilean society, generally speaking the latter's isolationism increased. Isolationism and rejection of the society seeking to incorporate them; the key principle of the morality of many Mapuches was not to *awinkarse*.

For their part, the Mapuches who had migrated to the cities learned that if their society was to recover what it had lost in the Pacification, they would have to use the structures of the Chilean state to their advantage; hence the appearance of the first Mapuche scholars, and the formation at the start of the 20th century of the first Mapuche organisations.

It can be said that the Mapuche movement proper began in 1910, with the founding of the Sociedad Caupolicán Defensora de la Araucanía. This fell within the context of a more general phenomenon of creation of associations for working people. According to José Bengoa, "it was the time in Santiago, and especially in Iquique and in the north of the country, of the *sociedades obreras* (working people's associations): friendly societies, craftsmen's associations, associations of various types for the protection of their members."[9]

The Sociedad Caupolicán was not isolationist, but rather integrationist and indigenist, seeking to forge alliances with sympathetic elements in Chilean society, "respectful integration", in Bengoa's words.[10] In an attempt to build bridges, the Sociedad's Onofre Colima declared the centuries-long battle with the *winka* to be over, in the following rhetorical words:

> "Now our lances are not tinged in the red blood of our enemies in horrific war, and today they fall from our hands to the ground, broken into pieces, before the great truth that we are all brothers."[11]

Other important Mapuche organisations were much more intransigent and uncompromising in their aspirations. In 1914, the Sociedad Mapuche de Protección Mutua was created by Manuel Aburto Panguilef, based on the cultural, territorial, religious and linguistic defence of the Mapuche. In 1919 Panguilef and others founded the Federación Araucana, which held several indigenist conferences in the years that followed, with the aim of recovering Mapuche traditions. At the congress held in 1935, one of the main resolutions passed, a highly uncompromising one, was to demand: "the provision of lands, the return of those that were usurped, the non-payment of taxes, schools under the control of indigenous people, a special department of the Agricultural Credit Bank staffed by Mapuches, the creation of indigenous courts with indigenous staff, the respecting of traditional customs by the state, the recognition of the Mapuche flag and the election of Mapuche representatives to Parliament."[12] Very few of these aspirations have been met even today.

In 1934 former members of the Sociedad Caupolicán founded the Corporación Araucana, according to Bengoa "the most important political organisation that the Mapuches had [in the 20th] century"[13], whose main leader was Venancio Coñoepán, an important figure in the history of Mapuche involvement in Chilean politics, being undoubtedly the most successful Mapuche politician, holding various government positions over three decades. In April 1940 Coñoepán took part in the First Interamerican Indigenist Congress, in Pátzcuaro, in Mexico. In a letter to his wife from Mexico, he wrote: "I have never been more convinced of the need to create an Indigenous Republic in Chile."[14]

In the course of the fifties, the indigenist line of this organisation strengthened, and in 1953 the Asociación Nacional Indígena de Chile (ANI) was formed, with a position on the left of Chilean political discourse.

Until the arrival of Salvador Allende, little was done by Chile's governments to return Mapuche land that had been usurped from them. Under the government of Jorge Alessandri (1958-1964), courts were set up to deal with land issues, but in practice very little land was returned. The frustration of many Mapuches at this resulted in the first *tomas* (land seizures). In 1962 the Law of Agrarian Reform was introduced, but this stated that land usurped from the Mapuche before 1946 would be allocated for public use. The INDAP (Institute for Farming and Stockbreeding Development) was formed, and this body did provide some assistance in buying seed, but this was strictly at individual and family, rather than community level.

Under the government of Eduardo Frei (1964-1970) Mapuche access to INDAP credit increased. In 1967 there was a new Law of Agrarian Reform, which led to some expropriations of land from large landowners by the government, but these were mainly in the central regions. The number of *tomas* increased in this period, not only by Mapuche communities, but also by poor *campesinos*.

Salvador Allende and the Mapuche question

It was under Allende's government (1970-73) that the number of *tomas* really burgeoned, with as many as 1,700 in his first year in power. It became clear that there needed to be a response from the government to what was already happening on the ground. Far from forcing through reform, Allende was merely trying to keep pace with the momentum of a process already underway.

In 1972 law no. 17.729 was passed, containing norms for the protection of indigenous lands and creating the Institute of Indigenous Development, authorising this organisation to expropriate land from private estates to the benefit of Mapuche communities. Between 1972 and September 1973, more than 70,000 hectares were transferred to Mapuche communities. In contrast with previous legislation, division of community land would only be permitted if 100% of the community members were in agreement on this.

The programme of Allende's Popular Unity government is very revealing about their view of the Mapuches. The programme promised the following:

> "Defence of the integrity and expansion of the indigenous communities threatened by usurpation and ensuring the democratic direction, so that

the Mapuche people and other indigenous peoples are guaranteed sufficient land and appropriate technical assistance and credit."[15]

Though these aims are estimable, Point 9 of the same programme stated:

"The technical assistance to the *campesino* sector will be free and will have special plans for credit, technical assistance and training for the more neglected groups, particularly the indigenous communities."[16]

This point betrays the fact that the framework within which the land reform was viewed was one of class, rather than of ethnicity. The Mapuches were members of the rural proletariat, not a separate ethnic group.

It was not supposed to be that way. On the Cerro Ñielol, the Mapuche's ceremonial hill overlooking Temuco, on 6 April 1964, the Pact of Cautín was solemnly entered into between Allende, when he was presidential candidate, and the Allendist Mapuches. In this Allende recognised:

"that the Araucanian people wishes to maintain and develop all those positive aspects of their traditional culture that enrich the store of national Chilean culture, such as their language, their legends, their religious ideas and their crafts ...."[17]

Even when trying to enlist Mapuche support for his presidential campaign, Allende seems to have been more interested in what the Mapuche could do for the nation, in terms of "enriching the store of national Chilean culture", than what he could do for them, in terms of recognising their rights and aspirations.

In 1971 a report, "La Cuestión Mapuche", was prepared by Alejandro Saavedra, published by the Institute of Training and Investigation into Agrarian Reform[18]. The report looked in depth at the situation of the Mapuches, suggesting remedies:

"The Mapuche economy [...] is a subsistence economy because it is structurally unable to develop and tends to maintain, or even worsen, the pre-existing living and working conditions. [...] Only by changing the structural conditions of this economy can a real process of economic development occur."[19]

The conclusion of the book is:

"[...] in order to resolve the "Mapuche problem", the government must reorganise the whole range of state action in relation to the Mapuche (economic, legal, educational, etc.) through a new policy, advancing towards the application of an integrated development programme and the organisation of a single administrative apparatus in their regard. "[20]

Though the report undoubtedly has what are perceived to be the Mapuche's best interests at heart, the solution is once again one of centralised action, of which the Mapuche are recipients, rather than the protagonists. This paternalistic attitude is not dissimilar to that of US anthropologist Louis C. Faron, whose book "The Mapuche Indians of Chile" appeared in the same period (1968), when he writes: "The Mapuches must become educated, not only in the three R's in Spanish, but to the prevailing system of values in Chilean society."[21]

A programme that was much more participatory, and much more aware of the contribution that Mapuche knowledge could make to Chilean society as a whole, was to be found in the area of public health. The "programme of intercultural health" was a programme, implemented by a medical team including Mapuche members in the area of Malleco and Cautín, which combined advances in Western medicine with elements of ancestral Mapuche medicine, emphasising the role of the *machi* in the curative progress.

The progressive nature of this programme becomes all the more evident when we see how dangerous it was perceived to be by Pinochet and his cohorts. Chilean historian Carlos Ruiz Rodríguez states that:

> "After the *coup d'état* of 11 September, the intercultural health team was cruelly persecuted: the generals of the coup considered that the activity they performed was highly subversive. They considered that if some left-wing professionals were working with the Mapuches, the most marginalised sector in Chilean society, then it could only be with the intention of stirring up revolt among them."[22]

By the time of the 1973 coup there were estimated to be 40 or so Mapuche organisations, ranging across the political spectrum, but many of these either disbanded or went underground, having been outlawed. To survive they would have to lie low and bide their time. Let us now look at the Argentine government's legislative attitude to the Mapuche.

The Argentine State and the Mapuche

In contrast with Chile, where legislation has been slow in recognising the existence of its indigenous peoples, Argentina has taken great care from its very beginnings to involve its original inhabitants in its national aspirations. In word, if not in deed.

In 1810 Manual Belgrano took it upon himself to devise new norms to guarantee the liberty and equality and the Guaraníes who had lived under the Jesuit régime. The General Assembly of 1813 eliminated such oppressive Spanish practices as the *encomienda* (forced labour and tribute to the *conquistadors*) and *mita* (forced yet paid labour, especially in mines) with most of this legislation drafted in Quechua, Aymara and Guaraní, as well as Spanish.

The Mapuches did not appear on these documents since at that time the area where they lived was considered to be beyond the southern frontier of Argentina.

The National Constitution of 1853 - which was in force till 1994 - established (in Chapter IV, part II, title 1, article 67, paragraph 15) that it is the responsibility of Congress "to provide for the security of the frontiers, to preserve the peaceful treatment of the Indians and promote their conversion to Catholicism."[23]

According to Sarasola, these few words summarise the three strands of the government view of Argentina's indigenous peoples, the recognition of the internal frontiers separating two worlds, the paternalistic spirit behind the expression "peaceful treatment", and the lack of respect for their religiosity inherent in the imperative of their conversion.[24]

The Conquest of the Desert also required some legal basis; Law 947 of 4 October 1878 sanctioned the campaign, but Law 1532 of 1884 also showed the "higher purpose" of the massacres under way, as it provided for the establishment of missions to assist the Indians by "drawing them gradually towards civilised life."[25]

There were elements of paternalism even in the midst of the attempts at the most progressive legislation. In 1904 President Roca's Minister of the Interior, Joaquín González, appointed the Spaniard Juan Bialet Massé to travel the length and breadth of Argentina to survey and report on the condition of the working classes in the "Interior", including its indigenous people.

Following a visit to El Chaco, Bialet Massé reported:

"The condition of the Indian is that of an incompetent, within the precise terms of civil law: he does not know the language of the country, he does not know how to read or write, nor does he have any idea of the legal relations, nor knowledge of the laws of the country, and barely of the most elemental ones of natural law. As a consequence, the existence is necessary of some institution to intercede for the Indians in their relations with society as a whole [...]."[26]

Though Bialet Massé's recommendations were not immediately implemented, the idea of the creation of an "institution to intercede for the Indians" was subsequently taken up with relish. Between 1912 and 1980, no less than fifteen different bodies were created by nine different presidents[27]. This would all seem to denote almost an excess of care; the truth is rather that the actions of these various bodies were erratic and mostly inconsequential, mainly due to confusion over continually changing jurisdiction.

The institutional process in terms of the indigenous peoples over the years could fairly be described as "one step forward, two steps back." For example, a small step forward was taken in relations between the Argentine state and its indigenous peoples with the creation of the *Consejo Agrario Nacional* in 1940, by Law 12.636, one of the aims of which was to hand over the ownership of land to the country's indigenous peoples, and to establish "the régime for the working of this land, also taking into account their customs and working methods" (art. 66). The steps back came three years later, as decree 10.063 of 28 September 1943 called for the incorporation of the indigenous peoples into "civilised life": "to this effect, the elementary instruction and the teaching of the Catholic religion must be imparted, as essential means of achieving this incorporation." Such dubious progress can also be said to have denoted Yrigoyen's periods in office.

Yrigoyen: progress and repression

It was the Radical Party government of Hipólito Yrigoyen (1916-1922) that recognised the valuable contribution of Argentina's indigenous peoples to society, rather than their perceived incompetence. The production of indigenous textiles was promoted to replace the unnecessary importation of foreign products, and article 135 of the draft bill for the Employment Code presented to the Chamber of Deputies on 8 June 1921 stated that "there will be no difference between the work of Indians and those of other workers." The draft bill was not passed, but its egalitarian aims were clear. The Yrigoyen government also made the first tentative attempts at expropriation to resolve the problem of indigenous territories, but these were soon reversed by Uriburu's 1930 coup.

Ironically, the country that was throwing its arms wide open to immigrants in the 19th century would come to see them as the source of all its ills before the 20th had come of age. Protection of the frontiers becomes an obsession, to the point of paranoia. An exponent of this obsession was Miguel Cané – in another irony, actually born in Uruguay - who drafted the xenophobic Law No. 4.144, the so-called "Residence Law", which the National Congress sanctioned on 22 November 1902, to authorise the Executive Power to expel foreigners from the country. In his words: "Honour and respect to the pure remnants of our native group (*grupo patrio*); each day, we Argentines diminish. Let us save our legitimate predominance."[28]

During the period that Yrigoyen presided over, the elite became ever more fearful that the working class immigrants arriving in the country were bringing dangerous elements with them, with subversive ideas such as anarchism and communism. They came to be associated with delinquency and disorder, and it is

Mapuche women demonstrate in traditional dress. Photo: IWGIA's archive

in this context that the nostalgic image of the noble gaucho, with his stoicism and simple, honest values, came to flourish.

During Yrigoyen's presidency, the culmination of the extreme reaction to immigrants and their dangerous ideas was the violent suppression of the strikes of the metal workers of Vasena in what became known as the *Semana Trágica* (Tragic Week) of January 1919, which resulted in the deaths of a number of workers, and the massacre of over 1000 rural workers in the far southern province of Santa Cruz in November 1921, meticulously documented by Osvaldo Bayer in his La Patagonia Rebelde. Many of the victims of this massacre were Chilean, and we may presume that many of them were Mapuches, whom the Argentines called *Chilotes*.

Such events foreshadowed the repression that was to come in the 1970s. US historian Sandra McGee Deutsch, who specialises in the history of the far right in Argentina, has written on the beginnings of the Argentine Patriotic League, the first example in Argentina of the state and private civilians working jointly for the purpose of repression. In her book Counterrevolution in Argentina, 1900-1932, Dr McGee Deutsch explains the aims of the League:

"It would stimulate the feeling of Argentinism among inhabitants of all religions, political parties, ages and income levels. League members would encourage the celebration of national holidays and award prizes for the best works on Argentine history, liberalism and social harmony, in order to counter anarchist propaganda. The group would instil love for the armed forces and convince the public that it was an honour to serve in the institutions that protected Argentine homes, order and liberty."[29]

The organisation was not only strong in Buenos Aires, but spread throughout the provinces, including Patagonia. There it was organised into brigades: local brigades, women's brigades, tradesman's brigades, these often promoted by the bosses to prevent the formation of trades unions, and even indigenous brigades, emphasising the threat to them of unfettered immigration.

Yrigoyen is not much loved by Argentina's indigenous peoples, also because it was his government that, with decree 7112 of 4 October 1917, established 12 October - the day of the "discovery" of America - as a national holiday, denominating it *Día de la Raza* (Day of the Race). The intention of the decree was twofold: to make a diplomatic gesture of friendship towards Spain during the fraught period of WWI, and to establish a spirit of unity in diversity in Argentina around the Spanish language. This is shown by this extract from the flowery text of the decree:

> "Therefore, it being eminently fair to consecrate the festivity of the date in homage to Spain, the progenitor of the nations to which she has given an immortal inheritance with the yeast of her blood and the harmony of her language, we must affirm and sanction the jubilant recognition, and the executive power of the nation: declares 12 October a national holiday [...]."

In the long term the intentions backfired, as each year the day is marked not only by celebrations, but counter-commemorations by indigenous groups, who consider Yrigoyen's decree racist and demand its derogation, and also rather guarded defence of the institution by its supporters.

Yrigoyen's two governments (1916-22 and 1928-30) saw a period of growth and modernisation in Argentina, with the appearance of the first motor cars, the development of the oil industry and the railway system. Yet as well as carrying the banner of progress, for the nation's indigenous people, the period also bore painful reminders of their past: such as in Chaco, on 19 March 1919, when in what is referred to as "the last malón", an indigenous group attacked Fortín Yunká, killing 16 occupants. In reprisal, Major Enrique Boy burned several indigenous settlements along the Río Pilcomayo to the ground. The context of the attack and reprisal was the fierce repression and exploitation of the local indigenous populations by commercial interests, such the quebracho timber yards in Chaco and the yerba mate plantations in Misiones. In a sense, the "Conquest of the Desert" was not yet over. Hence the ambiguity of the figure of Yrigoyen as far as the Mapuche are concerned.

Another attempt to encourage a spirit of interracial unity in Argentina came in the 1940s, during the anti-Yrigoyen Radical government of Roberto Ortiz. Unfortunately it was at the Mapuche's expense. It was a plan devised by Enrique Amadeo Artayeta, appointed the director of Francisco Moreno's Museum of Patagonia in 1940, to create what he called a "Tehuelche indigenous colony" in the territory of Santa Cruz. According to the plan, which was never implemented, an area would be established for "the procreation and conservation of the Tehuelche indigenous human race ... an autochthonous, exclusively Argentine race", counterposed with the "Araucanians", qualified as "Chileans." The purity of the Tehuelche race would entitle them to be Argentine, a truly bizarre idea in such a melting pot of immigration. Yet the thoroughbred Tehuelches would not have been allowed to practise their own "pure" religion:

> "The members of the colony will have to be baptised and belong to the Catholic religion, which would be fostered in them periodically and as far as is possible by members of our clergy."[30]

The plan was for domesticated Indians, the kind that pose for photographs in traditional costume, and show traditional deference to higher authority. Not the troublesome kind, like those of the Lof Prane.

Lof Prane: half a century of struggle

The Nahuel Pan Reservation was created by decree of 3 July 1908, in which the Argentine Government allotted 19 thousand hectares (extended to 21 thousand hectares by decree of October 1922) to "be occupied by the tribe of the native[31] Francisco Nahuel Pan", located in the "north east of the development of the *Colonia 16 de Octubre*, in the Territory of Chubut."

The allocating of this land was as a reward to the Mapuche-Tehuelches for expressing their desire to be Argentine citizens in the border dispute of 1902. Thirty years later, on 5 May 1937, the Argentine Government decided to "set aside those decrees", considering that "the purposes that were taken into account in ordering them have not been achieved, due to the absence of habits of work in the occupiers of same, who live precariously, revealing the absence of methodical work, order and morality and the absence of attention to the care of their properties, being undesirable elements that constitute a serious inconvenience for the settlers of that rich and prosperous zone." It is the last few words that reveal the motive for this decision: the area was potentially too rich to be left in the hands of mere "natives."

So the inhabitants of the reservation were forcibly removed by officials, calling them "thieves, idlers and drunkards"[32], and the reservation itself was divided up into plots that were shared out between the leading figures of the growing nearby town of Esquel.

With snow thick on the ground outside, I sat with Ana Prane in her warm sitting-room in a humble Esquel suburb, as the ritual *mate* gourd passed between us, and she told me of the history of her community. Ana is *werken* of the Lof Prane, and daughter of *lonko* Cipriano Prane, so she is responsible for keeping a record and recounting the trials and tribulations of her community's history.

She told me of the imprisonment after the Conquest of the Desert, and subsequent return:

> "*Lonko* Eduardo Prane, whose first wife had been killed in Choele Choel, remarried to a Mapuche - Lisa Llancaqueo - and other children were born. Their oldest son was Emilio Prane, followed by Cecilio Prane, Doña Julia Prane, and others. Their oldest daughter was a *machi*, María Prane. She married and had a large family, who were also part of the community."

She told me about the border dispute, and the government's pledge in a decree to recognise the area of Nahuel Pan as Mapuche-Tehuelche territory, an area amounting to around 22,900 hectares. Yet in 1937 the decree was ignored and all the community members were evicted:

> "The authorities not only sent the army in, but burned down their houses, right in front of them. *Lonko* Cipriano Prane, who was 19 years old at the time, was alone with his mother, because Emilio Prane - his father - was in Buenos Aires trying to stop it all. The ones who came already knew that the *winka* landowners that were coming to inhabit the southern area were in complicity with the State to arrange the eviction, to eject the people and nullify the decree that recognised that land as Tehuelche-Mapuche territory."

It was a family of Spanish origin, Amaya, previously owners of rice fields in Tucumán, who had pushed for the evictions. Gualberta Amaya was active in the Catholic church, and Lorenzo Amaya was no less than Argentine Minister of Justice, while Nicanor Amaya was a well respected doctor in Esquel. They had the support of their society friends and contacts. More than 200 families were thrown out onto the street, among them the Prane Community.

> "But Emilio Prane never let the injustice lie. Accepting all the consequences, he travelled by train, often secretly, he went on horseback from Chubut to Jacobacci, in the Province of Río Negro; he rode the boxcars of trains to

reach Buenos Aires with *werkens* from the other communities. They wanted to stop the eviction, yet they could not stop it because the agreement was in the name of the Nahuel Pan community. The Nahuel Pan brothers signed, because they were conned by the politicians, these landowners held a party for them and convinced them they should sign and hand over the community, this territory. They definitely didn't weigh up the consequences of what might happen to their own indigenous brothers and sisters, who were to end up on the street."

After being evicted, they went to live further east, in Lago Rosario, where they set up the community that still bears that name. The community nearly died out there. In despair, Emilio Prane killed himself by taking poison, worn down by the injustices he and his people had suffered.

In Lago Rosario life was tough, with a metre and a half of snow in winter, and horseback the only way to get around. One particular year, 1944, their animals died, and they had to find work elsewhere for food. The women had to resort to selling textiles and baskets. There were no doctors in the area, and one mother died during childbirth. Many of the community members decided to move to other places in the province, where they could find work, the women as domestic servants, the men as labourers. Those who stayed behind found it even harder. The younger generations regressed, because they had no access to education.

At the time *lonko* Cipriano found work on a cattle ranch owned by an Englishman, a certain Benjamin Cook. It was at about that time, in 1944 or thereabouts, that the land where the Pranes had lived went to the Defence Ministry. The Nahuel Pan community had their land returned – their reward for their complicity - but the claims of the other 8 communities were not recognised, and the land remained in the hands of the landowners.

In 1950 *lonko* Cipriano decided to leave the Cook estate and go with his two oldest children, Umberto and Marielita, to recover their land. In the years that followed, more children were born. He had ten children in all. The army did not allow him to build a house on the land he claimed, so he built it further up the slope. There he kept his animals, and pastured them lower down when the army were not around. He and his family stayed put.

"Two years later, they evicted him. He tells that a truck appeared. It was the army's. He was there with his family and other people from the community, who were there pasturing their animals for winter, lower down the valley. He was with his wife, and the army came, and bundled him into the truck. They beat him on the back and they took him and made him sign a paper. They demanded that he leave. So he had to abandon the land there and then, because of the extreme danger to his family."

And so they had to stay further up the slope, overlooking the land that was once theirs. For years they led a fragile coexistence with the army, playing cat and mouse with them. In the summer their animals pastured up in the hills, but in the winter they would go down onto the contested land. The place up the hill where they have their house is for summer pasture, very few hectares, where it snows heavily, and the animals die. The sheep, the cattle, or the goats all need a warmer climate. In the winter the army would usually stay away, because the weather was too bad for them to have any use for the land.

Perón the Tehuelche and the *Malón* of Peace

A chapter on the Argentine state's attitude to its indigenous population would not be complete without mention of the country's greatest demagogue, its most loved and hated figure.

Moira Millán is a Mapuche who does not hide her light under a bushel; she may be small, but she is passionately proud of her identity, and woe betide anyone who makes the mistake of disagreeing with her. Chatting to her son Juán, aged six, at the family home in Esquel, I asked him if his father is Mapuche. "No", he replied, "he's not Mapuche, he's Peronist." Maybe Juán will decide to become a Mapuche activist like his mother, or maybe he will be fired by the spirit of Perón, whose followers are often equally passionate and uncompromising.

Juán was named after President Juán Domingo Perón, known as the hero of the disinherited, the nationaliser of the railways, the enemy of the church. It is not widely known that the great man is claimed to have been part-Tehuelche himself.

In an article in the *La Nación* newspaper on 16 July 2000, journalist Enrique Oliva claims that, while they were in Caracas in 1958, Perón confessed to him that his mother was Tehuelche: "I feel very honoured to have Tehuelche blood, descending through my maternal line from those who populated Argentina centuries before the arrival of the colonisers."[33] Whether this claim is true or false, the fact remains that Perón was perceived by many of Argentina's indigenous peoples to be their President, the President of the dispossessed.

In Perón's first populist government (1946-55), for the first time large numbers of indigenous people received citizenship and the right to vote, thus swelling the ranks of Perón's Justicialista party. Although suffrage was clearly a step forward, indeed some were claimed to have been moved to remark "Perón has made us people", according to Morita Carrasco of the University of Buenos Aires, indigenous people were not necessarily freer as a result of this, as Perón "strengthened paternalism though one of its most perverse practices: political clientelism."[34]

Back in 1946, when Perón was second in command to General Edelmiro Farrell, shortly before becoming president himself, a group of Kollas from North-West Argentina arrived in Buenos Aires at the end of a long, gruelling march, known as the "Malón of Peace", to protest at the dispossession of their lands. They were received with military honours, accommodated in the old Hotel de Inmigrantes, and then summarily and forcibly sent back by train to their place of origin without any of their demands being met.

This episode is, I believe, indicative of an attitude on the part of the representatives of the state in its relations with indigenous peoples: that appearing to act to improve the latter's condition is more important than actually doing so. We have seen in this chapter that, to greater or lesser degrees, Allende in Chile and Yrigoyen and Perón in Argentina all attempted to present themselves as defenders of their countries' indigenous peoples, yet despite initial promises and high expectations, were unable to deliver any concrete improvement in conditions for the Original Peoples. Allende made the right noises in order to seek electoral support, but seemed to show no interest in Mapuche aspirations when in power; in any event, we will never know, as his experiment was cut short. Yrigoyen's period in office coincided with the political upheaval sparked by the Russian Revolution, and the immigrants so eagerly sought by Argentina in previous decades became a major problem for his government when they started to bring new "subversive" ideas with them, pushing the indigenous issue right off the agenda. The Mapuche were undoubtedly included in Perón's huge popular embrace, but there is little evidence that this was anything other than self-serving, the precursor of a "photo opportunity", a means of consolidating support, especially when viewed in the light of the treatment of the "Malón of Peace."

We can understand why it is that Fabián Pinta, *werken* of the community of Kuxaltuwe, near Cultral-Có, expresses a popularly held view among Mapuches when he says that "Now they no longer use the Remington, nor cut off ears. But they use something else: power and politics. The politicians are very hypocritical, because with one hand they welcome you and with the other they hit you."[35]

With the early seventies and the imposition of military rule, first in Chile then in Argentina, even the appearance of action in support of the Mapuche and the other native peoples of Argentina and Chile ceased. The coups of 1973 and 1976 marked a major step back for indigenous peoples' rights.

Notes

1   Gabriel Salazar, Historia contemporánea de Chile", Vol. II, LOM, Santiago, 1999, p. 137, cited in "Pacificación" by Luis Marciel O., contribution to the virtual congress on the Ethnohistory of the Mapuche by the Anthropology Dept. of the University of Chile (rehue.csociales.uchile.cl/antropologia/etnohistoria/simposio01/4.html).
2   These statistics are from "El proceso legal de abolición de la propiedad colectiva: el caso mapuche", by Jorge Calbucura (http://www.xs4all.nl/~rehue/art/calb1a.html).

3   Bengoa, *op. cit*. p. 372, cited by Jorge Calbucura in "El proceso legal de abolición de la propiedad colectiva: el caso mapuche", op. cit. The latter report has provided much of the information in this section.
4   "Historia de Chile", by Walterio Millar, p. 319, Zig-Zag, Santiago,1988.
5   Data from a report by Estanislao Gacitúa-Marió, of the World Bank, "Indigenous Peoples in Chile. Current Situation and Policy Issues", August 2000.
6   The lines are quoted in José Mariman, "Movimiento Mapuche y Propuestas de Autonomía en la Década Post Dictadura", Denver, USA 1997 (in the Rehue foundation website). The Spanish words are: "Las sangres de Valdivia y de Caupolicán, confundidas en una como regia alianza, dan al mundo una raza de soberbia pujanza."
7   José Mariman, *op. cit*.
8   I have borrowed the expression from Sara McFall, "Keeping Identity in its Place", Dphil Thesis in Social Anthropology, Oxford University 1998, p. 143.
9   José Bengoa, "Historia de un conflicto. El estado y los mapuches en el siglo XX", p. 100, Planeta, Santiago, 1999.
10 Bengoa, *op. cit*. p. 100.
11 Cited in José Mariman, *op. cit*.
12 Cited in Alejandra Krauss Valle, "El problema de los Mapuches exige una solución integral", article dated 22/5/2002, available on www.mapuche.nl. Alejandra Krauss is former Minister of MIDEPLAN.
13 Bengoa, *op. cit*. p. 98.
14 Bengoa, *op. cit*. p. 100.
15 Cited in "El pueblo mapuche y el gobierno de Salvador Allende y la Unidad Popular" by Carlos Ruiz Rodríguez, of the University of Santiago, p. 3.
16 Rodríguez, *op. cit*. p. 4.
17 Rodríguez, *op. cit*. p. 2.
18 A project by the Chilean Government with the United Nations Programme for Development and the UN Food and Agriculture Organisation (FAO), book published by ICIRA, Santiago, 1971.
19 Saavedra, *op. cit*., p. 89.
20 Saavedra, *op. cit*., p. 181.
21 "The Mapuche Indians of Chile", Louis C. Faron, Holt Rinehart and Winston, Inc. 1968, p. 109.
22 Rodríguez, *op. cit*. p. 14.
23 Carlos Sarasola Martínez, "Nuestros Paisanos los Indios", Emecé, Buenos Aires, 1992, p. 381.
24 Ibidem.
25 Sarasola, *op. cit*., p. 383.
26 Sarasola, *op. cit*., p. 384.
27 President Saenz Peña created the *Superintendencia de Misiones y Reducciones* (24/7/12) and the *Comisión Honoraria de Reducciones de Indios* (21/9/16) By decree.
    Pres. Ortiz created the *Consejo Agrario Nacional* by law (2/9/40).
    Pres. Farrell created the *Dirección de Protección del Aborígen* by decree (17/1/46).
    Pres. Perón created the *Comisión de Rehabilitación de los Aborígenes* by decree (11/9/53).
    Pres. Frondizi created the *Dirección de Asuntos Indígenas* (10/9/58), *Dirección Nacional de Asuntos Indígenas* (13/10/58) and the *Consejo Asesor de Asuntos Indígenas* (13/10/58), all by decree.
    Pres. Illia created the *Censo Indígena Nacional* by decree (27/5/65).
    Pres. Onganía created the *Servicio Nacional de Asuntos Indígenas* (9/5/68) and the *Departamento de Asuntos Indígenas* (7/7/69) by decree.
    Pres. Perón created the *Secretaría de Estado de Coordinación y Promoción Social* by decree (20/11/73).
    Pres. Videla created the *Secretaría de promoción y Asistencia Social* (13/5/76), the *Secretaría de Acción Social* (10/11/78) and the *Dirección Nacional de Promoción y Asistencia Social* (1/9/80), all by decree.
    Information based on Sarasola, op. cit. pp. 388-9.
28 Cited in José Feinmann, "La privatización del crimen", Página 12, 26/1/2003.
29 Dr McGee Deutch was interviewed by Clarín on 27/8/2000, "Genealogía de la derecha argentina."
30 Cited from an article by Osvaldo Bayer in Página 12 on 22/11/97, "Argentinos de raza pura."

31 The Spanish word used is "indígena", which has to be translated into "Indian" or "native", as no noun exists in English corresponding to the adjective "indigenous." The use of the word "tribe" ("tribú" in Spanish) is also interesting; I doubt whether the extended families of the first Welsh settlers of the area were referred to as "tribes."
32 These are classic insults used against Argentina and Chile's indigenous peoples; the theoretical underpinning of these racist slurs is discussed in chapter 10, "Cabecita Negra."
33 "Perón Tehuelche", by Enrique Oliva, "La Nación", 16 July 2000.
34 "El movimiento indígena anterior a la reforma constitucional y su organización en el Programa de Participación de Pueblos Indígenas", Morita Carrasco (http://lanic.utexas.edu/project/etext/llilas/vrp/Morita_Carrasco.htm).
35 Cited in the article "Gente de la tierra" on the website of the Argentine national Pastoral Aboriginal team - Endepa (www.endepa.org.ar).

THE JACKBOOT RETURNS:
THE MAPUCHE UNDER THE DICTATORSHIPS

"Indigenous peoples do not exist. We are all Chileans."
General Augusto Pinochet

It is hard for us in a liberal democracy to imagine the horror that is unleashed when a country's military sets about systematically destroying a section of its own population. Yet that is precisely what happened during the Pinochet period in Chile (1973-1989) and the period leading up to and during the "Dirty War" in Argentina (1976-1982). In chapter seven we see how the general repression affected the Mapuche in particular. We also see why many Mapuches – in contrast with the *winkas* - see these dictatorships not so much as an interlude, an aberration, but as an intensification of what went before and what was to come after. This view is supported if we consider the importance that the Argentine Junta devoted to commemorating the centenary of the desert campaigns in 1979, and the fact that in Chile, even in democracy, the "glories of the army" are still celebrated every year, even - sadly and ironically - by some Mapuches. Yet this is not to downplay the horror of the years of repression: when Leticia Veraldi became one of Argentina's thousands of "disappeared", for the "crime" of wanting to work with the Mapuche, for which they are still grateful to her today; and when Pinochet visited the Temuco area, bringing death to scores of Mapuches, exile to the luckier ones.

1979: the Argentine military's triumphalist centenary

Some have claimed that the horror of Argentina and Chile's *desaparecidos* was neither new nor unique, that their indigenous people were in fact the first "disappeared." Argentine writer David Viñas, who wrote the work "Indios, ejército y frontera" in 1982, during the dictatorship, is convinced that there are strong parallels between the planned extermination of the Mapuche in 1880 and the disappearances in Argentina. In both cases there was an attempt to create a new social, political and cultural order; what he calls "two disappearances in function of the need to eliminate all those who lay outside the rationalist power networks."[1]

Working on his book, Viñas could not help but notice the triumphalism that accompanied the celebrations of the centenary of the desert campaigns in 1979, which occurred during Videla's dictatorship, with the publication of commemorative books, plans of battles and even the minting of coins in "Homage to the Centennial of the Campaign of the Desert", all of which denoting a uniformity and a continuity of purpose.

Like the ideologues of the Conquest, such as Sarmiento, Echeverría and Alberdi, who spoke of nationhood and civilisation against barbarism and savagery, Jorge Rafael Videla also employed grand terms, yet his intellect was far more mediocre than his illustrious predecessors, according to his biographer, Vicente Muleiro[2]. Videla was the banality of evil personified: not eloquent, but able to take 30,000 lives to implement a policy, to accomplish a mission.

The generals were very interested in emphasising the similarities between Roca's "noble" endeavour and the mission they had taken upon themselves. But what was this mission? In the most Orwellian perversion of meaning, they claimed that by abolishing the Constitution and depriving thousands of life and liberty they were safeguarding the freedom of the republic. This was explained by the Commander-in-Chief of the Army, Member of the Military Junta, Lieutenant General Roberto Viola, in a speech on the Day of the Argentine Army, 29 May 1979[3], four days after Independence Day:

> "The worst thing is not the loss of life; the worst thing is to lose the war. For that reason, the Army, which today has restored the value of life, can say to the country that we have carried out our mission. [...] blameless families, affected by the pain, are also Argentinian. The Army knows this and feels this. Its only explanation is the liberty that our homeland entrusted to it for safekeeping."

So by killing, the army has "restored the value of life", and by repression it has safeguarded liberty; such chillingly oxymoronic statements are reminiscent of 1984's "freedom is slavery" or *Arbeit macht frei* on the gates of Auschwitz.

One clear example of the military's desire to create associations with the Conquest of the Desert was the "National Congress of History on the Conquest of the Desert" that was held in 1979 and in the town of General Roca. Yet despite the congress's clear intention to glorify the conquest and, by reflection, the dictatorship, it was not such a smooth ride down memory lane. Pursuing his own agenda, historian Rodolfo Casamiquela used the event to criticise General Roca and praise his disgraced predecessor, Juan Manuel de Rosas: he declared that Roca's state "had time to get to know at least the ethnic configuration of the north of Patagonia, and yet made war on the *caciques* as though they had all been Araucanians"[4]. In contrast, in Casamiquela's view, that pariah of the Argentine establishment, Rosas, had a much greater understanding of the indigenous people of the "desert." Casamiquela was speaking to deaf ears, as it was never the aim of either Roca or Videla's military junta to understand the Mapuche, only to eliminate them.

The city of Neuquén celebrated the centenary of 1879 with the construction of the Plaza de las Banderas, inaugurated in 1979, with its 33 flagpoles, representing the regiments that were present in the Conquest.

1979 also marked the 75th anniversary of the founding of the city, a further cause for celebration. A special publication was prepared to mark the recurrence, "Neuquén: 75 Años de Capitalidad" (Neuquén: 75 Years as a Capital)[5]. The book too was full of battle plans, together with a number of monographs by historians favoured by the régime. One such historian was Mirta Inés Ragio, a teacher at the Escuela Normal in Cipolletti, who stressed civil society's debt to the military:

> "Once the Campaigns of the Desert had finished, they left sowed behind them a new stage of greatness and prosperity for the Nation. But that great epic that allowed two-thirds of Argentinian Territory to enjoy the benefits of freedom and the republican norms of its political organisation was the fruit of numerous military expeditions carried out first by the Spaniards (1536-1810) and then by the Argentinians (1810-1917). This demonstrates to us that this is a secular battle that has occupied a lengthy period of our history (...)."

In her unquestioning devotion to authority, the redoubtable Ms Ragio is reminiscent of the character played by Norma Leandro in the Argentine film "La historia oficial", the history teacher who never questions the official history, and refuses to acknowledge the existence of the casual brutality of the régime with which her business man husband is associated until it is applied directly against her. Such unquestioning teachers saw it as their duty to monitor their students for signs of subversion.

The story of Leticia Veraldi, disappeared 4 July 1977

Schools were among the institutions where the power of the military was felt most strongly, and not only through the daily raising of the flag and singing of the national anthem. It was at their schools that Argentine youngsters, far from being safe, were at their most vulnerable, as an ill-advised critical comment by someone in a history lesson or during *educación democrática* (the highly ironic name given to the class we would call social studies) would mean they might be labelled a subversive.

For the "anti-subversive struggle" the Argentine territory was divided up into 5 zones, each of which was divided into subzones, and these in turn into areas, each with its own commanding officer and force of occupation. This was an army of occupation in its own country. In such a context, with a continuous, pervasive, indiscriminately violent military presence, all the communities could do was survive as best they could, fearful, more isolated than ever, their very existence denied by decree in some provinces. In her autobiography, Rosa Isolde Reuque Paillalef describes the pervasive fear of living under military rule:

> "Yes, people were scared, very scared. The fear was alive, you could almost touch it. "My dear", they'd say, "don't talk to that one, because look, that one was a communist, he had a red identification card." Or they'd say, "Look, that one's a snitch for the cops, this policeman always visits and he tells him everything." When I'd stay with someone, they'd always tell me the next day, 'don't tell anyone you slept here, don't mention me, don't write my name down anywhere'."[6]

There are very few Mapuches to be found on Argentina's lists of the disappeared, it is true, but this is because the military did not even accord them the dignity of considering them a threat. The report, *Nunca Más* (Never Again), by CONADEP, the National Committee for the Disappeared, does not list indigenous peoples as a category among the victims, who were listed according to their occupation or profession.

However, showing sympathy with the indigenous peoples was dangerous. The *Ruka*, the headquarters of the Co-ordinating Committee of Mapuche Organisations of Neuquén and other Mapuche organisations, was built in 2002. A smart, modern building in a poor suburb of Neuquén, it is the meeting-place for Neuquén's young urban Mapuches, the *warriache*. In the courtyard of the *Ruka* stands a commemorative wooden plaque, with the text carved onto it of which this is the translation:

> "The building that houses the *Ruka* was constructed with funds donated in memory of Leticia Veraldi, who was detained and disappeared in Cipolletti on 4 July 1977. She was 17 years old. She was active in her student centre and in the *Juventud Guevarista*. She wanted to work alongside the Mapuche. This donation and reparation is in homage to all those who were DISAPPEARED by the dictatorship. At the same time, it is a recognition of the *Coordinación de Organizaciones Mapuche* and all those who devote all their strength and the best of their lives to the struggle for the rights of people and peoples. 11-10-2002."

Wanting to work alongside the Mapuche was no crime, and was probably not even the reason why she was disappeared; this was most likely her extra-curricular activities at the Vicente López National College in the Province of Buenos Aires.

The Buenos Aires Centre for Legal and Social Studies (CELS) has published an extensive report, including eye-witness statements, on the disappearances during the "Dirty War", which enables us to piece together some of the circumstances surrounding Leticia's disappearance. The report describes the rationale behind the terrorising of schools:

> "[...] It becomes clear that the kidnapping of teenagers was part of a systematic plan that included the scrutinising of secondary establishments as such, and not only those occupying an important position on account of the number of future university students coming from them, or of the agitation registered during the period 1973/74. Beyond eliminating students who were actually or potentially involved in political movements, the aim was to destroy, under a cloak of terror, any possibility of the existence of extra-scholastic activities, whether ideological, trade union oriented, recreational or artistic, with the purpose of reducing the student to being a passive receptacle of cultural or doctrinal instructions.
>
> "The regimes founded on the doctrine of "National Security" were aware of the danger to the future of military dictatorships constituted by an education whereby each youngster is the protagonist of his or her own development as a person.
>
> Those responsible for this plan sought the complicity of the authorities and teachers in the establishments that fell under their gaze. We do not possess sufficient data to evaluate the importance of the collaboration provided to this end, nor to demonstrate the efforts of many teachers who attempted to safeguard the right of their students to be educated for democracy."

On 18 October 1976 persons who identified themselves to the Rector of the College as members of the Security Forces - an assertion that she checked by calling two telephone numbers that they provided - asked her for the records of students at the College, including sisters María and Leonor Zimmermann.

The visits were repeated throughout the week, during the course of which the men interrogated a number of students who were on the 1973 College student roll. One of those interrogated was Eduardo Muñiz.

When the youngsters told their parents about these interrogations, the latter presented themselves to the authorities, hoping to clarify matters. They were assured the teenagers had nothing to fear. So they continued to go to school as usual and to remain living in their respective homes. Which is where they were detained, at dawn on 23 October. The first to be taken was Eduardo Muñiz, then the Zimmermann sisters and a few minutes later, Pablo Fernández Meijide, María's boyfriend and a fourth year student at the College in 1975. They are all still missing[7]. A few hours later, the same group broke into the home of 16-year-old Leticia Veraldi, who had attended the Vicente López National College until the first months of 1976. She was not at home.

Leticia had managed to make it to Cipolletti, near Neuquén, and lie low for a few months with relatives, until the *milicos* finally caught up with her, and she was disappeared. Her file is No. 613 on the list of *desaparecidos* compiled by CO-NADEP.

Today the young Mapuche activists of the Neuquén Mapuche Co-ordinating Committee still draw strength from the commitment of the courageous *winkas* who risked - and in Leticia's case, lost - their lives in support of their struggle, and for the cause of tolerance and understanding between cultures.

In remembering the more than 30,000 *desaparecidos*, in a press release statement dated 24 March 2004, the young members of the Co-ordinating Committee made a point of remembering Leticia in particular:

> "As teenagers, we must make a special mention of Leticia Veraldi, who was detained and disappeared in Cipolletti on 4 July 1977. She was aged 17 and she dreamed of practising interculturality together with the Mapuche People. Her family has made it their commitment to help fulfil her dream, which today for us means strengthening and continuing our struggle as an Original People."

There are two Mapuches on the lists of the Argentina's disappeared. They are brothers José Francisco Pichulman Alcapan, aged 20, detained on 12 August 1976 at his home in Neuquén by a group of soldiers and seen for the last time alive by a guard in the Río Mayo detention centre, and Juan Raúl Pichulman Alcapan, aged 24, detained with his wife on 27 January 1977 in J.J. Gómez in Río Negro by a group of 20 to 30 people claiming to belong to the "combined forces." The brothers were from Chile, and they were disappeared through the collaboration between the Argentine and Chilean military regimes known as Operation Condor[8]. Like back in the time of Rosas and Bulnes, Argentine and Chilean military men were again working together to eliminate Mapuches.

Chile the neoliberal laboratory

Operation Condor was kept secret for many years by the military régimes involved in it. Ironically, the discovery of a different, wholly fictitious operation was used by General Augusto Pinochet to justify his coup. Plan Zeta was a supposed scheme to assassinate key members of the armed forces by persons loyal to Salvador Allende.

The Mapuche were claimed to be in on it, as the programme of intercultural health being implemented by doctors trained in Western medicine and traditional Mapuche healers in the 9th Region was presented as being highly suspicious, and so necessarily part of the alleged plot.

For the Mapuche, after the temporary improvements in the brief progressive parenthesis of Allende's popular government, on 11 September 1973 came the return of the stamping boot. With Pinochet the agrarian counter-reform began. The neoliberal ideology began to be executed in the countryside, with the return of land to estate owners who had had it expropriated, and the issuing of Decree-Law no. 701 of 1974, which authorised the National Forestry Corporation (CONAF) to provide subsidies for forestry expansion and to transfer land occupied by Mapuche communities to the forestry companies.

In 1978, with decrees 2568 and 2750, community property became private property; if just one member of a community requested this, then the land titles would become individual and protection of indigenous land would be lost. As a result, over 1,600 communities were divided, and 63,600 individual property titles were granted over 315,000 hectares.[9]

These reforms took a few years to devise and implement. The terror came almost immediately. And with it, the change for scores to be settled by the "wronged" landowners. According to Steve Stern, author of "Remembering Pinochet's Chile":

> "Landowners and other civilians supplied trucks and worked with *carabineros* to identify and locate troublemakers - that is, to take vengeance. More than in urban Santiago, the legacy of land invasions, official transfers of property and political conflictiveness had generated clusters of angry people ready and willing to work with the military forces and the *carabineros* to punish or execute individuals they considered subversives and troublemakers."[10]

Minutiae of repression

Iquique, Pisagua, Copiapó, Calama, Antofagasta, La Serena, Rancagua, Curicó, Talca, Linares, Cauquenes, Concepción, Victoria, Temuco and Valdivia. Places on a map, dots to be joined up to show a journey. This was the horrific itinerary of the Caravan of Death, a few months after the coup in Chile.

As the name suggests, the aim, apart from "dealing with subversives", was to paralyse society with fear. Chilean writer Luis Sepulveda describes this strategy:

"The true task of the Caravan of Death was to spread terror, unmistakable and unequivocal terror in the population and in officials with constitutional tendencies. The Caravan of Death made terror the sole method of the dictatorship, and it guaranteed the dominant class a dominated, quiet, socially disjointed country, submitting to the orders of the military. [...] In a Chile socially numb, with terror installed in every home, with the street forbidden during the curfew hours, it was easy to embark upon the first great neoliberal economic experiment, and it was also easy to declare it successful."[11]

Pinochet himself took the Caravan to Temuco, the "gateway to the Lakes", when he arrived by helicopter on 26 October 1973. He had declared that "in the zone of the Lakes there are extremists, so I have come to evaluate whether there is need to strengthen the forces or order another operation to exterminate them"[12]. Pinochet did not judge that normality had been established in the zone, as there were still some pockets of resistance, namely members of left-wing parties, trades union leaders and Mapuches. In that period, dozens of Pinochet's "extremists" were dragged away from their homes, often never to be seen again, or simply found shot in the street, in Temuco itself, in Pitrufquén, in Toltén, in Victoria.

In Puerto Saavedra, Mapuches Francisco Segundo Curamil Castillo, Mauricio Huenucoi Antil and Bernardo Nahuelcoi Chihuaicura were detained on the night when a contingent of soldiers from Temuco arrived in that locality. The next day their dead bodies were found by their families, riddled with bullets.

In Temuco itself, mainly *criollo* Chileans were murdered, while north of the city, in the small towns of Lautaro, Curacautín and Galvarino, it was the Mapuche population who paid the ultimate price, in the same kind of numbers as the dead of Temuco. In Temuco the victims were generally of extrajudicial executions, whereas in the Lautaro area they tended to be disappeared. The reason for this was simple: Temuco had detention centres, whereas Lautaro had fast-flowing rivers and plenty of open land for disposal of the bodies. The crime that these Mapuches had committed was occupying land that the local owners of large estates had their eyes on.

Other victims of Pinochet's "de facto" government were the thousands of Chileans, including Mapuches, who were forced to leave the country and go into exile, in Europe, North America and other Latin American states, in order to escape almost certain death.

Mónica Pilquil is a Mapuche who had moved to Santiago from Temuco with her parents. Her partner, by whom she was pregnant, disappeared after being arrested in July 1974. For three years she searched for him everywhere, in the police stations, hospitals, mortuaries, but could find no trace of him. Her position began to become dangerous when her links with anti-régime groups were discovered, so, with the help of CIME - The Intergovernmental Committee for European Migrations - she left for Europe and settled in Holland with her young son, marrying a Dutchman. She became a founder member of the Mapuche External Committee, founded in 1978, an umbrella organisation for the 600 or so Mapuches living in Europe. She now runs a bakery in the poor Santiago district of Cerro Navia.

Mónica describes her experience as an exile in the book "Flight from Chile. Voices of Exile":

> "I went to France first. It was so terrible to arrive there. Everything was so strange - it was like going from one landscape to another, a different world, people who talked differently. My sister and my brother-in-law had come to meet us, and then I remember that we slept in the home of some Chileans who lived in a big group there together in one house, because it was really expensive, I think. They rented the house for one family, then several got together, and there we were and I remember that my brother-in-law told jokes about Chile and people were really listening, like they were nostalgic to hear things about Chile."[13]

From France Mónica moved to The Netherlands, but she was always determined to return to Chile. That opportunity eventually presented itself with the return to democracy in 1990.

Mapuches and the glories of the army

As he slowly felt power slipping from his grasp, in 1988 Pinochet held a plebiscite, asking to be confirmed as President. To his dismay, the Chilean people voted "no."

You would think that after 16 years of de facto government, and Pinochet's reluctant retreat from power, the armed forces would be content to remain in the shadows, at least for a judicious period. Not so. Every year on the 19th September, they parade through Santiago to celebrate "The Day of the Glories of the Army", and representatives of the Mapuche people march with them. Many Mapuches are disgusted by the support given by members of their people to someone who has committed crimes against humanity

Reynaldo Mariqueo is another one of the dozens of Mapuches forced into exile in fear of their lives when Pinochet came to power. They were the lucky ones. Reynaldo was granted political asylum in Britain. He well remembers how tough the early years of his stay as a guest in this country were. No palatial home in Wentworth for him, just a modest house in Bristol. Reynaldo takes this view of the commemoration:

"As a Mapuche, like many brothers and sisters, it is totally offensive to me that they oblige our Mapuche children to parade during the celebrations of the Day of the Glories of the Army, just as it is for them to swear allegiance to the flag that represents the subjection of our people and the deaths of thousands of our ancestors. It is also humiliating for me that statues are put up in Mapuche ancestral territory to commemorate the bloodthirsty killers of our people."[14]

Though some Mapuches may downplay the support for Pinochet among their compatriots, it cannot be discounted so easily. In the 1988 plebiscite, even though the "no" vote won, interestingly it is believed that the majority of the Mapuches in the rural areas of Malleco and Cautín voted "yes", despite the repression that many of their *peñis* had suffered at his hands in the period 1973-75. The explanation usually offered for this is that it was functional and tactical, inasmuch as the policies of the dictatorship had favoured the cohesion of Mapuche communities, even assisting them in obtaining land titles (albeit not as "indigenous" communities as such, since for Pinochet these did not exist) and increasing access to electricity, whereas the supposedly more liberal governments, perhaps out of the best of intentions, were in fact detrimental to their interests. José Bengoa explains this in these terms:

"[After the Pacification] the Chilean authorities had the possibility of maintaining the social structure of Mapuche society; they had the possibility of handing over major land concessions, collective land title under the command of a *cacique*; the authorities had the possibility of allowing them a certain autonomous development. Yet what happened was precisely the opposite. Paradoxically, it was the military who fomented the maintaining of the community structure and the humanitarians, the liberals, the educators, the most pro-indigenous sectors, who fomented the dispersion and disintegration of Mapuche society."[15]

There are conservative elements in Mapuche society, just as there are in any society. Alejandro Saavedra Peláez is the writer of the book *Los Mapuche en la sociedad chilena actual*, which is in part a polemic against Bengoa's ideas on the Mapuche. Saavedra does agree with Bengoa, however, in identifying the existence of a clear right-wing Mapuche faction. In contrast with Bengoa, Saavedra believes that the Mapuche are not fundamentally different in political terms from the Chilean *campesino* and urban working classes, which he splits into three more or less equal groups, the conservative, the reformist and the revolutionary. The conservative Mapuches fall for the most part within the category of *Alessandristas* (followers of Jorge Alessandri Rodríguez, Chilean President 1958-64). According to Saavedra:

"Alessandrismo represented a failed attempt to maintain the existing society in those years [1960-73], modernising it and orienting it towards the right. This failure in relation to reformism and the emerging revolutionary tendencies was to incubate a movement, polarised towards the right, which would progressively orientate itself towards a military outcome."[16]

So it was that some Mapuches, fearing further unwelcome change to their way of life, preferred to characterise Pinochet as the devil they knew.

The desire of the military authorities to include Mapuches in their commemorations does not stem simply from the wish to further humiliate them, although there is undoubtedly an element of this. While often depicting modern Mapuches as godless and lawless degenerates, they have also often attempted to tap into the reservoir of courage and resilience that they represent as a people, or rather represented, as we are talking about the historical, rather than the actual people.

Pinochet himself, despite his violent persecution of the Mapuches, in their guise as dangers to national security, communist subversives and terrorists, was quite happy - by some accounts moved to tears - to receive the *toki kurá* (stone of command), presented to him on Temuco's Cerro Ñielol in 1986 by members of Mapuche who supported him. Some unconfirmed accounts place leading Mapuche politician Venancio Coñoepán among them. This act by Pinochet can perhaps be included within the "folkloric" view that the regime had of the Mapuche, which the Mapuche organisations, slowly growing in confidence, could take advantage of. According to Rosa Isolde Reuque Paillalef: "Our goal was not to be "folkloric." We weren't going to make a spectacle of our culture, turning it into a photo opportunity or using it for commercial gain. We weren't interested in making the dictatorship look good."[17]

By this time the extreme terror of Pinochet's early years in power had passed, and Mapuche organisations had already begun to re-emerge from hiding, the first being *Centros Culturales Mapuches*, created in 12 September 1978 as a response to Pinochet's decree 2568, which changed community property to private property, and linked with the Catholic Church. *Centros Culturales* was later to change its name to the *Asociación Gremial de Pequeños Agricultores y Artesanos Mapuche - Ad-Mapu*.

By the early eighties Ad-Mapu was becoming increasingly influential, and in 1981 its leaders organised a *nguillatún* outside Temuco, with several thousand people present. Due to its inability to establish any form of dialogue with the dictatorship, it was accused of coming more and more under the wing of the communist party, which led to a number of schisms later on. We will look in detail at Mapuche organisations in the return to democracy in the next chapter.

"The struggle of man against power is the struggle of memory against forgetting"[18]

In November 1984 the Argentine Commission of Disappearances - CONADEP - issued its report, *Nunca Más* (Never Again), on human rights abuses by the armed forces during the Dirty War. Since then the document has become an all-time best-seller in the country.

The report states that throughout the country there were 340 different places where torture was carried out. It is intended that each of these places of infamy will have a plaque outside it, indicating for what purpose it was used.

Yet as visitors to La Plata drive down the coast along the Avenida Martínez de Hoz, they may find it odd that the family of the dictators' Economy Minister and inventor of the *plata dulce* scam that ended in galloping inflation should be honoured with a place among the pantheon of famous men whose names adorn the city's major roads. We must not forget that this "Chicago boy" is a member of a famous Argentine dynasty, and that generations earlier another member of this illustrious family, also called José Martínez de Hoz, had founded the *Sociedad Rural*, the landowners' organisation that lobbied for the Conquest of the Desert.

José Martínez de Hoz the younger must have believed that he would never be truly forced to go away when, on leaving the Ministry of Economy in 1981, he menacingly remarked: "I am not saying farewell, I am just saying see you later." We can only hope his wish is not fulfilled.

In Chile many monuments stand to mark the atrocities committed under the all-seeing eyes of Pinochet (as he himself declared in October 1981: "Not a leaf moves in Chile if I don't move it - let that be clear"). There is the Park for Peace in Santiago, which during the dictatorship was a torture centre, known as Villa Grimaldi, and the Park of Peace in Temuco, inaugurated in April 2001.

One of the most moving memorials is a carved wooden cross, erected in remembrance of the 15 agricultural workers that were massacred in Liquiñe, near Villarica, a month after the coup. Liquiñe is an area in which many Mapuche families cultivated crops for their own subsistence, supplementing their income with seasonal work in the forests. Prior to the military coup, agrarian reform had spurred the community to organise itself and take a greater role in local decision-making. Training programmes were set up and steps taken to improve infrastructure by building schools and constructing roads.

Soldiers arrived in the area immediately following the coup, and along with *carabineros*, began mass detentions on September 18. On October 10, 1973 a military patrol arrested 15 men. Some were members of the Revolutionary Campesino Movement (MCR), while others were members of the farm workers' union. Others had no political affiliation whatsoever. After futile efforts to determine the whereabouts of the arrested men, one of the families pooled money to send a brother to Santiago, believing that all prisoners were held in the National Stadium. After several fruitless days outside the Stadium, he returned to Liquiñe without any news. It was later found out that the 15 men had been shot on the Villarica bridge and thrown into the Toltén river.

Perhaps the best way to render the clinical, systematic way that Mapuches were killed, with the methodical approach of the scientific experiment, is simply by giving a list of the names of the victims. Such a list has been compiled by the Spanish human rights NGO Equipo Nizkor, using information from Amnesty International.[19]

There are 88 names on the list; the first is Carlos Aillñir Huenchual, a farm worker aged 57, who was killed by extrajudicial execution in Temuco in November 1973, and the last name is Oscar Romualdo Yuufulén Mañil, also an agricultural worker, aged just 18, disappeared from Lautaro in June 1974.

Every one of these victims deserves to have his or her story told. As this is not possible here, we will tell one story, no more or less special than any of the others, the story of José Ignacio Beltrán Meliqueo, name eleven on the list.

José's story

José was married with 6 children, and worked as a farm labourer near Lautaro, in the Manuel Levinao Community. He is said never to have been involved in any political activity.

On the afternoon of 15 October, after having tea with his family, he went into town. While in Lautaro, at around 3pm, he was detained by police officers Domingo Campos Collao and Enrique Ferrer Valeze and taken to the police station. He was not unduly alarmed, as they were acquaintances of his. According to Steve Stern, "In the agrarian settings and provincial towns where *carabineros* were a familiar part of the lower middle class landscape and local kinship networks, how many people guessed wrong about the Chile they thought they knew?."[20]

José was probably not aware that some days earlier, on 4 October 1973, his cousin José Andrés Meliquén Aguilera and a friend, Sergio del Carmen Navarro Schifferli, had also been taken from their homes and detained by the same officers. Had they given his name under torture?

 The following day his wife, María Celinda Melihuén Mellado, went to the police station to report her husband missing. She was told that he had been interrogated there, but had been released. He never returned home, and was never seen alive again.

It would take the return to democracy for any light to be shed on this shadowy episode, and thousands of others.

Notes

1   Viñas was interviewed by *Acción Digital* on 15/07/03 (www.acciondigital.com.ar).
2   "He is surrounded by big words such as God, Fatherland, Family and Army, words that he cannot explain, that he cannot develop. It is amazing that such a banal man completed such a major genocidal task": Vicente Muleiro, in an article "Tras la personalidad de Videla" on BBC Mundo. com, 23rd March 2001.
3   Cited in the report of the Inter-American Commission on Human Rights, 1980, case number 2271 (www.iachr.org/countryrep/Argentina80eng/chap.3c.htm).
4   Cited in Vezub, *op. cit*. p. 37.
5   Published by Editorial Sur Argentino, Neuquén, 1979.
6   Rosa Isolde Reuque Paillalef, "When a flower is reborn. The life and times of a mapuche feminist", Duke University Press, 2002, p. 109.
7   www.geocities.com/CapitolHill/Senate/1137/desaparecidos/cels_4.html
8   Information from the Nunca Más website (www.nuncamas.org/investig/buscados/buscados_04.htm) and from "Terror sin fronteras: Chiloens víctimas de la Operación Condor" by Róbinson Rojas (http://www.rrojasdatabank.org/condor2.htm).
9   Data from a report by Estanislao Gacitúa-Marió, of the World Bank, "Indigenous Peoples in Chile. Current Situation and Policy Issues", August 2000.
10 Steve J. Stern, "Remembering Pinochet's Chile", Duke University Press, 2004, p. 72.
11 Luis Sepulveda, "La infame historia de la infamia", Le Monde Diplomatique, Chile edition, March 2001.
12 Cited in the Punto Final report, "Pinochet también comandó una Caravana de la Muerte", by Ana María Olivares (www.puntofinal.cl).
13 "Flight from Chile. Voices of Exile", by Thomas Wright and Rody Oñate, 1998, University of New Mexico Press.
14 From "Mapuches accused of being anti-patriotic by nationalist and racist Chileans", a press release by Mapuche International Link dated 30/9/98.
15 Bengoa, *op. cit*., p. 341.
16 Alejandro Saavedra Peláez, "Los Mapuche en la sociedad chilena actual", LOM Ediciones, Santiago, 2002, p. 95.
17 Rosa Isolde Reuque Paillalef, *op. cit*. p. 112.
18 From "The Book of Laughter and Forgetting", by Milan Kundera, Faber & Faber, London, 1982.
19 The information on José Ignacio Beltrán Meliqueo comes from the Memoria Viva website on Chile's Disappeared (www.memoriaviva.com) and from details kindly provided by Roberta Bacic, co-author with Durán Pérez and Pérez-Sales of "Muerte y desaparición forzada eb la Araucanía"; Roberta was a member of the Chilean Truth Commission, and ran the WRI programme "Dealing with the Past."
20 Steve Stern, *op. cit*., p. 81.

NEW TREATMENT OR SAME OLD TRICKS?
THE MAPUCHE IN THE RESTORED DEMOCRACIES

The subject of chapter eight is the painful return to democracy, and the two states' difficult balancing act between the need for reparation and the need for reconciliation, and the requirement to unearth the truth without reopening old wounds.

Also considered in this chapter is the relationship between state bodies and Mapuches. The early nineties saw the emergence of many new Mapuche organisations, particularly in Chile, and the Chilean state created CONADI, the Commission for Indigenous Development; as to this body's success, the jury is still out. Likewise the Commission of Historical Truth and a New Relationship, which was supposed to herald a new dawn of relations between the state and indigenous people. The equivalent to CONADI in Argentina is INAI, the National Institute for Indigenous Affairs, which has also so far mainly excelled in paying lip service to Mapuche aspirations.

Chile's long silent march of reparation

For all societies of the world death has a special significance, and the Mapuche are of course no exception. For them death is a major painful event, but one necessary in life.

The Mapuche believe that imminent death is presaged by the sighting or hearing of certain forms of natural phenomena: the song of certain birds or the presence of certain insects. It is also announced in *pewma*.

The *eluwún* is the ceremony the community performs to send off the member of the *lof*. It consists of a social ritual, in which the whole community participates on the last day of the vigil, when food and drink are shared out, and there are invocations for the deceased person to have a peaceful journey.

The place of rest, the *eltun*, is a space of great importance, as it symbolises the reunion of the deceased person with his *mapu*, his reintegration with the land.

Burial of José Beltrán in 1992. Photo: courtesy of Roberta Bacic

When the body is laid in the earth in the *eltun*, the belongings - clothes, jewellery, ornaments - are deposited too. *Mapugetuy* is an expression denoting the transmutation of the person from the state of *che* to the new state of *mapu*, becoming earth. The *eltun*, is the space where the spirit may return to communicate with descendants and reorientate, teach, warn and continue teachings to new generations.

Democracy had returned to Chile. Rumours had been circulating for some time about "illegal inhumations: nameless graves in Lautaro Cemetery, where it was suspected that victims of the repression had been disposed of. One marked "NN (*ningun nombre* - no name) was particularly suspicious.

Eventually, in 1992, forensic anthropolists were called in to examine and identify the remains being found in the Lautaro area. They worked tirelessly for seven months. The grave marked "NN in Lautaro Cemetery was exhumed, and several bodies were found, including that of José Beltrán.

The police officers involved in the detention and subsequent disappearance of José Beltrán, his cousin and friend were interviewed, but they would only confirm that in 1973 they had been policemen stationed in Lautaro, and denied any involvement in or knowledge of the detention and disappearance of the three victims.

The Beltrán family was told that the state would take care of the cost of the burial. Undertakers chose the best coffin - money was no object.

José remains were collected by his relatives from the Lautaro Courthouse, and the hearse was slowly and solemnly accompanied to the family's house in the

Manuel Levinao Community, where it was placed outside the house for the vigil by relatives and friends.

After the vigil came the most intimate stage of the burial, when the ox cart carried José coffin to the *eltun*, with only his relatives walking beside the remains on this stage of his journey.

For the final burial, José relatives were rejoined by friends, government officials and members of NGOs, and his closest relatives lowered the coffin into the grave.

Mapuches do not believe that death separates them from their loved ones. In the case of José Ignacio Beltrán Meliqueo and his family at least, the final violent separation of disappearance had been averted.

Democracy had returned to Chile. The sceptics among us would say that Pinochet was able eventually, albeit reluctantly, to stand down because his job was done, as the repression had been sufficiently internalised by Chile's citizens, and the structures of control only required the occasional fine-tuning. This is certainly the view of a number of Mapuche organisations, those who have borne the brunt of post-Pinochet repression. According to a report by the Aukache organisation of Buenos Aires:

> "The Chilean state is using the same laws and repressive apparatus that was designed by the military dictatorship. From late '98 to mid-'99, for instance, more than 100 people were arrested, on repeated occasions the Chilean police and private the guards of the landowners have hit, tortured and threatened with death the members of various communities and non-indigenous people showing solidarity with their struggle. It has also been reported that several murderers who belonged to the National Intelligence Office (DINA, Pinochet's secret service) are today working in the landowners' armed groups."[1]

A reminder of how cruelly negligent the Chilean army can still be came in May 2005, when, in what became known as a "snow tsunami, 45 young army recruits – many of them Mapuches – were killed when they were caught in a freak snowstorm during drills on the Antuco volcano. The body of Mapuche Silverio Avendaño Huilipán was the last one to be found, two months later.

Although the repression has continued, less openly and more privately, since 1990 the Chilean state has endeavoured to identify and pay its debt to the victims of the dictatorship, including Mapuches. The recovery and reburial of José Beltrán is just one example of that process in action.

The new government that came to power in March 1990, under President Patricio Aylwin, realised that there were deep wounds that needed to be healed. *Muerte y Desaparición Forzada en la Araucanía: Una Aproximación Etnica*, by Teresa Durán Pérez, Roberta Bacic and Pau Pérez Sales, an important work for those wishing to understand these wounds and the healing process, says the following:

> "The political repression caused great damage and pain. The consequences of what happened affected families, communities and the whole country. Furthermore, what happened was denied and the truth of the facts was experienced as something private, producing a distortion of reality itself. However, the denunciation of the facts by the human rights groups, the various organisations that resisted the dictatorship, international solidarity and the weakening of the ruling government, among other factors, meant that through elections (a very ingrained practice in our country) an end was put to almost 17 years of military government and a civilian one took charge.
>
> With the coming to power of the first President, there was a huge ceremony in Santiago's National Stadium, during which he undertook to face the problem of the violations of human rights and recognised the disappearances, executions, political imprisonment, exile and other deterrents used by the military government. Because of this and other signs and manifestations, a large number of citizens had expectations that what they had lived through would be recognised and that the new government would repair, as far as possible, the damage caused."[2]

President Aylwin perhaps had good reason to wish to make amends. He had supported the coup that brought Pinochet to power, no doubt expecting the reins to be handed over to him once Allende was removed and order was restored. That process took 17 years.

By Supreme Decree no. 355 of 25 April 1990, the President set up the National Commission of Truth and Reconciliation. The Commission formed work groups, gathered together the information compiled by the human rights organisations and other documentation, and travelled all over the country to work, through the provincial government structures - a fact that aroused resentment and suspicion among many who had suffered as a result of the actions of these same structures - and drew up a report in 3 volumes. As a result of the report, the National Congress approved law 19.123 of 8 February 1992, which created the National Corporation for Reparation and Reconciliation, which was empowered to pay compensation for economic damages, provide pensions for relatives of victims, medical and education facilities and exemption from military service. It was from the National Corporation for Reparation and Reconciliation's pot that the funds came to pay for José Beltrán's funeral. Neither the victims' families nor their organisations were consulted on how to set up the commission. Let us briefly look at some of these organisations.

Auki Wallmapu Ngulam: The Council for All Lands

The period when Pinochet felt his grip on power loosening coincided with the formation of one of the Mapuche's most important organisations. In late 1989 came the creation of *Auki Wallmapu Ngulam* (The Council of All Lands), formed by socialists who had split from the main body of Ad-Mapu because they were strongly against voting in the 1988 plebiscite, which they considered corrupt and fraudulent. Their rally cry was "half the people voting, half the people fighting for their rights. They sided with the latter half.

Mapuche historian José Mariman refers to the organisation as "fundamentalist[3], and indeed it is traditionalist inasmuch as it claims its authority from the traditional figures of *lonkos*, *machis* and *werken*. Its aim is to establish a political authority for the Mapuche, which would be autonomous from and run in parallel to the existing state authorities, although exactly how these two systems would operate in parallel has not been clearly explained. It claims that the effect of the Chilean political parties on the Mapuche movement has been "neutralising, and led to the instrumentalisation of Mapuches within the parties' own power games.

Although closing themselves off from contacts with Chilean political parties, over the years *Auki Wallmapu Ngulam*, and particularly their charismatic leader Aucán Huilcamán, have sought to establish contacts with international organisations, particularly under the auspices of the United Nations.

When asked in 1999 whether he expected to find sympathisers in the international community, Aucán answered:

"What role do they play? It is relative, and can be more or less decisive. For example, disseminating information abroad about the situation of the Mapuche in Chile is not a bad thing, because the Chilean state does not recognise the existence of another people, only Chileans. It is very positive that there are bodies that highlight hidden situations, as is the case of the Mapuche and the indigenous peoples generally. Chile is the only country in South America that does not have constitutional recognition of indigenous peoples. It could be said to be the most retrograde state in America. It is the most anti-indigenous state."[4]

In recent years *Auki Wallmapu Ngulam* has become increasingly sidelined by the other Mapuche organisations; this is mainly attributed to their tendency to "go it alone and not work with other groups. The organisations representing young urban Mapuches consider them too traditionalist. Pedro Cayuqueo, editor-in-chief of Azkintuwe magazine, summed them up as follows: "Aucán and *Auki Wallmapu Ngulam* have a traditional vision of the Mapuches, of the countryside. They are another generation, and there has been a generational change[5]. This generational change is what Rosa Isolde Reuque Paillalef jokingly refers to as the split between the "pot-bellied" line (*línea guatona*) and the "long-haired" line (*línea chascona*).[6]

Although *Auki Wallmapu Ngulam* are more marginalised now, the Mapuches have no shortage of other organisations to represent them. There are umbrella organisations, such as the *Coordinadora de Instituciones Mapuches* (CIM) or the more confrontational *Coordinadora Arauco-Malleco*, women's organisations, such as the *Corporación de Mujeres Aukiñko Zomo*, urban and students' organisations, such as *Resistencia Mapuche*, organisations representing specific ethnic identities within the Mapuche mocvement, such as *Identidad Territorial Lafkenche* and the *Consejo General de Caciques Williche de Chilo*, and organisations based abroad, such as Mapuche International Link in the UK. New organisations are born as quickly as older ones become irrelevant. The state counterpart of the many Chilean Mapuche organisations is the one body set up to address their concerns, CONADI.

CONADI, the solution or the problem?

In April 1987, Pope John Paul II made his one and only visit to Chile. He visited Temuco, where he took the time to address a large crowd and to meet with representatives of the Mapuche people. This is an extract from his address:

> "I know that [...] in the life of the beloved Mapuche people there are many difficulties and problems. You have often been the object of injustices and exclusions. But do not allow yourselves to be seduced by those who offer tempting and illusory solutions to your problems, as are hatred and violence, or that of the unjustified abandonment of the countryside and your own values, often to find yourselves with an even more precarious and difficult life." [7]

Within a couple of years of this speech, another frail old gentleman was removed from the centre stage of Chilean political life, as democratic government returned to Chile.

The Pope's visit seemed to tweak the consciences of Chile's Catholics, such as new Christian Democrat President Patricio Aylwin, and catalyse them into activity to improve the situation of the Mapuche. In 1990, keeping to a commitment he had made in signing the Nueva Imperial Agreement of 1989, he halted the division of Mapuche land that had gone on under Pinochet and created the Comisión Especial de Pueblos Indígenas (CEPI), with the purpose of realising programmes and projects for the development of the indigenous peoples of Chile.

This organisation proposed a body of laws that, when submitted to Parliament, was transformed into Law 19.253, the law by which the National Commission for Indigenous Development (CONADI) was established.

Article 1 of the law states:

"It is the duty of society in general and the State in particular, through its institutions, to protect and promote the development of the indigenous peoples, their cultures, families and communities, adopting adequate measures to these ends, and to protect indigenous lands, to provide for their adequate exploitation, their ecological equilibrium and to support their expansion."

At the same time as the creation of the state agency CONADI, an Indigenous Land and Water Fund was established. This fund was to be used to buy land, which would then be returned to those communities that had laid legitimate claim to them. From 1994 to 1999, approximately 112,000 hectares of land were purchased, to the benefit of 27,000 families.[8]

Other funds were set up to benefit Chile's indigenous peoples, such as the Fund for Indigenous Development, in charge of financing plans and special programmes to support the development of indigenous peoples and communities, and the Culture and Education Fund, to foment, promote, administer and execute programmes dedicated to recognising, respecting and protecting indigenous cultures.

Another very useful fund was the National Programme to Support Indigenous Students in Higher Education, which was used to finance the establishment and maintenance of indigenous student halls of residence, which has become a real lifeline for Mapuche students away from their communities. There are nine student residences (*hogares*) in Chile today, one in Iquique, one in Santiago, three in Concepción, three in Temuco and one in Punto Arenas, but they cannot keep up with the demand and are bursting at the seams; such pressures have led to open conflict between Mapuche students and the authorities, discussed in chapter 10. Adán Cheuquepil, a journalism student who runs the *Hogar* in Santiago, explains the problem:

Peñis (Mapuche brothers) are constantly arriving looking for a roof and they stay a month or two until they find somewhere else. There must be at least a hundred of us here who need a place to live to be able to study, and the place is only built to house 25." [9]

Although some progress had been made in attempting to cater for the needs of the nation's indigenous peoples, it is significant that there has not been any constitutional recognition of their existence, nor the ratification of ILO Convention 169, which recognises and extends the collective rights that have been denied to all nations without states.

Since its inception, to say that CONADI has been beset with problems would be an understatement. In the Nueva Imperial Agreement, the indigenous organisations had been led to believe that it would be an indigenous agency, and that it would have clout. In fact it is now widely believed that the government has undermined it, making it powerless, with preference being given to big business interests close to the government.

A clear indication of this came when Domingo Namuncura, the Mapuche National Director of CONADI from 1996, was dismissed in 1998 because of his opposition to the Ralco Dam Project, which we will consider in depth in chapter ten.

When she was interviewed for this book in her office in Santiago in December 2001, Cecilia Alzamora, CONADI National Communications Officer, explained some of the tribulations and machinations of her agency:

> "CONADI has little influence over government policy. It is dependent on Mideplan [the Ministry of Planning and Cooperation], which is funded by the Ministry of Finance. As it is a technical body, its influence is relative. When the director is politically close to the President, he has more influence. In such cases he is sometimes not very popular with the Indians. [Ricardo] Lagos designated the current director.
>
> [Eduardo] Frei sacked the previous director, who was against the Ralco Dam. Frei had been an entrepreneur, with links with the companies working in Ralco, so he supported the dam. Rodrigo González, who was put in place by Frei, was actually physically attacked, with indigenous women throwing plates and eggs at him. This was very bad for his image, so he in turn resigned.[10]
>
> CONADI is currently being investigated by the courts for corruption. Mideplan has ordered a restructuring, an increase in CONADI staff, internal controls and a review of processes for acquiring land. There is plenty of money at stake, so people are "vulnerable; corruption may occur. The process is that a community claims a certain piece of land, so the owner agrees to sell to CONADI, but at an artificially high price. They know CONADI has lots of state money, so they hike up the prices. You might call it systemic corruption."

So there is widespread scepticism among the Mapuches about the usefulness, and even about the good faith, of CONADI. One director, Edgardo Lienlaf, was forced to resign in March 2002 due to pressure from within the government over his supposed support for "violentist" Mapuche groups, and because he clashed with the director of Mideplan, on which CONADI depends, Jaime Andrade.

When asked how her relations with the Mapuche people were, Alejandra Krauss, Mideplan Minister from 2000 to 2002, replied: "sometimes good, sometimes not so good. The problem is the lack of trust; it is hard to make them believe you, to believe that what you are saying is the truth.[11]

There is also a widespread perception that the government is attempting to neutralise the conflict with the Mapuches, by simply throwing money at the problem on the one hand, and by the age-old strategy of divide and rule on the other. This is the view of Alejandro Herrera, director of the Institute of Indigenous Studies at the *Universidad de la Frontera*, Temuco, criticising a Mideplan development programme called *Orígenes* (Origins):

> "A large number of the officials currently working on the programme are indigenous - in many cases the leaders of indigenous organisations. This is clear in the Mapuche case. This does not contribute to the strengthening of the indigenous organisation concerned and, less still, to the strengthening of the movement. On the contrary, it creates mechanisms of division within the communities and conflict within the indigenous organisations, particularly if we consider the large remunerations available." [12]

Mapuche communities are suspicious of their fellow Mapuches on government bodies, often accusing them of *awinkarse*. The Mapuche identity of someone perceived to have not behaved in the interests of their people can sometimes even be withdrawn by their fellows. In any event, the climate is one of suspicion. The criticisms of corruption within CONADI reflect badly not only on the body itself, but also on the Mapuche communities involved with it, who are accused of being "in on the scam. This is because if they occupy a piece of land, rather than negotiate, the process of land transfer can be speeded up and more money will be forthcoming from CONADI[13]. The rather sordid reputation that CONADI has acquired is in stark contrast with the high-minded aspirations of the new commission set up by President Lagos back in 2001.

Is it really a New Relationship?

In January 2001 President Ricardo Lagos formed the grandiosely titled *Comisión de Verdad Histórica y Nuevo Trato* ("The Commission of Historical Truth and a New Relationship), charging it with reporting on the "historical truth of Chile's indigenous peoples from independence till today and proposing a new relationship, which could lead to constitutional or legislative reforms or new government policies.

The Commission was to be chaired by former president Patricio Aylwin, with subcommittees chaired by such eminent figures as José Bengoa, jurist Carlos Peña and economist Felipe Larraín, and including prominent Mapuches such as activist José Llancapán, representing the urban Mapuche population.

The Commission has issued copious documents, over a hundred to date; it has certainly been busy. Its first major report was issued in October 2003. This report accepts that the State has ridden roughshod over its original peoples' rights and makes a series of proposals to serve as a basis for the preparation of public policy in relation to the indigenous peoples. These focus on political and territorial rights, and the election of their representatives to the National Congress and their presence on regional and municipal governments, their participation in the drafting of the laws and programmes affecting their peoples. The report also discusses a series of reparations, constitutional recognition and the creation of a Council of Indigenous Peoples.

These proposals are momentous indeed, but it remains to be seen whether they will be implemented, or whether the Commission will prove to have been nothing more than yet another talking shop.

It is hard to find Mapuches who wholeheartedly and unreservedly support the Commission. After the report's publication, even one of the Commission's Mapuche members, José Llancapán, expressed his fear that its findings would not be acted upon: "I'm worried it will have no practical implication. The last word is with the Executive.[14]

From its very beginnings, some Mapuches have been suspicious about its motives and doubtful about its prospects. Reynaldo Mariqueo has disparagingly referred to it as the *Comisión de Verdad Histórica y Nuevo Maltrato* ("The Commission of Historical Truth and a New Mistreatment)[15]. When interviewed in February 2002, Adolfo Millabur, the outspoken Mapuche Mayor of the town of Tirúa, was also scathing on this subject:

> "I have been invited many times to be photographed shaking hands with the President, but this is just a game of images, I have always refused. It is a way of dividing us. There are always Mapuche puppets, used when the politicians offer patch solutions, aspirins, to solve real problems.
>
> We think there will be no change in this Chilean classist, racist mentality on the part of the government and big business, until they know our history. There is so much violence that is hidden. We must first write a version of history that is truthful. How did those who have the land get to be legal owners without being the legitimate owners? The Minister of the Interior only knows about the Mapuche from the newspapers and from the history books, who only mention us in negative terms, how can he act on our behalf?
>
> Two days before they formed the commission, they invited Aucán Huilcamán, Alfonso Reiman[16] and myself to join. We wanted first to find out what it was all about: its scope, powers, rules, etc. They could not explain. So the commission was formed with pseudo-representatives who don't represent anyone, who are linked with the political parties. We said they could go to hell."

It has taken time for Chile to overcome the trauma of the Pinochet years, and the various initiatives of the new democratic governments have shown that there is a will on their part to improve the Mapuche's lot, and people of good faith who wish to do so. Yet the Mapuche are still waiting for deeds, not just fine words, of which the official history is already full. And on the ground, there are still fierce battles going on, as we will see in chapter ten. Is the reality post-dictatorship in Argentina any different for Mapuches?

Argentina's indigenous institutions: INAI and CAI

In much the same way as in Chile the return to democracy after the dark years of dictatorship brought with it a promise of improved conditions for the Mapuche, so in Argentina. Nothing good could have been expected of Argentina's "military caretakers, who were keen to emphasise the continuity between the conquerors of the desert and themselves. The election of Radical President Raúl Alfonsín brought higher hopes.

Just as Chile's President Aylwin created CONADI, Alfonsín was responsible for establishing the INAI, the National Institute for Indigenous Affairs. The INAI was created under Law 23303 of November 1985, in these terms (article 3):

> "The National Institute for Indigenous Affairs may, by itself or in conjunction with national or provincial bodies, co-ordinate, plan, promote and execute short-, medium- and long-term programmes for the full development of the indigenous communities, including health, education and housing plans, the awarding, use and working of lands, the promotion of farming, livestock and fisheries, forestry, mining, industry and crafts, the development of the commercialisation of their products, especially autochthonous ones, on both national and foreign markets, social services [...]"

This was, in short, the promise of a very complete support and development package.

Unlike Chile, Argentina also ratified the International Labour Organisation's Convention 169 of 1989, with Law 24071 of 1992. The reform of the National Constitution in 1994 went even further; in its article 75, paragraph 17, it establishes that it is the responsibility of the Argentine Congress:

> "To recognise the ethnic and cultural pre-existence of the Argentinian indigenous peoples. To guarantee respect for their identity and the right to a bilingual and intercultural education; to recognise the legal personality of their communities, and the possession and community ownership of the lands they traditionally occupy; and to regulate the delivery of other land that is suitable and sufficient for human development; none of this land will be alienable, transferable or subject to encumbrances and seizures. To

assure their participation in the administration of their natural resources and the other interests that affect them. The provinces may exercise these powers concurrently."

If the Argentine Congress were to fulfil all the tasks that it is charged to in this article, then there would be little point in writing this book, or half of it at least, as the Mapuche and Argentina's other indigenous peoples would be totally safeguarded in fact and law. The reality, as we will see in the next chapter, is somewhat different.

The reforms also had an impact at provincial level. In 1984 the *Consejo Asesor Indígena* (CAI - Indigenous Advisory Council) was created by the Río Negro Provincial Government, bringing together representatives of the indigenous communities scattered throughout the province. During the first democratic government after the dictatorship, the CAI collaborated extensively with the provincial government. In 1988 Integral Aboriginal Law no. 787 in Río Negro provided for increased participation of indigenous organisations in the decisions that affected them. Provincial Governor's decree no. 310 recognised the existence of the *Coordinadora del Parlamento del Pueblo Mapuche*, an umbrella group for the Mapuche rural and urban communities of Río Negro.

Things are far from perfect, however, as ultimately it is always the governor who decides. In contrast with the centralised Chilean system, in Argentina the provincial governors wield considerable power, and it is at their discretion whether they do so to the benefit of those they supposedly serve. In the Province of Neuquén, Governor Sobisch, who is suspiciously cosy with the oil companies active in the province, recently decided - in Decree 1184 of 2002 - that he himself would be the only authority able to decide which indigenous communities would be granted legal personality (those who behave themselves) and which would not, or would have it taken from them (those causing trouble). This decree met with wholesale condemnation from Mapuche organisations, NGOs, and even the Catholic Church, in the person of the Bishop of Neuquén, Marcelo Melani. Yet, unfortunately, what Governor Sobisch says goes. And he is certainly no friend of the Mapuche.

Fine words falling on deaf ears

Irrespective of events on the ground, fine words and good intentions still proliferate in Argentina, as in Chile. On 11 January 2003, in the midst of the electoral manoeuvres of the various candidates for President, the then incumbent President Duhalde made an important statement about indigenous land claims that was virtually ignored by the Argentine media, who were obsessed with the intrigues of the campaign under way. Visiting the province of Misiones, he called in at the Los Pocitos Guaran community, where he made the following speech:

> "[The Guaraní] claim their culture, their spirituality, and this is why we have come. We have provided them with some land that we have purchased, but we need much more land. It is possible to enable them to find their true culture, which has little to do with the culture of the white man. We have to look at them with our own eyes and listen to them, and understand that their problems are not solved with European thought and culture, which is the majority one in this country. Their specific requirements are the same as those of their ancestors: to live according to their culture, and not the white one, which has always sought to assimilate them. They want other things, they want those forests where they can obtain their remedies and they want to live as their ancestors did."[17]

Once he had finished speaking, the journalists present immediately pushed their microphones and tape recorders towards his face, eager to grill him about the election prospects of his Justicialista party colleague Néstor Kirchner. He was not asked one question about the content of his speech.

In August 2005 Néstor Kirchner himself, now President, met with Mapuche leaders when on a visit to Zapala. They presented him with a document containing their "historical demands, such as for the State to formally recognise that the country's first genocide began in 1870. There are no reports as to what Kirchner said to them, but *Clarín* reported on the Zapala visit by concentrating on a spat between Kirchner and Neuquén Governor Sobitsch, its only acknowledgement of the Mapuche presence being the comment that "the most colourful aspect of the event was the presence of the Mapuche aborigines"[18], showing that for the newspaper the purpose of indigenous people would seem to be primarily to provide a touch of the exotic (see chapter 12).

This incident speaks volumes about the relationship between state, media and Mapuche today, with the latter "colourful" yet totally voiceless, unable to find a mouthpiece to articulate their concerns. And these are many and profound, as we will see in the next chapter.

Notes

1 The report, entitled "The Guluches respond to the call of the land, is dated 23rd April 1999. (linux.soc.uu.se/mapuche/mapu/aukache990423.html).
2 Chapter 15, "La Ley de Reparación, in "Muerte y Desaparición Forzada en la Araucanía: Una Aproximación Etnica, by Teresa Durán Pérez, Roberta Bacic and Pau Pérez Sales, Ediciones LOM, Santiago, 1998.
3 José Mariman, *op. cit*. p. 2.
4 Interviewed in "El Grito Mapuche, by Aníbal Barrera, *op. cit*. p. 55.

5   Interviewed in Temuco on 9/12/01.
6   Rosa Isolde Reuque Paillalef, op. cit., p. 168.
7   Cited in Alejandra Krauss Valle, "El problema de los Mapuches exige una solución integral, article dated 22/5/2002, available on www.mapuche.nl. Alejandra Krauss is former Minister of MIDEPLAN.
8   This according to Estanislao Gacitúa-Mari, in a report for the World Bank, "Indigenous Peoples of Chile. Current situation and policy issues, August 2000, p. 175.
9   Quoted from the article in *La Tercera*, 11/6/2000, "Difícil situación enfrentan hogares indígenas.
10 This happened on 5 July 1999, at the Hotel Nicolás in Temuco, when González met with representatives of 22 communities and Aucán Huilcamán of Auki Wallmapu Ngulam. He was actually kicked and punched by Juana Calfunao, of the Paillalef community.
11 Interviewed in the Mujer supplement of La Tercera newspaper, 24/3/2001. (mujer.tercera.cl).
12 Interviewed in El Siglo on 11th September 2002; text available on the for Kolektivo Lientur website (www.nodo50.org/kolektivolientur/).
13 My thanks to Sara McFall for this insight.
14 Quoted in the magazine *Qu Pasa*, in the article "¿Nuevo trato?, 7 November 2003.
15 Speaking at the Patagonia Conference held at Manchester University in September 2005.
16 President of the Asociación Ñankucheu of Lumaco.
17 Reported in "El Territorio, 12th January 2003.
18 *Clarín*, 6/8/05, "Kirchner esta vez viajó a Neuquén y criticó a Sobisch."

RESOURCES AND RESURGENCE

PART THREE

PUEL MAPU: CONFLICT TODAY IN CHUBUT, NEUQUEN AND RIO NEGRO, ARGENTINA

Chapter nine begins the third and final part of the book, and is devoted to how Mapuches live in Argentina and Chile today. This chapter presents the situation of Mapuche communities in Argentina today; specifically, it looks at a number of the communities in the provinces of Chubut, Neuquén and Río Negro, and the problems they face, most dramatically in their relations with multinationals such as Repsol and Benetton, but also with local estate owners with designs on their land.*

Marici Weu!

> "A long time ago, a *lonko* was fighting for freedom, to keep his people's freedom. Due to an act of treachery, many of his warriors were massacred and he said that for each defeated Mapuche, ten more would rise up. He was the *lonko Leftraru* (Lautaro).
>
> For this reason we cry "Marici weu!", because for each evicted person, there will be ten more who will come to take back that land. Because for each repressed person, ten more of us will rise up."
>
> Mauro Millán[1]

Marici Weu (we will win ten times over) is the Mapuche battle cry, their affirmation that they exist as a force to be reckoned with. After all, their resilience is legendary; they were able to resist against the rapacious Spanish conquistadors for 350 years before finally capitulating.

Though their past battles do sometimes appear in the school history books, their present battles usually take place far away from the media gaze. They do not make easy reading, as the sheer extent of the violations of the Mapuche's rights, and the systematic rigour and callousness with which these violations have been carried out, are presented in detail. But all is not despair, and Mapuches do not like to be portrayed as the victims, the passive recipients of their fate, but rather as the protagonists of their own destiny. Hence their battle cry, the life-affirming shout: *Marici Weu!*

These have been troubled years for Argentinians. Governments have come and gone; some very hurriedly indeed, as the words *cacerolazo* and *corralito* have been dramatically added to the nation's political vocabulary. Now with President Kirchner firmly installed, signs are showing of a cautious economic recovery and a tentative optimism about the future.

Now the tourists are finally returning to Buenos Aires, attracted by the excellent exchange rate offered by the peso. Even if the tourist brochures still tend to concentrate on the tango and polo, it would be a mistake to think that Buenos Aires and its pastimes are all there is to Argentina, although many who live there – and plenty who do not - are convinced it is. Outside of Buenos Aires are the vast expanses of 22 provinces, the "interior", which have provided the wealth of the country with their raw materials, and have borne the brunt of the country's various downturns.

There are also indigenous faces in the metropolis, as it is a magnet not only for the people of Argentina's northern provinces, but also those of neighbouring countries, Paraguay and Bolivia. Yet in contrast with Santiago, which is now home to nearly half Chile's Mapuche population, Buenos Aires has not attracted Argentina's Mapuches in significant numbers. They are concentrated in the provinces of Chubut, Neuquén, Río Negro and Buenos Aires, as distinct from the Federal Capital itself. Most live in the cities and towns, where they have to deal with the problems of being urban Mapuches, which we discussed in chapter one.

In this chapter we will be looking at those Mapuches who live in the communities, the *lof* or *lofche*, and the very real threats they face on a daily basis to their land, their culture, their health, and even their lives.

As Argentines sit in their kitchens and living rooms, bemoaning the current state of their country or heralding another new dawn, their animated conversations are invariably accompanied by the one object and custom that they have inherited from the peoples who welcomed their ancestors - *mate*. The ritual of the shared *mate* gourd, which circulates, its contents of bitter tea drunk in turn by those present, by sucking through a *bombilla* (tube and strainer), is common to the houses of the haughty and the humble, from Paraguay to Tierra del Fuego. It is a metaphor for shared identity in a region scarred by separation.

A journey to the Mapuche communities under threat

Our journey begins in Esquel, in the province of Chubut. An appropriate starting point, if only because this was the place where US travel writer Paul Theroux ended the ambitious train journey that resulted in his book "The Old Patagonian Express." Theroux did not deign the communities there worthy of his interest, so he opted to go home:

> "The Patagonian paradox was this: to be here, it helped to be a miniaturist, or else interested in enormous empty spaces. There was no intermediate zone of study. Either the enormity of the desert space, or the sight of a tiny flower. You had to choose between the tiny or the vast. [...] There were no voices here. There was this, what I saw; and, though beyond it were mountains and glaciers and albatrosses and Indians, there was nothing here to speak of, nothing to delay me further."[2]

So Theroux went off on his way, in search of other siren shores to arouse his curiosity. We shall dwell a while, since we know that here there is indeed something to speak of. Theroux found no voices, but in fact voices there are, and many are angry and demanding to be heard.

There are estimated to be over six thousand Mapuche-Tehuelches in Chubut, out of a total Mapuche and Mapuche-Tehuelche population in Argentina of around 50,000, and a total indigenous population in Argentina of between 800,000 and 1 million, in approximately 800 communities.[3]

The town of Esquel has a population of 28,000, the majority of whom (perhaps 60-80%) are, at least partially, of Mapuche-Tehuelche origin. Despite this, there are very few people with indigenous surnames occupying administrative positions in the town. Instead, the incumbents tend to have sound Spanish or Welsh surnames, the latter because of the significant colonisation of Chubut by the Welsh in the 19th century.

Esquel is very much a military town, which perhaps explains in part why social mobility there is very restricted. It still has the atmosphere of a frontier outpost, and it is home to a regiment of the mountain infantry and to the 36th battalion of the police.

Scattered around Esquel, up into the Cordillera and over on the plain, are the communities of Fofo-Cahuel, Cushamen, Rinconada, Vuelta del Río, Costa del Ñorquinco, Cañadón Grande, Costa del Lepá, Nahuel Pan, Prane, Sierra Colorada, Lago Rosario, Cerro Centinela, Pocitos de Quichaura, El Moye, Bajo la Cancha, Barrancas, Huisca Antieco and Tramaleo. In the province of Chubut as a whole, there are at least 80 Mapuche and Mapuche-Tehuelche communities. They do not appear on the official maps.

The *Nguillatún*, the heart of a community

What is a *lof*? It is a group living in the same geographical area, ranging between a handful of households belonging to an extended family and hundreds of people belonging to a number of families interrelated by marriage. Traditionally *lofs* have

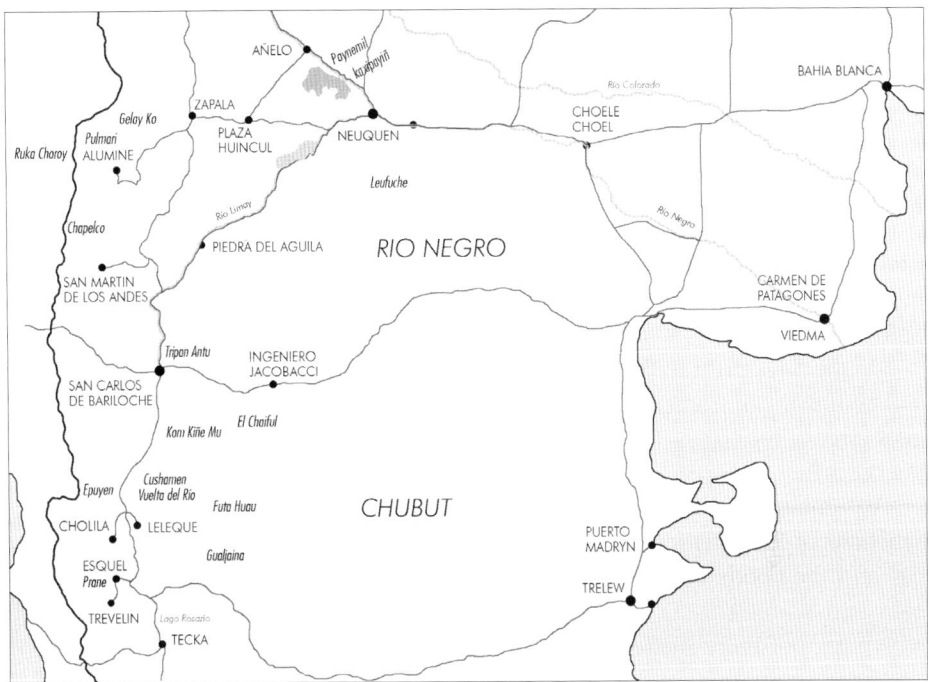

Mapuche communities in Chubut, Neuquén and Río Negro

been organised along patrilineal lines, with women leaving their own communities to live in their husband's, though this is less rigidly kept to today. The *lonko* is the traditional head of the community.

In the UK, the church is generally taken to be the heart of a village. In a *lof*, the heart is not so much a holy place as a ritual. It is the *nguillatún*, the rogation ceremony that links the members to the community, the community to the land and nature generally, and the living with their ancestors. In the *Puel Mapu* it is known as *kamarikún* or *kamaruko*, but the ceremony is essentially the same.

Until very recently communities celebrating the *nguillatún* have tended to be rather secretive about them, conducting them in private, and being reluctant to allow the presence of *winkas*. In the ceremony they ask for a good year, with pasture for the animals and health for all. They may be held annually, although these days most communities tend to hold them once every few years (and some not at all).

Among the Pewenche, the *nguillatún* is held in February, on a date set by each community, but generally after the harvest of the nuts from the *pewen* (araucaria, monkey-puzzle tree). Part of the festivities involves the drinking of *mudai*, a *chicha* (strong liquor) made from the fermented *pewen* nuts.

In agricultural communities the celebration takes place at harvest time during the full moon, when the moon gods give fertility to the fields. In the areas of Neuquén, Río Negro and Chubut, where the communities base their subsistence on sheep and goat farming, the rogation rituals are usually held in March, when it is the fertility of the sheepfolds that is propitiated.

A flat field is chosen, where a ritual space is mapped out in the shape of a "U" open to the east, the cardinal point considered sacred, as it is there that the sun rises, and life itself is believed to originate. In the centre of the enclosure, the sacred space, the *rewe* is erected. The word *rewe* has been translated variously as sacred place, trunk, altar and ladder, and its meaning contains aspects of all of these. In the *Gulu Mapu* it is a sacred tree (often cinnamon) or a *prawe* (stair or ladder), whereas in the *Puel Mapu* it is built with branches of the *colihue, lenga, maitén* and other trees of the area.

On the days prior to the ceremony, pillows, blankets, beds, clothes, food, tables and chairs are all transported to the ceremonial site. During the *nguillatún*, which lasts three or four days, the families live in *ramadas*, shelters built from branches for the purpose.

A number of communities generally participate in the *nguillatún*. One of the functions of the ceremony is to consolidate the relations between these communities and the bonds between the community members. During the ceremony the men and women wear their best clothes, the horses have their best harnesses, which are normally made of silver. The event evolves through an alternation of ritual dances, orations and sacred songs. Horses are ridden in circuits (*troya*) around the holy space (*awun*) at breakneck pace, with sometimes as many as 80 or more galloping horses and riders taking part. This awesome spectacle probably had the function of frightening away evil spirits, and still clearly marks the boundary of the ceremonial space. The site chosen for the *nguillatún* must necessarily be sufficiently flat to enable the *awun* to take place.

Offerings are made to the *ñuke mapu* (mother earth) of *mudai, mate*, tobacco and the blood of animals, which are scattered on the earth. In the past animals were ritually sacrificed, but more commonly nowadays their ear is cut to draw some blood, rather than killing them. The aim of the offerings is to mediate between the Mapuche and the upper levels of the cosmos, propitiating the supernatural forces and preventing the ancestors from being captured by evil spirits (*wekufu*), so ensuring the continuation of the agricultural cycle.

In the *Gulu Mapu* the event culminates with the climbing of the *rewe* by the *machi*, where, in an entranced state, she asks for the spirits to meet the desires of the community.

The first and last event on each day of the *nguillatún* is the dancing of the *choike purún*, the dance of the rhea, in which the feather-wearing participants dance in circular movements, nodding their heads and flapping their ponchos, simulating the movements of the ostrich-like bird. The fact that this opens and closes each day's proceedings is an indication of the circularity of the ceremony, reflecting that of the seasons, a circularity that is also expressed in the physical shape of the *kultrun*, the ceremonial drum.

In short, the *nguillatún* attempts to give order to the cosmos, spatial order through ritually reconstructing the community, the cosmos and the Mapuche territory, and temporal order, through the repetitive nature of the ritual, indicating a continuity between life, death and rebirth. The inability to conduct the *nguillatún* is felt by a community to be a disruption of natural balance and order that is potentially catastrophic for its existence[4]. Such an inability is felt profoundly by the Prane community.

Lof Prane: horses against tanks

We have seen in previous chapters that the members of the Lof Prane have been engaged in a century-long battle with the Argentine state and army over the land in the Nahuelpan reservation, handed over to them in 1902 and taken away again in 1937.

Since 1952 they have lived within sight of their land, on less hospitable terrain higher up the mountain slope. The Lof Prane is an example to Mapuche communities in Argentina, as, despite tremendous odds, it has never ceased to be a *lof*, and has maintained its authority figures, the *lonko* and the *werken*, and has endeavoured to continue to conduct the age-old Mapuche ceremonies in the time-honoured manner. It is this that makes it a *lof*, and not just a collection of a few houses.

When I visited Esquel it was August, the town was covered in snow, and even walking down the street was a major ordeal, as most of the roads slope and no salt or grit had been put down, apart from around the army base. José Prane, *Lonko* Cipriano's son, told me that the previous day he had found cattle that had died standing up, frozen to the spot. Community life is not a pastoral idyll.

During our interview in her home, *werken* Ana Prane told me proudly that it is thanks to the determination of her father that the *lof* is still together. Now he is old and frail, 86 years old, and his struggle has been taken up by his children:

> "He has been a good father, he has taught us a great deal, and we continue to reconstruct his culture gradually. Although we have a *winka* part [their mother is non-Mapuche], we always give precedence to our indigenous culture. We have never been upset about people calling us "Indian"; they can call us what they want. We have continued the fight together with the *lonko*, by his side, and we have seen him suffer and sometimes even weep, for his animals, because of all the suffering and abuse. We have also heard his *pewmas* (dreams); sometimes he would talk in his sleep of his great poverty, and his dream of returning to his land, to die there and leave his remains beside those of his grandfather, with his father in that land that saw him born and welcomed him and sowed his roots."

For half a century now the Pranes have been in the same frustrating situation: believing they have a moral right to the land that they were promised but that was taken away, yet having to tolerate the de facto presence of the Argentine army on that land.

The situation is further complicated by the fact that the army has attempted to make money out of the land in question, by letting it out to local landowners, or at least tolerating their presence there, presumably in return from some undisclosed favour. Between 1981 and 1982, local landowner Omar Yague kept his livestock there, until the army evicted him. In 1995 it was the turn of Esquel businessmen Said Bestene to lay claim to the land.

Out of the blue the army appeared in October, apparently acting on behalf of Mr Bestene. October is the lambing and calving season, and the soldiers removed all the Pranes' animals from the land, dumping them physically outside the fenced-off area. As a result of this manhandling, several of the pregnant and young animals later died.

The community managed to obtain a protective measure from the court, yet the army has still continued to carry out manoeuvres whenever they have felt like it. They appear, carry out some manoeuvres, launch some missiles and then return to their base is just 17 kilometres away.

Over the years Argentina's various governments have occasionally toyed with the idea of returning the land. Deputy Alberto Herrera, representing the province of Chubut, supposedly had the intention of presenting a bill requiring the return of the land. Whatever his intention was, nothing came of it.

ILO Convention 169, which Argentina agreed to ratify in 1984 but only did so in 1992, would seem to sanction the return of the land to the Lof Prane, as in article 14 it states: "The rights of ownership and possession of the peoples concerned over the lands which they traditionally occupy shall be recognised."

The clearest statement by a politician in favour of the Pranes came from President Carlos Menem, in 1999, before ending his mandate, when he announced that he would be signing a presidential decree to return the land. The decree was never drafted. Despite such dashed hopes, Ana says that the community has not been disheartened:

"Indigenous communities don't need pieces of paper saying "this is a title to land." We were born here and believe that we are part of the land, that we don't need the land to enrich ourselves or to exploit it, but rather we have the land, she is our mother, we are her children. Because we are part of this territory, we are entitled to have it respected. We need it to perform our spiritual ceremonies, we need the *chenke* (cemetery) where our *lonkos* lie, where Don Eduardo Prane lies, to be available to the community, because it is a very special place, it is a place of great *newen* (natural power) for us, and neither the army nor any landowner has ever been able to keep that land from us. Our *newens* are there."

In September 1999 the community decided to build their *rewe*, to mark out their *leufún*, the flat sacred place to hold the *kamarikún*. The ceremony took place on 20 September, after which the community built the *ruka*, in October, to indicate their intention to remain as a permanent presence in the place. The army would not be allowed to return.

In 7 January 2000 the army duly reappeared, with the intention of carrying out more manoeuvres. Ana believes the *newens* were working in the community's favour, that the *lonkos* who are buried in that earth were summoning sympathetic souls, as it just so happened that a group of youngsters belonging to Buenos Aires human rights organisation Horneros, including photographer Andres Kudacki, were in the area; they were meeting with the 11 October Organisation, on their way to the Pillan Mahuiza community further south. They were quickly able to come and act as human shields to support the community's stand. Kudacki took some stunning photos of José Prane galloping to cut off the path of an advancing tank.

In the stand-off that followed, the people stood their ground, so the army eventually backed down and retreated.

A couple of days later the *lof* members held a march through Esquel as far as the army base, accompanied by over a hundred supporters. Lieutenant Colonel Preto Armandi invited the community representatives in and said that he would undertake not to return to the land, and to reach an agreement so that the manoeuvres would not happen again.

> "He appears to have kept his word, but since then a few strange things have happened to the community members, so we do have our doubts. There have been odd incidents, such as a car being burned out and people being threatened by unidentified people. I am a *werken*, but I have children and I don't want them harmed, and I don't want to subject them to danger, so I understand that I must bide my time until the *newens* tell us it is time to go out and fight again.
>
> We have made great efforts to recover our culture. Thanks to the national state, we have almost lost our identity; we have to pay for every journey the teacher makes - kilometres and kilometres - to come and teach our children, out of our own pockets, because the state never gives us anything. It doesn't even give us the possibility to maintain our territory, to hold our ancestral ceremonies, to recover our culture, nothing.
>
> We are waiting for the day when we can live in peace in our territory, when *lonko* Cipriano Prane, as in his *pewmas*, can remain forever in this territory, so his *newen* will some day shine on his grandchildren, on his descendants, as those of his ancestors did."

Let us hope that the quiet dignity and determination of this gentle lady will be rewarded. She and her community have the *newens* on their side, but their struggle is not over yet, and their opponents are implacable. In Esquel's local newspaper, *El Oeste*, the landowner who occupied their land in the early '80s, Omar Yague, published an open letter addressed to "professionals and lawyers", offering his own interpretation of the issues involved:

> "[...] private property is democracy and culture, and it must be taken into account that the Argentine Army is the army bequeathed to us by General San Martín. How can it be that intruders such as the Pranes can be allowed to insult our armed forces? Respect and culture must exist, all civilised acts state this, and I say to you, Sirs, as professionals, I know that in law you may defend a murderer, but rules of ethics and principles must exist in society in order for rights to be defended, otherwise we will fall into barbarism, and you will be the accomplices. "[5]

The Prane community cannot even count on the support of all the other Mapuche communities in the area. Sergio Nahuel Pan, *lonko* of the Nahuel Pan community - the community that has most benefited from circumstances, as of the original 9 *lofs* they are the only one that has held onto legal title over their land - had this to say about the Pranes' claim:

> "What these people say are lies. The Nahuel Pan community has never been bothered by the actions of the Army. On the contrary, we have been helped by the Army and they have never troubled us. This land was handed over to my grandfather, and [...] many other families came to live here, but with my grandfather's provisional permission."[6]

Once again that age-old strategy of divide and rule is being used here, offering more or less preferential treatment to the different communities in order to make them fight against each other. The Nahuel Pan community have benefited from favouritism from the army, and would not want to bite the hand that feeds, whereas the Prane have received nothing so they have nothing to lose. For now the unity of the *mate* gourd is still no more than an ideal.

Futa Huau: from schoolhouse to storehouse and back again

160 kilometres northeast of Esquel, in the area known as the western plateau, is the Mapuche-Tehuelche community of *Futa Huau* (*Cañadon Grande* in Spanish). Some twenty-five families make it up, those who resisted the continuous evictions, to-

gether with those who eventually returned home after turning their backs on the poor neighbourhoods of the cities.

The history of Futa Huau is very similar to that of hundreds of original communities. They arrived, at the end of the 19th century, from different parts of the *Wall Mapu,* to their current location. They had been pursued by the Argentinian and Chilean armies, some from the Río Colorado area, others from Azul (province of Buenos Aires) and others from the *Gulu Mapu*.

Gradually the landowners' wire fences advanced, cutting down the community space. In 1980 Said Bestene – the Esquel businessman whose name we also encountered in connection with Lof Prane – obtained a temporary interest-free loan from the educational department of the provincial government and appropriated provincial school No. 76, which stood inside the community, along with 1000 hectares belonging to it; he used the land to keep livestock and horses and the building as a storehouse. It is ironic that he took the school and land for himself, as the understanding he had reached with the education department was that his role was to safeguard it temporarily to prevent it from falling into the "wrong" hands.

The school had been built on the community land, thanks to donations of materials from individuals, and it was the army - in its guise as benefactor, this time - that constructed it. It was closed – apparently arbitrarily - after less than a year of operation, without the community's consent. At the same time a boarding school opened dozens of kilometres away, which all the children of the community were required to attend.

The years passed and the families of Futa Huau repeatedly laid claim to the land, each time more forcibly, each time they were evicted more violently. In 1997 they occupied the premises of the Autarchic Institute of Colonisation and Public Works (IAC) in Esquel, a department of the provincial government. The officials committed themselves to resolving the matter, but nothing came of it. The pattern is a familiar one.

In April 1998 the community recovered the school building and in September they removed the fencing around the 1000 hectares. Following these actions, they were accused of usurpation, but were finally acquitted, after a lengthy legal process.

Alcira Sánchez was born in Futa Huau in 1954. She studied at the community school, when the walls of the building were made of mud, and her teacher was a certain José Luis Rosso from La Pampa. When she was eighteen years old, she was evicted, along with her family, but she returned and today she is *kona*, a name that used to be reserved for warriors, but nowadays is given to the community members most active in defending their rights.

I asked Alcira what condition the land was in when they decided to return to claim it:

"There were no houses left where we are now; they had knocked them all down. There was just the school and a few of the old people scattered around.

> The school was just the walls and roof. Bestene had even taken the doors. Because the old people didn't speak out, Bestene took everything, even their water."

Even the cemetery had been fenced off, so the few community members who had remained had had their spiritual link with their ancestors severed. In 1998 they finally decided to act. Alcira managed to overcome her fear.

> "The recovery was tough and frightening. Several were afraid and left. I said: 'I'm not leaving. If I have to fight the *milicos*[7], then I'll fight them'. And I stayed with the youngsters. We already had the clubs ready.
> They filled the place with *milicos*. 'What are you going to do?', we said; 'we're not fighting anybody, we're just claiming what is rightfully ours'."

Alcira says she found the inner strength to fight because for a number of years she had been *piuchen*, a child who represents one of the *newens* during the *kamarikún*. She knew the *newens* were on their side.

Rubén Antipan is the oldest of Alcira Sánchez' nine children. He is just over thirty and well knows the diaspora to which Mapuches are condemned in their own territory, as he has lived it as a daily reality. In 2001 he returned definitively to his community. After losing his job in Esquel, he had no reason to stay in the city.

Like the rest of his community, he is convinced that the struggle carried forward in Futa Huau must remain in the memory of his people and serve as a driving force to keep going.

> "We followed all the legal procedures and, as the legal system did not respond, the community decided to act. In September 1998 we invited some other communities - Vuelta del Río, Costa de Gualjaina, Sierra de Gualjaina, Gualjaina - and we decided to take down the fencing around a thousand hectares."

It seems the action was needed in order to prompt the government and the justice system to respond. They must have felt some pangs of conscience, because the court returned the school building and the land to the community.

Even with the land returned, life is still tough:

> "Today we continue to demand that the government keep their commitments to the community, such as the commitment to help us repair the school. The community recovered it so that it would run again, so that it would be authorised for teaching again.
> The community's children still have to go to School 137, in Costa del Chubut 70 kilometres away, which is a boarding school. One of the requests

we have made is for a vehicle to transport the children. Not having a vehicle, in the wintertime it is too difficult to go to visit the children. You can't even go on horseback, because the road is impassable.

They made a commitment to repair the road. They did part of the work and then left it. If we had a vehicle we could collect the children on Friday afternoon and return them on Sunday afternoon.

We also asked for a health centre. Because from here, in winter, if somebody falls ill it is very hard to get to Gualjaina, which is 80 kilometres away."

The processes are very slow, and things do not change overnight. But the people of Futa Huau have shown that they are prepared for a struggle. They have managed to regain their identity as a *lof*, and the authority of the *lonko*, Agustín Sánchez, who is now re-established as the interlocutor for the civil authorities.

Futa Huau is another story of a community that has refused to abandon its traditional way of life, despite the enormous pressures upon it to do so. At Futa Huau community life is tough, but its inhabitants are optimistic about the future. Despite the wind and the aridity of the soil, they say that in recent years the rains have increased and the pastures have improved. They believe this is due to their recovery of their ancestral form of community life, their *nguillatún* ceremonies and their territory. Gradually, the balance between the different elements of nature, the *newens*, has been restored.

As I write in a hot sticky English July, in Futa Huau the wind blows chilly, the snows have arrived and the residents must remain there, isolated until the thaw. But in spite of the inclemencies of the climate and the aridity of the land, Futa Huau has demonstrated that when dignity takes root, nothing can stop it growing.

Vuelta del Río, Lof Curiñanco and the tainted colours of Benetton

The Mapuche-Tehuelche community of Vuelta del Río lies inside the Cushamen Reservation, 40 km from El Maitén, near Leleque, midway between San Carlos de Bariloche and Esquel. The Reservation was created in 1899 to relocate some of the remnants of the Mapuche-Tehuelche peoples who survived the genocide of the Conquest of the Desert.

Since 1957, when the Provincial State of Chubut was created, successive governments have issued titles to property inside the reservation to *estancieros* (the owners of large estates) and non-Mapuche individuals, disregarding state law and the status of the occupiers of the land.

In 1991 the Benetton brothers purchased eight large estates totalling nine hundred thousand hectares in Argentina, seven of these territories located in Patagonia. Approximately nine hundred thousand sheep are raised and pastured on these estates, providing the multinational with about six thousand tons of wool a year.

Among the land to which Benetton purchased titles was that occupied by the Vuelta del Río community. They did not evict all the residents; they allocated a small plot for some of the families to live, known as the Company Reservation, thus mimicking government policy and terminology. 30 families, around 150 people, live there. The community has lived from sheep rearing for as long as they can remember, but this is now impracticable in view of the inadequacy of the land and the fences that the Italian "owners" have had had put up.

The land in the Leleque area that Benetton had purchased was the very same land that the Argentine Southern Land Company acquired following the Conquest of the Desert. Benetton bought the land titles dating back to 1896. The Mapuche believe their entitlement predates this, but have no documents to prove their case.

In 1999 Argentine national newspaper *Clarín* reported that the company had also diverted the course of the River Lepa, a tributary of the River Chubut, to improve the quality of the grazing land for their famous Merino sheep. All this was done without any environmental impact studies being carried out, or any consideration of the effect on the populations living downstream. The community are now deprived of access to the river, which makes their land much more prone to drought than before. Ronald Macdonald, the administrator of one of the estates, has stated that "fishing is not prohibited, as the river is the property of the state. However, it is forbidden to walk along its banks, as the land is private property."[8]

In recent years there have also been claims that community members are exploited on the Maiten and Leleque estates as low cost labour, receiving a salary of around $150 a month for working from dawn to dusk. In March 1998 these claims were investigated by the INAI, the Argentine National Institute for Indigenous Matters, and the Chubut Under-secretary for Labour, but no further action was taken.

At 8.40am on 2 October 2002, twelve policemen in riot gear accompanied by dogs raided Santa Rosa, near Leleque, a plot of land recovered by the Curiñanco family. At that moment Atilio Curiñanco was in the fields and his wife, Rosa Rúa Nahuelquir, was inside the rickety house they had built on the land. When she refused to allow them entry, the police ordered her to leave. Subcommissioner Pérez, in charge of the operation, warned Rosa that if she resisted they would take her away in handcuffs. He told her: "nobody can meddle with them (the Benettons), because they're the ones with the most money."[9]

The Curiñanco's precarious corrugated tin dwelling was completely dismantled by the officers. They then proceeded to seize Atilio and Rosa's belongings, and consequently take away their livelihood: their work tools, their plough and a pair of oxen.

Following the operation, a police caravan was positioned permanently at the property, occupied by two uniformed policemen and a civilian, identity unknown. The operation was ordered by the Investigating Judge of the Court of Esquel, José

Oscar Colabelli, all with great alacrity, considering the court's lethargy in dealing with comparable accusations by communities against landowners, which can spend years gathering dust in some cupboard somewhere.

In February 2003 a protest demonstration was held in Leleque outside the Benetton's estate in support of the Curiñanco family, with about 150 Mapuches and supporters present. Following this, Mauro Millán, *werken* of the 11 October Organisation, was arrested and charged with "crimes against private property." The charges were subsequently dropped, but it seems reasonably clear that this was an attempt to warn him off.

Mauro is a founder and high-profile member of the 11 October Organisation, who lives in Esquel and struggles to make a living as a silversmith, selling his wares at local craft fairs. Over the years, he and his family have received a large number of threats and financial inducements, sticks and carrots, to try to persuade him to abandon the cause. They only make him more determined than ever to see it through to the end.

Mauro has this to say about the Curiñanco case:

"There is no doubt that the case of the Curiñanco family is very important, because they planned to return to the land to work it, to generate an independent income and release some of the tension caused by overcrowding in the poor neighbourhoods of the towns.

When we say 'return to the land', we are talking about arable land, we don't want to return to the desert, to live among the stones. And the State doesn't look kindly on this kind of solution, because it means it has to return land. The government of the province of Chubut has a spirit of mutual cooperation with the people who are oppressing us. Returning land means touching the interests of powerful people, the landowners who have invaded us and stolen from us, and are now part of the political leadership of this province. When this type of solution is suggested, the government does everything possible to prevent it from becoming a beacon for the desperate people in the poor neighbourhoods."[10]

Since the demonstration in February 2003 things have progressed and then regressed for the Curiñanco family. When Judge Colabelli was removed from office, there were signs that the legal proceedings to decide on the ownership of the land in question would place the validity of the land titles of the Argentine Southern Land Company, dating back to 1896, in doubt. Then on 31 May 2004 came the decision: the land is Benetton's.

Attilio and Rosa are strong willed, and they will not give up easily. They have appealed against the decision; they also know that the courts are only one of a number of ways to pursue their aims. So they decided to take the fight to Benetton. They visited Italy in November 2004, accompanied by Mauro Millán and their lawyer Gustavo Macayo. They met with Luciano Benetton himself in Rome, with Nobel Peace Prizewinner Perez Esquivel acting as mediator. There Benetton offered to donate 2,500 hectares of "his" land in an unspecified area of Patagonia to the Mapuche communities, an offer which Rosa and Atilio rejected, so he suggested offering it to the Argentine state instead. The Curañincos want the return of the land near Leleque, no more and no less. In July 2005 Benetton bought 11,000 hectares in the area of Piedra Parada, near Gualjaina, to be "made available to the province of Chubut in line with the proposal made months ago."[11] The struggle between the media-sensitive multinational and the determined Curiñanco couple continues.

In 2000 Benetton inaugurated their Anthropological, Archaeological and Paleontological Museum in Leleque. A tourism website for Patagonia[12] has the following to say of the museum:

"The museum is the result of the will and passion of Pablo Korchenewski, who has devoted his whole life to gathering testimonies on the peoples of Patagonia, and Carlo Benetton, who is so fond of the natural beauties of this land that, in 1991, he acquired the Argentine Southern Land Company, who, thanks to their tradition in top quality wool producing sheep breeding, have been part of the history of Patagonia since the 19th century."

An admirable enterprise, then. Not according to the 11 October Organisation, who in a press release dated 12 May 2000, commented on the event in the following bitter tones:

"Present at the inauguration were the Governor of the Province of Chubut, officials, representatives of the Roman Catholic Church, millionaire foreigners from various countries, scientists, historians and the national and international media. Of course they needed the token indigenous face for such an event as this, which is why they resort to Mapuches with no self-respect, who willingly hire themselves out for the circuses set up by these *winkas*. Among these "brothers and sisters" was "Tehuelche" lawyer Rosa Chiquichano, the woman who is always sent for on such occasions."

Mauro and his fellow activists may not be being entirely fair to Rosa Chiquichano. She has followed the path of education – she is a qualified lawyer – and of working within the local political system of Chubut rather than challenging it, to the extent that she has been elected a deputy in the Chubut Provincial Assembly. On 28 May 2004, a couple of days before the decision in favour of Benetton was issued, she used the forum of the assembly, during a debate on environmental matters, to speak in favour of the Curiñancos:

"The defence of human rights, the defence of life with dignity falls within the defence of the environment and within what is known as sustainable development, and sustainable development means quality of life and quality of life means work, education, housing and health. That is, the quality of life sought by the Curiñanco family in Santa Rosa, in the area of Leleque, so that they can keep on working their hectare of land, just a tiny plot, in comparison with all the land at the disposal of the Benetton company. With this decision they will be able to choose the way of life they have had from the time of their ancestors."[13]

The case of the Curañinco family, and the Vuelta del Río community, in their legal battle with the Benetton company, has become something of a test case for relations between the Mapuche and the state. It will show whether the legal system is capable of resolving disputes of land ownership impartially or whether, as many Mapuches suspect, the judges and *latifundisti* (large estate owners) have always had only each other's interests at heart.

Paynemil and Kaxipayiñ in Neuquén: Repsol and the stink of oil

The province of Chubut, associated with sheep breeding since the 19th century, has more recently developed as a centre for tourism, both national and international, with the east coast promoting the attraction of the whales and sea mammals of Peninsula Valdes, and the mountains in the west offering ski resorts such as San Carlos de Bariloche and La Hoya near Esquel.

The province of Neuquén also has its ski resorts, such as San Martín de los Andes and Junín de los Andes, in the south west of the province. Now dinosaur fossils are also providing the stimulus for the burgeoning tourist sector for the province.

One of the largest dinosaurs to be discovered in the world, purported to have weighed 100 tons, is *Argentinosaurus Huinculensis*, which was discovered near Plaza Huincul in 1993. Also in 1993, in El Chocón, car mechanic Ruben Carolini discovered the remains of *Giganotosaurus Carolinii*, which was named to commemorate its discoverer.

Although dinosaurs have belatedly brought some degree of prosperity to the region, greater economic wealth has come from what we might consider to be a by-product of dinosaurs - and of other flora and fauna of the Jurassic, Triassic, and Cretaceous periods - oil.

There are 50 Mapuche communities in the province of Neuquén, totalling 11,000 or so people, without counting all those individuals or families of indigenous origin living mainly in urban and suburban areas.

In June 1996 Mapuches were among the thousands of residents of Cutral Co and Plaza Huincul who took to the streets and set up roadblocks to protest against the severe consequences of unemployment in the town after YPF, the formerly state-owned company, had closed down its refineries there. The gendarmes were called in, and in one of the clashes that followed a young woman, Teresa Rodríguez, was shot dead. This uprising became known as a *pueblada*, and marked the beginnings of a slow crescendo of popular revolt that culminated in the events of December 2001 in Plaza de Mayo, Buenos Aires. It was the discovery of oil in 1918 that caused Cutral Co and Plaza Huincul to be born as towns, just as it is now the closing down of the refineries that is killing them.

About 100 km north of Neuquén, and north-east of Cutral Co, is Añelo, which was officially founded in 1915 on the site of one of the forts that formed a line of defence in the Conquest of the Desert. Over recent decades the area has changed its economy from being predominantly one of horticulture and animal breeding - particularly goats - to oil production.

Close to Añelo is the huge complex of the Chocón-Cerros Colorados, which supplies hydroelectric energy to places as far away as Buenos Aires. Yet it is a dirtier form of energy that is causing the greatest problems to the Mapuche communities of the area. The communities concerned are Paynemil and Kaxipayiñ, which are located in the area of the so-called Mega Processing Plant of Loma de La Lata, also now known by the corporate abbreviation LLL.

The plant covers 100 hectares of land, and was purchased by Repsol-YPF from the provincial government. In exchange for this purchase, the company agreed to construct a methanol plant in Cutral Co-Plaza Huincul, thus generating new employment in that devastated area.

The LLL plant, one of the largest in Latin America, is the point of departure of the $440 million Mega Project being implemented by Repsol-YPF in partnership with U.S. Dow Chemical and Brazilian Petrobras. The plant separates methanol from ethane, propane, butane and petrol; then the liquid gas is transported by pipeline to Bahía Blanca on the east coast, to be used to feed Dow's and other petrochemical plants in the region. The dry gas is transported by pipeline via Bahía Blanca to Buenos Aires, for domestic and industrial use.

The Mega Project was opposed not only by the Mapuches, but also by ecological and human rights groups and the local Catholic and Methodist churches.

Another gas pipeline is also planned, this time commissioned by Gasoducto del Pacífico. Again starting at LLL, this pipeline with run over the Argentinian-Chilean border across the Buta Mallin Pass, through Pinto and Leonera, and end in Concepción and Talcahuano in Chile. From there the gas can be shipped abroad, principally to the USA and Mexico.

I talked to Verónica Huilipan, fellow *werken* of Jorge Nahuel at the Co-ordinating Committee of Mapuche Organisations in Neuquén, about what the effect of the presence of the oil companies has been on the lives of neighbouring Mapuche communities:

*Mother and child from Kaxipayiñ and Paynemil communities protest against Repsol.
Photo courtesy of the Coordinating Committee of Mapuche Organisations in Neuquén*

"One of the worst effects is what I would call "petrodependence", namely the way oil has come to dominate all aspects of the communities' lives. In the past, when two men out on horseback met in the fields, they would inquire about each other's health and that of their respective families. Then the conversation would move onto the animals, the fields, the climate. Now the sole topic of conversation is oil: pipelines, contamination, leaks. They have changed our language."[14]

The *Lof* Kaxipayiñ and *Lof* Paynemil are located between the Río Neuquén and Lakes Los Barreales and Mari Menuco. The members of the former community are descendants of Juan Kaxipay, who settled there at the end of the 19th century, and the latter community dates back to the same period. Their main activity is and has always been small-scale livestock farming. Together the communities consist of 24 families altogether, with 100 or so members.

Since the 1960s they have suffered invasions by various oil concerns, and no less than 80 oil wells are bleeding the community areas dry.

Following the construction of the gas separation plant and oil pipelines, the vegetation began to dry up. They discovered too late that oil sludge was being poured into the fields without any treatment, causing many of their animals to die.

Paynemil was recognised as a reservation in 1964 and obtained title to the land in 1990-91, while Kaxipayiñ only achieved recognition in 1997 and in 1998 the official commitment to establish title to part of the land claimed by them.

In 1992/93, despite having provoked serious erosion of the soil and contamination of the air, land and water for almost 20 years, the operator agreed to pay the Paynemil community the derisory sum of $700 to $900 per month as easement, and not a cent to the *Lof* Kaxipayiñ.

Following contamination of the surface water, pumps were then provided for the community to draw up water from a depth of 4 metres. In 1996, when this water too became contaminated, a judge ordered the provincial government to bring them water in barrels, in return for payment. By this stage, various members of the community had lead in their blood and mercury in their urine that were double the levels considered safe.

In May 1997 the provincial government of Felipe Sapag transferred 106 hectares to YPF, at 300 pesos a hectare, some of which were occupied by families making up the Kaxipayiñ community. The community opposed the sale, claiming property rights over 6,180 hectares of the land, on the basis of ancestral entitlement, also recognised by a resolution by the Department of Social Development and Provincial Law 24071.

Both communities are now enclaves inside the heart of a 36 thousand hectare oilfield, with the largest reserves in the country, generating $35 million per month for the company and $4 million per month in royalties to the provincial government (data from 1996).

Meanwhile there has been a catalogue of serious accidents affecting the communities. In a letter to Provincial Government Minister Gorosito, dated 25 April 2001, they reported the following incidents: a significant spillage from UAM plant 2/3, belonging to the French company Total (an associate of YPF), which poured out at least 30 cubic metres of contaminating effluents; the leakage of toxic products that reached the Río Neuquén, following the perforation of a pipeline; the collapse of a tower owned by the company Pride (a Repsol-YPF contractor), which killed one worker and subjected others to serious risk; the explosion and demolition of a tank with a capacity of tens of thousands of litres, which was empty of liquids but full of gases, due to welding being carried out during the night in the vicinity without even the most elementary safety measures being in place.

In recognition of Repsol's 'excellent' work in the area, on 28 December 2000 the Argentine Economy Minister extended their LLL concession for a further 10 years, in return for the annual payment of 80 million dollars. This was in contrast with the attitude of the governors of the Provinces of Salta, Mendoza and Santa Cruz, who announced that they would not agree to any extensions before the reform of the Hydrocarbons Law.

Mapuche organisations point out that the concession was granted to YPF when this was still a state company, and that it was granted in violation of ILO Convention 169, ratified by the Argentine Government, as we mentioned above. Article 15 states:

> "In cases in which the State retains ownership of mineral or sub-surface resources or rights to other resources pertaining to lands, governments shall establish or maintain procedures through which they shall consult the [indigenous and tribal] peoples, with a view to ascertaining whether and to what degree their interests would be prejudiced, before undertaking or permitting any programmes for the exploration or exploitation of such resources pertaining to their lands. The peoples concerned shall, wherever possible, participate in the benefits of such activities, and shall receive fair compensation for any damages which they may sustain as a result of such activities."

When multinationals are criticised in campaigns, it is curious how often they then set about cleaning up their sullied image, rather than their act. Repsol/YPF's efforts at greenwash have been impressive and wide-ranging. Through the YPF Foundation, formed in 1996, they provide funding for education projects, museums, libraries and even dental health campaigns. The Foundation's mission statement is:

> "To promote, stimulate, participate in and intervene in initiatives of an educational and cultural nature, and especially in the promotion of scientific

research and the professional and technical training of the young generations."

In 2001 Repsol arranged for local children in the provincial capital of Neuquén to paint murals on the walls of their headquarters to commemorate the International Declaration of Children's Rights; the various paintings were to represent the rights that children are supposed to have. On 12 October, Columbus Day, 20 or so youngsters from Neuquén belonging to the urban Mapuche youth organisation *Tayiñ Rakizuam* (Our Thoughts) arranged a demonstration outside Repsol HQ. They held banners and shouted out slogans pointing out that the children of the communities also have rights: to clean air, good health and uncontaminated soil. Within minutes 50 or 60 police piled out of riot vans. First they demanded to speak to the "leader" - most of the children were aged 10 to 14 - then scuffles began, and finally the kids were chased away, during which many of them were beaten. The speed with which the riot police were mobilised offers incontrovertible proof, according to Aukan, one of the youngsters who was on the demonstration, that "it's Repsol that runs the city."

On 1 November 2001 a study commissioned by the Mapuche Communities of Paynemil and Kaxipayiñ from the German scientific testing company Umweltschutz Nord was presented at the National University of the Comahue in Neuquén. According to the study, the presence of cadmium, arsenic, lead and mercury in the bodies of the members of the Paynemil and Kaxipayiñ Mapuche communities was well above the values considered normal. The report affirmed that the remnants of heavy metals in the area investigated were 700 times higher than those permitted by national legislation. As well as having direct effects on people, due to their capacity to accumulate biologically (skin irritation, cancer, congenital defects, damage to the nervous system and bone marrow, anaemia and leukaemia, allergies, asthma, stomach problems), the heavy metals resulting from the extraction of oil also damage food cycles in ecosystems.

The contamination caused by the mining affects not only the Mapuches but, if it continues, could affect the whole region, since the rivers Neuquén and Negro are very close; more than 400,000 people are supplied with water from these rivers.

In November 2001, the company that provides bulk drinking water to the families of the Paynemil Community suspended the supply, because the Ministry for Development would not take responsibility for billing. For their part, Repsol have cut off the electricity supply to the communities. So these two communities find themselves in the situation of being beside a river and on the water table that they have used for a century, yet having no drinking water, and being on the country's largest oil reserve and beside a large hydroelectric power station, and having no gas or electricity.

No one could doubt the dramatic nature of the situation and the events unfolding at LLL, but some politicians seem to be confused about who the victims are and who the culprits. A protest by the two communities outside the Repsol headquarters in Neuquén was subsequently discussed at a session of the Provincial Government held on 3 May 2001. Commenting on the demonstration, Deputy Julio César José Falleti, of the centrist, regionalist Movimiento Popular Neuquiño (MPN), who had supported the privatisation of YPF, stated what he considered to be the most serious aspect of the previous day's events:

> "[...] Yesterday I believe that the history of the Province of Neuquén was marked by a fact that must be absolutely repudiated, because not only were the installations of a highly important company that has greatly benefited the Province of Neuquén attacked, but also the highest emblem of our Fatherland was assaulted: the Flag of the Argentine Republic, the Flag that is held dear by all Argentines as the most heartfelt symbol of our sentiments. Yesterday a group of hot-heads lowered the Argentine Flag, soaked it in a petrol tank and then raised it again. Mister President, our flag must never be soaked by anyone!"[15]

What seems to be most striking here is the MPN deputy's singular lack of a sense of proportion: the negligence of multinational companies motivated more by considerations of profit than by environmental or health safeguards has led to destitution and illness in the local indigenous community, and potentially large-scale consequences to the ecosystem, yet the deputy is more concerned over an affront to the flag.

Lof Casiano: the familiar pattern of expropriation in Río Negro

As with our reports on today's major conflicts in the provinces of Chubut and Neuquén, in Río Negro too the point of departure has to be the Conquest of the Desert. The Conquest arrived in Río Negro with more destructive force than in Chubut and Neuquén, decimating the communities, therefore making it more difficult for them to recover their original values, such as language, religious celebrations and ancestral forms of organisation.

Despite the enormous extension of the province, approximately 20 million hectares, there are only 11 indigenous communities in the reservations, and those with approved legal status can be counted on the fingers of one hand. The vast majority of the Mapuches in the Province of Río Negro therefore live spread out throughout the territory and in the urban centres.

Just as the 11 October Organisation was formed to provide representation for the Mapuche-Tehuelches of the urban centres and the communities of Chubut, and the Co-ordinating Committee of Mapuche Organisations to represent the urban and rural Mapuches of Neuquén, so the Mapuches of Río Negro have an organisation to represent their interests: the C.A.I. (*Consejo Asesor Indígena* - Indigenous Advisory Council), which was formed in 1984.

A valuable source of information for an understanding of the conflicts in Río Negro Province is the paper presented by Dr. Darío Rodríguez Duch, who has worked tirelessly in support of the Mapuche communities in Río Negro, at the conference held in Buenos Aires on 6 and 7 December 2001 on the rights of indigenous peoples, entitled "The territorial conflicts of the *Lof* Mapuche in the Province of Río Negro"[16]. In this, Dr Duch explains a mechanism for the usurpation of Mapuche land that has often been repeated, in Río Negro and elsewhere, to the point of being a formula for appropriation; the text is worth quoting at length:

> "In these situations, in which one of the parties always enjoys considerable disparity of forces compared with the other, in terms of both economic might and the possibility of access to information, the plunderers, generally influential money-grubbers with a certain knowledge of the area and contacts at local political level, had various strategies available to them for the frequent cases in which they wanted to extend their land possessions and this land was occupied by the descendants of the ancient inhabitants of the location.
>
> In many cases the plundering was violent. There would be no beating about the bush, since "with Indians you have to proceed like the Europeans do when they hunt boars, you must not take pity on them" as General Roca said. The task would be begun by using threats. For this armed thugs were used to do the dirty work and bring about the actual eviction, in the best style of a cowboy movie. There have been many historically documented cases in which these armed men have gone too far and brought about the deaths of the lawful owners of the land.
>
> A subtle variant of this first system was the night-time advancing of the wire fences by these money-grubbers, who were the only ones who could pay an army of people to put up kilometres of wire fencing in a single night. When the *peñi* woke up with a wire fence just a few metres from his house, taking almost the whole field away from him, his first and natural reaction was to cut the parts of the wire that most bothered him or his animals, or to break the padlock of some improvised gate that had been put up. The response would be immediate.
>
> In a matter of hours the money-grubber would arrive, accompanied by several policemen, who would issue a bill of indictment for criminal damage. As the *peñi* found himself unable to hire a lawyer, he would be detained for days, until a judge eventually resolved to release him. When he returned home, he was left with a small part of his original field, since it was now all fenced in more permanently and substantially by the other person.

The *peñi* would then set out on a long pilgrimage around the public land offices, making fruitless accusations, which always received the same negative, more or less disdainful answer from the officials concerned.
Two thirds of the Anecón Grande and Cerro Bandera Reservations, both created by National law at the beginning of the 20th century, were lost in this way."

In the south west of Río Negro Province, near the town of Ingeniero Jacobacci, are 5,000 hectares of land that between 1885 and 1969 were occupied by several generations of the Casiano family, part of the Mapuche Lof El Chaiful.

In 1969, through the deception of a supposedly unpaid debt, the landowning Abi Saad family succeeded in evicting the Casianos without the involvement of the legal system.

In 1988 the Casianos lodged an official claim to the land before the Río Negro Provincial Land Office. Incredibly, the Office managed to misplace the documentation, included in which was supposedly an eviction order against the Abi Saad family in favour of the Casianos. Due to the paralysis of the officials, at great personal expense and sacrifice, the family travelled to Viedma, the provincial capital, some 800 km away, only to be told that the documents were either in Jacobacci, or in Bariloche!

The CODECI (Council for the Development of Indigenous Communities), the organisation responsible for ensuring that laws safeguarding indigenous peoples are respected, was called upon to support the claim; this they did, but with insufficient commitment to make a difference. Not for the first time, Mapuches had been damned by faint help.

In April 2000 the community was outraged to find that the tomb of Agustín Casiano, grandfather of *werkens* Marta and Delfina Casiano, which lies in the community cemetery in the contested land, had been desecrated by Alfredo Abi Saad.

Finally, exasperated, following the inaction of the authorities, and with the support of CAI and other solidarity groups, in December 2000 the family decided to occupy the land, as a way of bringing pressure to bear and as a de facto reclamation. CAI have also supported the continued exploration of legal means to resolve the issue: sixteen years on, the missing dossier containing the eviction order against the Abi Saad family is still being sought, but it has not yet re-emerged.

Meanwhile the threats against the Casianos continue. On 7 August 2004, following the radio programme "La Escuela en Marcha", in which presenter Jorge Fernández had interviewed Fidel Guarda of the Lof Casiano and Marcelo Cayumil of CAI, he was accosted by Edgardo Abi Saad, who allegedly said to him:

> "Why do you get involved in this land business? Why do you give airtime to these shitty Indians? If they hold that meeting in Quetrequile, I'm going to shoot the shit out of them all!"

Fernández immediately reported the incident to the police. The meeting that Abi Saad referred to is the convening of the many groups and individuals who support the Casianos, due to be held a few days after the programme.

The issue is gradually attracting a high profile nationally. Even Nobel Peace Prize Winner Adolfo Pérez Esquivel has clearly declared his support for the Casianos. In an open letter to the Río Negro Provincial Governor dated 2 July 2004, he wrote:

> "Once again, the Mapuche people must suffer plundering and violence to the benefit of the interests of the powerful. This is the case of the Lof Casiano, who are threatened with eviction from their ancestral territory, which is to be returned to the landowner Abi Saad, and so the policy of marginalisation against our Original Peoples continues. In this way not only our National Constitution, but also ILO Convention 169, are being systematically violated.
>
> Señor Governor, how much longer must our Mapuche brothers and sisters suffer the policy of discrimination and impunity?"

Only time will answer that question. In the meantime, the news was announced in November 2005 that, after 16 years of dispute, the government may at last be planning to return the land to the Lof Casiano. So not every story of the Mapuche in Argentina leaves a bad taste in the mouth; let us close this chapter with what appears to be another piece of positive news.

Ancalao: when is a battle won?

It was with surprise and joy that supporters of the Mapuche read, in the issue of Argentine national newspaper "Página 12" of 1 March 2000, that: "For once, the Mapuche communities of the south of Argentina have won a battle, after decades of seeing the land on which they are settled despoiled. In a landmark decision, the Río Negro Courts have prevented two investors from fencing off a field located in the south of the province, of which they possess title of ownership, accepting an appeal presented by the Ancalao indigenous community, in which it is affirmed that the land has historically belonged to their people."

Cause for celebration indeed. All the more so, if we consider that the person who had transferred these lands to the Ancalao Mapuche community was Julio Argentino Roca himself, the butcher of the Conquest of the Desert, when he subsequently became Argentine President.

The only problem is that encroachments, furtive sales and the use of legal process against the community still continue. The media spotlight - to the extent that one report in one newspaper can ever constitute a media spotlight - will never be kept on such remote communities indefinitely, and as soon as it is switched off or directed elsewhere, dark forces recommence their work, spreading their thriving, invasive roots like knotweed.

Notes

*   NB: The information contained in this chapter was obtained from interviews and from the archives of the Co-ordinating Committee of Mapuche Organisations in Neuquén, the Mapuche Centre in San Carlos de Bariloche and the 11th October Organisation of Mapuche-Tehuelche Communities in Esquel.

1   The quote comes from a speech by Mauro to an assembly of Mapuches and supporters outside the Benetton estate, Chubut, to protest at the eviction of the Curiñanco-Nahuelquir family from the land they had claimed on that estate. The speech is on the video/CD "Marici Weu", 2003, produced by Gente de la Tierra/Indymedia Video.
2   "The Old Patagonian Express" by Paul Theroux, p. 429, published by Cape Cod Scriveners Co, 1979.
3   The figures are obtained from taking the averages of statistics from various sources, including ENDEPA (Equipo Nacional Pastoral Aborigen de la Iglesia Católica) and INAI (Instituto Nacional de Asuntos Indígenas).
4   The information on the *Nguillatun* comes primarily from Sara McFall, "Keeping Identity in its Place", Dphil Thesis in Social Anthropology, Oxford University 1998.
5   Letter published in "El Oeste" on 17/01/00.
6   Quoted from an interview that appeared in an article in "El Oeste", entitled "Nahuel Pan family denies Prane declarations", dated 10/01/00.
7   *Milico* is a pejorative word used in the Southern Cone of Latin America for policemen and soldiers. Because of their association with dictatorships in Chile and Argentina, they often command fear and loathing rather than respect.
8   The quote is from the Italian magazine "Avvenimenti", January 1999 issue.
9   According to a press release by the 11th October Organisation (mapuche.info.scorpionshops.com/mapu/MapuTehu021003.html).
10 Mauro Millán was interviewed in Esquel on 16th December 2002.
11 Azkintuwe, 28 July 2005.
12 www.interpatagonia.com/paseos/leleque/.
13 The transcript of the Session (952) is on www.legischubut.gov.ar/SES952.HT.
14 Interviewed in Neuquén, January 2002.
15 Translated from the official transcript of the session.
16 "Los conflictos territoriales de los Lof Mapuche en la Provincia de Río Negro", available in Spanish on http://www.pueblosindigenas.org/duch.htm.

GULU MAPU: CONFLICT TODAY IN BIO-BIO, ARAUCANIA AND THE LAKES, CHILE

Chapter ten is devoted to the main issues involving the Mapuche in Chile today. It looks at the battle of the Quintreman sisters - who in many ways embody the Mapuche struggle – to prevent the construction of the Ralco Dam, which will inevitably destroy their way of life. A clash that is equally damaging in its effects and implications is that between Mapuche communities and the forestry companies; the latter's influential media friends have assisted the attempt to portray the Mapuche as "terrorists", whereas it is often they who are the victims of extreme violence and of a compliant legal system. The chapter closes remembering Alex Lemun, gunned down by the police.

The place where the world ends

"The land where the world ends" is the meaning of the word Chile, in the Aymara language. And indeed, it is hard to find a description of Chile that does not refer to the remoteness of this slender country very early on.

Within this remoteness, the areas where the Mapuches are in conflict with the multinationals and the state are even more remote, since they are far away from the national capital, Santiago. It is often affirmed that it is in Santiago that the most popular sympathy is to be found among *winkas* for the demands of the Mapuches; this is perhaps not surprising, because Santiago is well away from the frontlines of conflict.

More importantly, Santiago is where all the major decisions are taken that affect the Mapuche. Politically, Chile is divided into twelve regions, but the power structure is highly centralised, with everything passing through Santiago and its government ministries and departments, with all their political affiliations and rivalries.

In Santiago traditional indigenous dress would be frowned upon, with its implications of backwardness, the very antithesis of the aspirations of a modern state. Yet, paradoxically, this supposed backwardness is central to the promotion

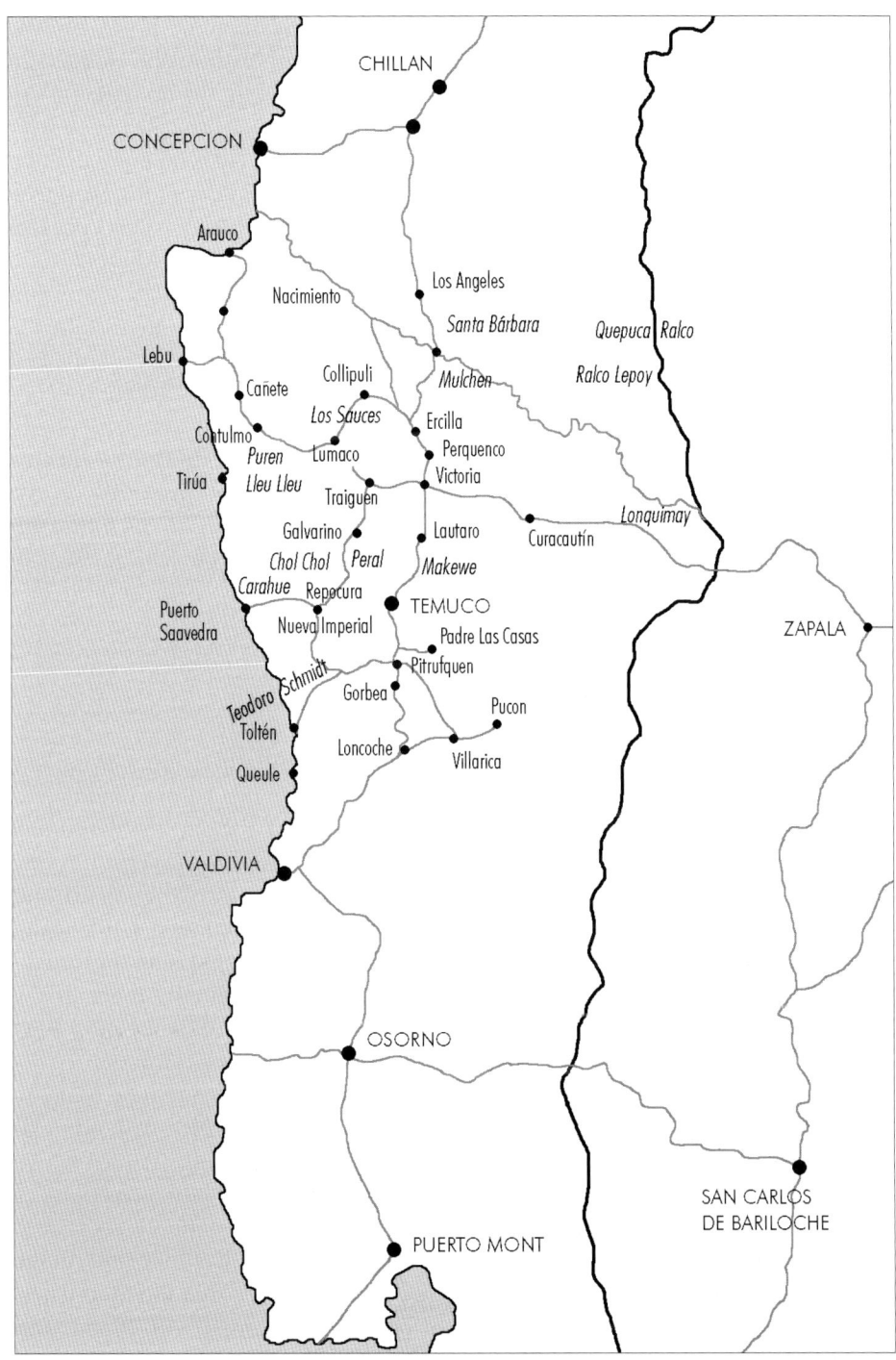

Map of towns in Bío Bío and Araucanía where communities are in conflict

of modern Chile, particularly in its guise as a tourist destination. If you browse through any travel book on Chile, you are almost sure to find the photo of a Mapuche woman in full traditional dress somewhere among the images.

The 1992 Census reveals that no less than 44 percent of Mapuches aged over 14 who declare themselves as such live in Santiago, some 400,000 plus, making up over 10 percent of the capital's population. Of the remainder of the Mapuche population, the majority is split between the 9th Region, Araucanía (144,000, 15.5 percent) and the 8th Region, Bío-Bío (125,000, 13.5 percent). 38,000 Mapuches, 26 percent, live in Temuco, the regional capital. This is indicative of a significant migration towards the cities, mainly due to the land's inability to sustain the population. The 2002 Census gives much lower Mapuche population figures, but there are reasons for this to do with the wording of the questions asked; we consider the census issue in chapter 12.

Though we will touch upon the situation of Chile's urban Mapuches in this chapter, and elsewhere in the book, here we will concentrate primarily on the Mapuches living in communities and in and around the small towns in the 9th Region, the sounds of whose clashes with the powers that be echo loudest in Chile's regional and national press.

Araucanía: Gateway to the Lakes

Geographically the Region of Araucanía is distributed into three main areas. The Andean area is dominated by the summits of the volcanoes Lanin, Llaima and Lonquimay. Access is difficult, as the stone roads are not always passable; small communities are scattered over the area. The central valley is traversed by the Pan-American Highway, the region's main road; here is Temuco, the capital, and the other main cities, Angol, Collipulli, Victoria, Lautaro, Pitrufquén, Gorbea and Loncoche. The area of the lakes (Villarrica, Calafquén, Caburga) is an intermediate stage between the mountain range and the central valley. Finally, there are the lowland areas of the coast, which are not very fertile and sparsely inhabited. Several large rivers run through the region, such as the Cautín and the Toltén.

Temuco is the capital of Cautín province and the Araucanían region, lying on the River Cautín. It was founded in 1881 after the land on which it stands was ceded by Mapuche leaders. The Cerro Ñielol, the hill overlooking Temuco where the copihue, Chile's national flower, grows in abundance, is now considered a national monument, and has been the site of many events of symbolic resonance for Temuco's Mapuches. It was on the Cerro Ñielol, on 10 November 1881, in the early hours of the morning, in the area known as *La Patagua*, that the Mapuches' *tokis* gathered around a *toki-kura* (stone of command) stained with blood, and decided to turn over the land so the city could be built.

A century later, the Cerro Ñielol was the site of a *nguillatún* held on 12 October 1999, in solidarity with the march of the Lafkenches and Pewenches to Concepción in protest against the celebration associated with Columbus' "discovery" of the Americas.

The hill is a versatile resource, serving the purposes of the most diverse interest groups. For instance, it was the site of the presenting of diplomas to 138 women belonging to 12 different Mapuche communities, to mark the completion of a course on Nutrition and Medicinal Plants organised by Forestal Mininco - about whom a great deal will be heard later in the chapter - showing the supposed commitment to conservation and development of this multinational forestry company.

General Augusto Pinochet himself was presented with a *toki-kura* on the Cerro Ñielol in 1986 by the Mapuche leaders who supported him. He was ousted with a general election that swept Patricio Aylwin to power in March 1990 in a wave of optimism. At the beginning of this new period of transition, Aylwin declared: "my government wishes to establish a different relationship with the indigenous peoples of Chile" and also spoke of "the recognition of the Indigenous Peoples as part of the diversity of Chilean society."[1]

Despite these noble sentiments, the truth is that today, a decade and a half later, the battle lines are still drawn. The Mapuche still experience the hostility of many sectors of a society that is still polarised. According to Juana Paillalef Carinao, director of the Mapuche Museum in Cañete, and a Mapuche herself: "Today Chile is still divided between Pinochetists and non-Pinochetists, between Mapuches and non-Mapuches. One local person opposed to the museum here said that he would line up the Mapuches and machine-gun down the whole lot of them!"[2]

We saw in the previous chapter that the Mapuches of the *Puel Mapu* are under threat on many fronts; if anything, the much more numerous Mapuches of the *Gulu Mapu* are even more threatened. More of them are killed, more injured, more arrested and imprisoned. In Chile it has above all been the advance of the forestry and hydroelectric companies south of the Bío-Bío river that has posed the greatest threat to the Mapuche communities, accompanied by the systematic violence of the state's security forces and private militias.

Against this advance, two elderly sisters have stubbornly stood their ground.

Symbols of the struggle: the *ñañas* against the dam

The *ñañas* (elder sisters) concerned are Nicolasa and Berta Quintreman, aged 65 and 79 respectively, who have come to speak for and symbolise the battle to prevent the construction of the Ralco Dam, part of the ambitious project for a huge complex of hydroelectric dams on the Bío-Bío River that would wash away the Mapuche communities that have been in the area for hundreds of years.

The Ralco Dam is not the only "megaproject" in the region. The Temuco bypass is another major scheme involving relocation of entire Mapuche communities, with no less than 23 communities affected directly by this "tumour established in Mapuche territory", as it has been called by Chilean anthropologist Jaime Soto Navarro[3]. Another major highway is planned between Concepción and Puerto Montt, passing through Lafkenche and Williche territories, also involving the cutting down of a swathe of the coastal forest. Then there is the bridge over the Chacao Channel, which will disrupt the way of life of the Williche People of the Island of Chiloe. Serious though the implications of these projects are, the Chilean government's landmark project, supposedly marking a watershed in relations with the country's indigenous peoples, is undoubtedly the Ralco Dam.

We interviewed Nicolasa Quintreman at her home on 25 January 2002. Against a background of cocks crowing in her yard, she uttered these defiant words, which she has surely repeated countless times to the many activists who have beaten a path to her door:

> "I was born and grew up here. My family has always lived here. My great grandfather said that Pewenches are buried where they lived; with the dam, all this will be lost. Why are we leaving our *Ñuke Mapu* (mother earth) without support? It is like killing your own mother. This is why we fight to the end; we are Mapuche-Pewenches. Endesa wants to sell the river to another country, but the river runs like the wind, and nobody stops the wind. They say we are crazy, drunk, dirty, but we are proud, we don't want handouts, we just want our land."

Reacting to the resistance against the project, that same Patricio Aylwin who heralded a new dawn of relations between the state and indigenous peoples is reported to have said that "five families cannot hold up the progress of the country."[4]

The Ralco project, devised during Pinochet's régime, is one of South America's many hydroelectric projects (Brazil alone plans 10 new hydro-electric dams in the Amazon region), and is the brainchild of the Spanish company Empresa Nacional de Energía (Endesa). The battle against the construction of dams in the Upper Bío-Bío region has already been lost, since back in 1996, following rubber-stamping by Eduardo Frei's government, Endesa built the Pangue Dam, with funding from the International Finance Corporation, the private sector lending arm of the World Bank. Frei himself inaugurated the Pangue Dam on 6 March 1997. In an article that appeared in *Resurgence* magazine, US environmentalist Penny Cabot wrote:

Photo of Nicolasa Quintreman by Grace Livingstone

"With only a loan agreement from the World Bank to adhere to and no environmental codes to keep them in line, Endesa were able to forge ahead with their plans, causing irreversible environmental damage. They took whatever land they wanted to build Pangue, which was completed and the reservoir secretly filled in September 1996, drying up the river and breaking a 1991 law. Flying high above the dam was the flag of Chile. Alongside it flew the flag of engineering company Swygto-Koppers. President Frei, a hydraulic engineer by trade, apparently divested himself of a major shareholding in this company before taking office."[5]

Despite Endesa claiming at the time that Pangue was a stand-alone project, events since then have made it all too clear that it was a dress rehearsal for the bigger performance that is Ralco.

There are a number of Pewenche communities living in the Upper Bío-Bío area affected by the dam. Primarily the communities of Ralco-Lepoy – to which the *ñañas* belong - and Quepuca-Ralco, but to a lesser extent others such as Malla Malla, Trapa Trapa and Quallaqui. These communities have existed in the area for centuries, and as their mobility has been increasingly limited by the expansion of the Chilean state to the west and the Argentine state to the east, they have gradually been pushed into their own forced ecological niche, that of dependency upon, verging on symbiosis with, the *pewen*, the staple for both themselves and their animals. If they were to move away from the area, they would literally cease to be Pewenche, the people of the *pewen*.

The lives of the members of the Mapuche communities affected by the dam project would never be the same again. In an article for the magazine *El Canelo* from 1997, Patricia Bustos describes the beginnings of this epic clash between tradition and "progress", when the community members found out that their sacred places, their orchards, cemeteries and meeting places would be totally flooded, and that they would have to move to other lands. On theirs a huge dam would be built: Ralco:

> "Their first reaction was bewilderment, and then came amazement. Amazement on account of the unsuspected benefits that were offered them in exchange for their homes. Housing, drinking water, electricity, animals, roads, bridges and schools. Help and training to increase their productivity, grants, tourism in the area, promotion of organisation and participation in communities, among many, many other benefits. The decision was in their hands, and the dilemma was a huge one. The possibility of improving their precarious living conditions, but in exchange for giving up a history, traditions and a whole way of life in Ralco. In spite of the doubt, most said no to what the businesspeople and technicians referred to simply as relocation."

In recent years the project has moved inexorably forward, despite the growing opposition from the Pewenche communities in the area and an increasing number of environmental and human rights organisations. The Chilean National Indigenous Commission resoundingly criticised the project in the following terms in its report to the United Nations Commission for Human Rights (Geneva, 15 April 2002):

> "The Ralco project […] is a typical case of the management of indigenous policy in Chile, since from the very beginning the project, which is a representative expression of the model of development being driven by the post-dictatorship governments, met with the determined opposition of the Mapuche-Pewenche communities, with the solidarity of environmentalist groups and wide sectors of Chilean and international society. […] The fact that the project is still going ahead demonstrates quite clearly that indigenous law, environment law and the National Corporation of Indigenous Development (CONADI) are worn out and useless tools for defending the interests of the indigenous peoples of Chile."

In fact the project and the government attitude associated with it go totally against the provisions and recommendations of Chapter 26 of the Action Plan for Sustainable Development (Agenda 21 of the Rio de Janeiro Conference), a document that the Chilean government claims to have supported and approved without reservation.

For the Mapuche floods, earthquakes, prolonged droughts or other calamities are the result of an imbalance in the forces of nature, which they attempt to correct with the convening of a *nguillatún*, their response to a crisis, whether political or natural. In recent years several *nguillatúns* have been held in the Upper Bío Bío to counteract the perceived disruption of the *newens* caused by the Ralco Dam.

The government evidently deems development to be a priority over environmental considerations. It would be tempting to paint the Chilean government as heartless, but the truth is that it finds itself in a real dilemma. It has made commitments to defend the environment and Chile's indigenous peoples, but Chilean society is desperate for energy. Endesa expects the 570-MW dam complex to meet 20 per cent of Chile's electricity requirement, but that requirement is increasing fast. In Santiago alone, the demand doubles every decade. The government must find a way to meet the country's energy demands, even if it means inconveniencing what it considers a few indigenous families. After all, endlessly on-tap energy is what a modern nation is all about, even if the social and environmental price is sky-high. As Juana Paillalef Carinao of the Mapuche Museum in Cañete put it succinctly: "we struggle to defend nature, they struggle to defend the economy."

According to Chilean Law 19.253, which is binding, no land can be bought or expropriated from indigenous communities by non-indigenous persons; the only means of acquiring indigenous land is through a land swap (*permuta*), authorised by CONADI. When Mauricio Huenchulaf, a Mapuche director of CONADI let it be known that he was opposed to the dam, he was removed from office and replaced with a more compliant director. Carrots and sticks were then employed to persuade the families to move to other land that had been set aside for them, such as El Barco, higher in the mountains, and El Huachi and Santa Laura, 80 km away. By May 1997, thanks to the temptations of the swap, with added sweeteners provided by the Pehuen Foundation, a charity set up by Endesa subsidiary Pangue S.A., only five of the 98 families were still holding out against the *permuta*. According to Sara Imilmaqui Aguas, of *Mapu Domuche Newen* (Women with the Force of the Land), a women's organisation opposed to the dam, the division between families here is between "those who believe the land is priceless, and those who think that land has a price, but it is a high one."[6]

That winter many of the latter group, who had originally agreed to move, found that they had sold their land too cheaply, when the higher land was covered in over a metre of snow, making it impossible for their animals to live there. So, having originally signed up to the scheme, they then publicly declared their change of mind.

Endesa even managed to recruit Berta's own 22-year-old son to their side; in early 2002 he was headhunted by them, clearly for strategic reasons. It is very saddening and disappointing to Berta that her only heir would willingly hand over her 7 hectares of land to Endesa.

The response of Nicolasa and Berta to the entreaties and injunctions of Endesa has been first to concede and then recede, to back down then back-pedal, to such an extent that it has been almost impossible for the observer to understand where exactly things stand, who is leading the strange dance. After all, as Berta has famously said, "talking is not swapping."

In early January 2002 it was said that they received $20 million from Endesa, in exchange for a signed undertaking to negotiate (called a pre-agreement), having already turned down an offer of a million dollars and 70 hectares. Yet on 5 January a press conference was held by Mapu Domuche Newen to deny that the sisters had swapped their land. In February 2003 Nicolasa was said to have reached agreement with Endesa over the *permuta*, and it was passed on to CONADI for approval. Yet six months later she was still leading the anti-dam campaign.

It has been difficult for those involved in the anti-dam campaign to work together, not least because of language problems. The language of Nicolasa and Berta is *Mapudungun*, and they struggle to express the concepts of their language in Spanish, just as Spanish speakers who are not fluent in *Mapudungun* struggle to understand them.

According to Sara Imilmaqui:

"The *ñañas* don't understand this Western language. It is very difficult to speak the Western language if you speak another language. Hilda Riquelme[7] and I don't speak *Mapudungun*, so it is difficult for us. Their language is based on other concepts. What they want is quite clear to them: loving the land, the rivers, is spiritual, not ecological, it is more profound."[8]

When Berta speaks on the dam issue in Spanish, her words are punctuated with the invocation in Mapudungun *mapu ñuke mapu chau* (mother earth father earth). Her and her sister's spirituality is also not understood by the members of Chile's official faith. When the sisters protested in front of the house of the newly invested cardinal, Monsignor Francisco Javier Errazuriz, in March 2001, they were received by one of his bishops, who promised to pass on their message to the cardinal. Nicolasa said that the bishop treated them "like fools, and never understood our vision of mother earth. If they really believe in the god who gives us light, they will decide in our favour. But we want that to be soon."[9]

The Pewenches and GABB, the Action Group for the Bío Bío, the umbrella organisation for those against the dam, have attempted to act to oppose the project both through the law and through direct action. They even attempted to sign up Hillary Clinton to support the campaign. Despite concerted attempts by the Chilean authorities to keep the former First Lady away from them, a group of ecologists led by Nicolasa Quintreman managed to meet her briefly in Santiago on 19 April 1998, on the occasion of her visit to Chile for the Second Summit of the

Americas. During the meeting, Nicolasa explained to Hillary how she was one of the people threatened with being unavoidably displaced from their ancestral lands, and gave her a gift of some handmade wool socks from the Pewenche and a copy of the report by the lawyers of International Federation of Human Rights (FIDH). "That was the highlight of the meeting", said one of Hillary's assistants[10]. It is not known whether Mrs Clinton has been able to devote any time to assisting the campaign since their meeting, or whether she has worn the socks.

El Mercurio, one of Santiago's daily newspapers, with an editorial line consistently hostile to the Mapuche, has published many articles that neatly invert the reality of the situation south of the Bío-Bío, alleging that Mapuches have caused the problems they face through land-grabbing, violence and arson:

> "Attempts have been made to accommodate the indigenous demands with more property and more money, yet they continue nonetheless and are expressed with new land occupations and new attacks. This social conflagration cannot be put out with offers of more and more land."[11]

If the press have been against them, the police have not been sympathetic either. When the two elderly sisters took part in a blockade of the dam area on 18 February 1999, they were even charged with assaulting military personnel. Their supporters were not oblivious to the humour of the absurd accusation:

> "We believe it to be very bold of Chile's armed forces to accuse us of mistreating special forces policemen holding firearms, bullet-proof vests, shields, helmets, batons and tear gas, during the incident."[12]

Nevertheless, such charges, and repeated violence on the part of the police, have undoubtedly had the effect of scaring off some activists who would otherwise have become more involved in the campaign. Foreign activists have been detained and deported, such as Marc Serra i Torrent, a Catalan journalist, who was deported in March 2002, effectively gagging him and preventing him from revealing anything further about the situation.

The Ralco Dam is very much a test case for the policy of the Chilean government in relation to the country's indigenous peoples, indeed the report of the International Federation for Human Rights referred to it as such in its report following its investigative mission to the region in July 1997, going on to state in its conclusion: "the IFHR urges the Chilean authorities to fulfil their obligations, both national and international, to find a solution that respects effectively and fully the rights of the Mapuche-Pewenche peoples."[13]

Rodolfo Stavenhagen, UN Special Rapporteur for Indigenous Peoples, visited the area of conflict in early 2003, in the same period when the Interamerican Commission for Human Rights of the Organisation of American States enjoined the Chilean government to act in the interests of the Pewenche families involved in the conflict.

Finally, on 16 September 2003, a Memorandum of Agreement was signed between Endesa and the *ñañas*, in which it was agreed that the disputed land was to pass over into the possession of the former. Endesa have now completed the dam and flooded the area. Ralco is one of the largest roller-compacted concrete dams in the world, covering an area of 3.5 thousand hectares. So far Endesa have not fulfilled their promises made in the memorandum of Agreement. Now the area is flooded, the ground where the *nguillatún* were held to attempt to conserve a balance of the forces of nature lies under 1.2 billion cubic metres of water.

In August 2005 Berta Quintreman and members of the Quepuca-Ralco and Ralco-Lepoy communities visited La Moneda to formally protest to the government. Socialist Party Deputy Alejandro Navarro, who accompanied them, stated: "The Chilean State signed a commitment before the Interamerican Commission of Human Rights, facilitating the agreement and resolving the problem of the Upper Bio-Bio with the Ralco project. That is, the Quintreman sisters and the Pewenche women signed this agreement that committed the Chilean state to be guarantor that Endesa would complete the various stages of the delivery of benefits to the families affected. This guarantee has not been met, since the 67-hectare property given to Berta Quintreman has no water and is infertile."[14]

A Desert of pine and eucalyptus

From floods to deserts, it seems that encounters between international capital and Mapuches tend to leave extreme environmental consequences.

It is a platitude often heard in Chile that the legislative structure of domination established by Pinochet's dictatorship has not been dismantled, even if Grandpa[15] himself has now retired into the shadows. Opinions differ as to whether this structure is a strait-jacket restricting the progressive actions of the *Concertación* (Reconciliation) governments, or whether it provides a convenient justification for the acceptance by them of Pinochet's economic model, and even its fine-tuning.

We saw above that many of the megaprojects now being implemented were devised during the dictatorship. It is also true that in the forestry sector, the low wages, strike bans, violent suppression of protests, lack of legal protection for workers, and, last but not least, the laws allowing the irreplaceable age-old forests of holm-oak and rauli beech to be chopped down, all date back to Pinochet's time in power. The General also returned all the land that had been expropriated by the Allende government to be used by the indigenous communities to the "original" landowners; much of this land has now ended up in the hands of the forestry companies, particularly in the areas of Arauco, Lumaco and Purén.

According to data in the Statistical Yearbook for Latin America and the Caribbean produced by the Economic Commission for Latin America, cited by *Le Monde Diplomatique*[16], between 1976 and 1997 there was a 53-percent increase in the area of forestry being exploited in the 8th and 9th Regions, the Mapuches' traditional homeland, a total of 1,677,000 square kilometres.

Adolfo Millabur is one of only three Mapuche mayors in Chile, and – despite his slight physique and personable, unassuming manner - is certainly the most outspoken. He has used his position as mayor of the small coastal town of Tirúa to challenge the power of the forestry companies head-on. These are his accusations:

> "They produce no resources for the local communities and provide no employment for local people in the region. They pay no taxes of any kind. Quite the reverse: under decree 701 they are subsidised by the state, which refunds the capital they invest in proportion to the area under cultivation. Their trucks and heavy machinery destroy roads with no thought for the people who live here."[17]

Yet, as we mentioned at the beginning of this chapter, Forestal Mininco devote a great deal of time and money to convincing the community that they are working for their good. Their magazine, *El Buen Vecino* (The Good Neighbour), goes to considerable lengths to explain the extent of their good works and good intentions.

In year 2, issue 6 of the magazine, they answer their own question "What business are we in?" in these terms:

> "Every time we use some of the products obtained from wood, such as paper and exercise books, pencils, chairs, tables, blackboards, among many other products, it is thanks to the fact that there has been a production process that has enabled this material to be transformed into the different elements that are so useful to us."

The good works of Forestal Mininco also extend to safeguarding the environment. According to their website (www.mininco.cl/medioambiente.htm):

> "Forest plantation is the main ecological contribution made by CMPC[18]. The use of thousands of hectares of eroded land *that were of no use* and now have vigorous trees means wealth for the country and help in keeping the environment clean." [my italics]

The truth about the ecological benefits of growing pine (mainly *pinus radiata*) and eucalyptus (*eucalyptus globules*) - these are the species that are mainly planted by

Mininco and the other logging companies, on account of their fast, high yields - is more complex, as one might expect, with the disbenefits balancing if not outweighing the benefits. According to a report by Washington College and the University of San Francisco on reforestation with eucalyptus and pine in Ecuador[19], the advantages are the halting of erosion, rapid growth and economic value, since the wood from these trees can be regularly harvested. The disadvantages are that both species dry out the soil and cause it to become acidic, thus reducing biodiversity, since acidic soil makes it hard for autochthonous species to grow, and decreasing overall biomass, which even works to limit the biomass of the eucalyptus and pine themselves.

The Mapuches living in communities have no doubt about the effect of pine and eucalyptus on their land and livelihood:

> "Now the area around here is too dry, at other times of the year it floods. The plantations of pine and eucalyptus are drying out the land; our wells are drying, so we have to go to the river for water."
>
> *Fernando Movil Urbina,*
> *of the Buchahueico community near Lumaco* [20]

> "Our community has no water, not even for our animals, no medicine for the *machi*. We cannot find our traditional remedies any more; they don't grow. Pine and eucalyptus are drying out the land."
>
> *Julio Ñanculeo*
> *of the Anadela community outside Lumaco* [21]

The less sustainable the land becomes, the more Mapuches are driven off it and into the cities in search of work. So in a sense the very infertility of the land is slowly working to the benefit of the timber companies, as it is depleting the opposition to them.

The forestry companies of course deny such claims. We asked José Manuel Rebolledo, area manager of Forestal Arauco for Cañete, to respond to accusations that pine and eucalyptus dry up and acidify the soil during an interview in his office just outside Cañete on 14 December 2001:

> "There has been some talk of lack of water, acidification of soil. I say this is a myth. It is due to climate problems, lack of rain. The process is not cyclical, which would enable us to predict rainfalls. It rains half the amount it rained 100 years ago. Besides, eucalyptus consumes only half the water of local varieties."

Having said that, Señor Rebolledo went on to explain how the company attempts to minimise the acidification that the plantations do not cause:

"This is a young sector; the oldest plantations are 35 years old. Originally 2500 trees were planted per hectare. Now we plant 1500, or even 800; the plants are spaced out more, so they allow in more light, and do not affect the flora and fauna to the same degree. The forest is not dark, so does not create the same level of acidification today as in the past."

The damage to the plants may not be due to the dryness and acidity of the soil caused by pine and eucalyptus alone, but possibly also to indiscriminate use of pesticides. After the autochthonous species are cleared, they begin to recover in the short term, so the forestry companies allegedly use chemical defoliants, some of which are prohibited in other countries, to protect the exotic species from the native ones.[22] One case of such use is described by Chilean researchers Ruperto Ramos and Rodrigo Catalán:

"... They began to fumigate the pines in this place on account of a destructive larva that they claimed attacked the pines. Light aircraft arrived there to fumigate. But the pines were not touched much by the pesticide, most of it fell upon other fields that it was not supposed to touch. The smell of the pesticide that the planes discharged from that height reached here. It affected the water too, most of the streams that arise there and the streams come down here, where there are more families..." [23]

When we put it to Señor Rebolledo that respiratory deseases in the Mapuche communities may have been caused by the use of pesticides, he said that he had never heard of this happening.

An equally serious accusation, made by the Arauco-Malleco Co-ordinating Committee of Communities in Conflict, is that the forest fires that affected 53,000 hectares of native forest of southern Chile in the month of February 2002, started deliberately by persons unknown, were associated with the forestry companies. This environmental catastrophe could thus be seen as being prompted by the forestry companies' desire to expand while conveniently sidestepping – by clandestine action - the laws protecting native species such as monkey-puzzle, *coigue* (southern beech) and rauli beech.

The Mapuche's problems due to the presence of the forestry companies are not just caused by the dryness of the soil, but by something much more alarming for the communities. The introduced species have drastically reduced the presence of the medicinal plants, the *lawen*, which are used by the *machi* for remedies and also to ward off malignant spirits. The disappearance of the *lawen* indicates an imbalance in the *newen*, the forces that link the Mapuche individually and collectively with their land. According to English anthropologists David McKinnon and Sara McFall: "Actions that damage the capacity of the people to relate with their territory in this way, receiving the *newen* in its multiple expressions and fortifying it in its daily form of existence, threaten the culture in its entirety. From various perspectives, the expansion of the plantations of exotic species within Mapuche territory could be interpreted as such a threat."[24] If the *lawen* are no longer to be found by the *machi* today, how will they be able to pass on their skills in identifying them to the next generation? The communities believe they are fighting for their very survival as a people.

Communities in conflict

Around 500 Mapuche communities are in conflict with forestry companies over land. Stated in those terms, the fact does not seem so shocking, but numbers alone do not render the extent to which rural society south of the Bío-Bío River is at war with itself over land.

Not all these conflicts are stand-off situations, with the forestry companies holding the land and the communities vainly claiming it. Many are in a continual state of flux, with the communities, impatient at the inactivity of the authorities, regularly reinforcing their claims with de facto occupations. Within the space of one month, April 1999, seven *fundos* (the Spanish name given to properties in the countryside) were occupied by members of the communities claiming them: Cuyinco, Tranicura, Rucañanco, Pidenco, Santa Rosa de Colpi and Hacienda Lleu-Lleu.

More often than not, the occupiers are forcibly removed by the police, and usually arrested. Yet amazingly, in the face of abundant evidence to the contrary, the representatives of the forestry companies regularly claim that they are on good terms with the communities. José Manuel Rebolledo talks of the company's relationship with them:

> "We are open to talking to Mapuches, if they want access to the sea, for example, for fishing, or to collect forest fruit or firewood. We have a team of forest rangers, who may be Mapuche or non-Mapuche; this is the first contact. Then there is an authorisation from the manager. They need something, so by talking we can reach agreement. Three or four years ago there were problems, now we sit round a table and sort it out. We always try to establish a dialogue. We do not have one dialogue with 20 communities, because each community has its own particular issues, each has a different objective; they are never organised enough to approach us as a group."[25]

This is the stereotypical image popularly given to the Mapuche in Chile, as disorganised and argumentative, unable to work in concert to achieve an objective. Always implicit is the paternalistic attitude whereby "if only they would co-operate more, then we'd be able to help them."

Señor Rebolledo's words were circumspect on the subject of how the company came to own the land.

> "We have been in the area as a company for 32 years; we have been the fifth owner of this land since the Mapuches. The first owners (1905-1910) may have tricked them, done something fishy, made them sign or place their thumbprint; but we bought legitimately."

Let us give the example of one community - Esteban Yebilao - to show the contorted process through which one particular piece of land came to be in the hands of Forestal Mininco[26]. The community is located in Choque Alto, near Tirúa, and claims a total of 400 hectares, 100 of which held by Forestal Volterra and 300 by Forestal Mininco. The land concerned was rented out by settler Arnaldo Ebensperguer to the community *lonko* Esteban Yebilao, and 400 hectares appear in Ebensperguer's name in a document from 1930. During the process of Agrarian Reform (1967-1973), he handed over the land to the Corporation for Agrarian Reform (CORA) for the establishment of a *campesino* settlement. The Corporation later handed over the land to the National Forestry Corporation (CONAF) to be planted with trees, a decision that met with the community's approval. Yet after the military coup, the CONAF handed over the land to Forestal Mininco, who in 1992 sold 100 hectares to Forestal Volterra. Mininco cannot be accused of stealing the land from the community, yet the process whereby it came into their possession is dubious to say the least.

Since the return to democracy, attempts have been made through CONADI to return some of the land to its rightful owners. The government provides CONADI with funds to purchase land from the forestry companies, land which is then returned to the communities.

Señor Rebolledo is happy with the process, and says that relations with the communities are good and mutually beneficial:

> "We are working with the communities. They recognise that this land is ours, but that the land was unjustly taken from them. They want the state, through CONADI, to return the land to them; we have 11 situations of this kind.
>
> We have generated 4,000 jobs in the wood sector, and 3,500 jobs in the industrial side, e.g. cellulose and manufacturing. Previously we did not employ Mapuches; now we want at least 50 percent of the people working in the wood sector to be of Mapuche origin. We also work to encourage leisure, camping, Mapuche food, textiles, knowledge of woodland fruits, fungi. They have the knowledge, but we are managing the resources through another company. We don't want people to migrate to the city, but to remain in the country."[27]

Though the forestry companies clearly approve of the process of sale through CONADI, the communities are still sceptical; even those who have benefited from the initiative, such as the Buchahueico community near Lumaco. According to their *werken*, Fernando Móvil Urbina:

> "They took land from us during the dictatorship, now we are recovering it. The forestry companies are in the middle. Through CONADI we have recovered some land, but very little. Our grandparents owned this land, and one day we will recover all of it. We should not buy the land, of course, because it's ours. The state is having to pay huge amounts of money to individuals. We need machinery to work the land, because even if the state buys land for us, through CONADI, it's completely dry. Over recent years we've managed to survive by selling a few animals, by growing a little food."[28]

The reader will recall from discussion of the Ralco Dam dispute above that the Chilean press, particularly the *El Mercurio* newspaper, has been far from sympathetic to the Mapuche in their struggle, indeed going so far as to call them and their supporters eco-terrorists. This is also the case in their conflicts with the forestry companies. While *El Mercurio* has turned a blind eye to the damage to the communities caused by aridity, acidification fumigation and forest fires, it has been keen to highlight the violence they have used in pursuit of their goals. The newspaper has been fiercely critical of CONADI's land purchasing scheme, particularly with regard to the transfer of the *fundos* Alaska and Ginebra to the Ignacio Queipul community of Ercilla and the communities of Collipulli respectively, as a result of the uncompromising, proactive attitude of the communities concerned. An article entitled "Government rewards intransigent Mapuches" begins with the following paragraph: "Indians who have occupied properties, provoked fires, destroyed machinery and attacked workers have been rewarded with land by the government."[29]

The Head of Mideplan at the time, Alejandra Krauss, was unpopular with the newspaper because she rubber stamped these deals, even though when she took up the position she had supposedly stated that she would not favour "violent" Mapuche groups; the communities themselves, on the other hand, considered her too remote, as they claimed she never left her comfortable office in Santiago to come and see the situation for herself. Krauss (2000-02), has been succeeded by Jaime Andrade, Andrés Palma, and, since 2004, Yasna Provoste; all have suffered from the apparent lack of desire to see the situation for themselves. Were they to have visited the region, the Mideplan Ministers would have found a situation of escalating violence.

Delinquents, terrorists and foreign infiltrators

A worrying development in 2002 was the reporting of the supposed existence of a vigilante paramilitary organisation known as the "Hernán Trizano Squad." This squad was named after the mercenary of Italian origin who fought in Cyprus, Russia and the War of the Pacific before combating alongside Cornelio Saavedra in the Pacification of Araucanía, and later with an irregular army supporting José Bunster in the colonisation of the region. A statue commemorating this famous "Mapuche-hunter" stands in Avenida Balmaceda in Angol. The new group, named in honour of Chile's Buffalo Bill, as Trizano was also known, is supposedly once again fighting alongside business interests in the region to suppress opposition from its indigenous people. The existence of any organisation of this name has been denied by Jorge Correa Sutil, Minister of the Interior.

The communities have not only been persecuted unofficially. The level of violence and oppression against them from the forces of law and order gives the impression that the whole region is under a state of siege. Though the use of the law against the Mapuche is as old as the Chilean state itself, with peaks during the Pacification and the Dictatorship, the use of the law against them under the new democracy dates back to 1992, when a series of symbolic land recoveries were followed by the detention of 100 Mapuches by the police. Since then it is not only the men who have felt the full force of the law: María Isabel, of the Corporation of Mapuche Women *Aukiñko Zomo* (Voice of Women) of Temuco, claims that "since 1997 many women have even had to give birth in Chile's prisons. We are presented as delinquents for defending our lawful rights."[30]

Chilean politicians are concerned about the exacerbation of what has become known euphemistically as The Mapuche Question. More than anything, they seem to be principally concerned about the effect of the conflict on the image of Chile abroad. They must have been worried when a scathing article appeared in prestigious French newspaper *Le Monde Diplomatique*, dated November 1999, highlighting the racism and brutality employed by the police and paramilitaries:

> ""Pigs", "dogs", "Indian scum", "Indian bastards." The methods and language of Chile's police and paramilitary *carabineros* have changed little since the day in September 1973 when President Salvador Allende was overthrown and thousands of Popular Unity militants were imprisoned. On 18 and 19 February this year, 43 Mapuche Indians, militant ecologists and their student supporters, were arrested in the provinces of Bío-Bío and Traiguén. The brutal repression that led up to the arrests - a search for supposed "terrorists" - left more than 30 wounded. In March the situation deteriorated. A hundred arrests, a dozen wounded and losses estimated at

several thousand dollars followed the operations of the paramilitaries and private guards employed by forestry companies to "deal" with the Mapuches' claims to their ancestral territories."[31]

Such articles have prompted calls for action. For example, Eugenio Tuma, an MP from the Partido por la Democracia, wrote the following in an open letter to President Lagos in 2001:

"In your capacity as Head of State, you know better than anyone that a conflict of this nature threatens the international image of Chile, the reliability of the country for investors and the image of its government."[32]

Voices further to the right in the Chilean Parliament believe the very unity of the Chilean state is under attack. To quote Jorge Martínez Busch, the former Commander-in-Chief of the Navy, now a Senator, speaking on 16 June 1999:

"All these [Mapuche] communities and groups receive international support. It is clear that there are pro-Mapuche organisations (such as the Belgian American Indian Committee, Mapuche International Link, of Holland, the Ñuke Mapu Documentation Project, of Sweden, the Mapuche Interregional Council, of England) that, in combination with the actions of Chilean citizens with Mapuche roots, will lead to a worsening of the conflict, if spaces are opened up that directly attack national unity."

Such a view gained further ground in April 2003, with the publication of the book "La Cuestión Mapuche", published by the right-wing Instituto Libertad y Desarrollo (Freedom and Development Institute), particularly the chapter by Andrés Benavente and Jorge Jaraquemada dealing with the "political connections of Mapuche groups." Commenting on the furore provoked by the publication of the book, the *El Diario Austral* newspaper of Temuco, owned by the *Mercurio* group, stated that the thesis of the chapter is that "the mobilisations and acts of violence that have occurred in the zone are the fruit of its own dynamic, inspired by the radical indigenism arising in Mexico during the Zapatista insurrection, the objective of which is to create situations of ungovernability. Even worse, the mobilisations aim at the creation of armed social groups."[33] Mapuche organisations, particularly *Aukiñ Wallmapu Ngulam*, were quick to affirm that their claims are just and their methods peaceful.

Such accusations were not new, however. Back in December 1997, when three lorries loaded with timber were burnt in an arson attack, the then Minister of the Interior, Carlos Figueroa, said that these were "acts of terrorism", stating that the government was aware of a history of subversive infiltration in the Mapuche community, implying links with ERP (the People's Revolutionary Army).[34]

When on 9 June 2005 landowner Jorge Luchsinger was attacked by masked men and his house on the Fundo Santa Margarita, near Temuco, burnt down, he did not hesitate to "identify" his masked assailants: "They were from the Coordinadora Arauco-Malleco ... professional terrorists."[35] Luchsinger has made unsubstantiated claims that he has been the victim of 22 incendiary attacks.

Newspapers have not been slow to repeat such claims. Back on 30 December 1999, an article in the magazine *El Siglo* had made the outrageous claim that the Mapuche Inter-Regional Council had associated with Nazi organisations. And in an article in *El Sur* on 13 January 2002, Héctor Ruiz Arias claimed that Mapuche organisations had "links with websites of armed organisations." This claim was repeated as recently as June 2005, when *El Diario Austral* had the following headline on Sunday 19: "Terrorism on the Web."[36]

These are curious inversions of reality whereby organisations whose primary role is to report and denounce violence against Mapuche communities are accused of inciting the violence themselves and fomenting revolution and Mapuche nationalism.

Meanwhile, prominent Mapuches accuse the state of spying on their political organisations. According to Juan Pichún, *werken* of Temulemu community: "The government talks about preventing crimes, about anticipating possible criminal acts in the Mapuche area, but we are political and social organizations. The Mapuche are a social movement that is being investigated today as through it were a terrorist movement. I find it shameful that in Ricardo Lagos' democracy the government is conducting these espionage operations against our communities"[37]. And espionage may prove to be only be the thin end of the wedge, as past event has shown.

A people under siege: violence against the Mapuche

In late January and early February 2001, the small town of Tirúa in the Arauco region, with a population of less than 10,000, came under martial law. Special units of *carabineros* from Arauco were drafted in to reinforce local units, apparently believing intelligence reports that Mapuche actions against Forestal Arauco were imminent; specifically, they had been informed of a planned attack on a crop-spraying plane in the company aerodrome.

The quiet fishing town had to suffer the frightening and surreal spectacle of armed patrols and tanks crawling along its streets. Despite the bizarre situation in which they found themselves, the workers in the municipal offices attempted to carry on as normal. It may be no coincidence that it was Tirúa that was chosen for this show of force, since its mayor is Mapuche-Lafkenche Adolfo Millabur, Chile's first indigenous mayor.

By now Mayor Millabur has become used to such provocations. Interviewed for this book on 4 February 2002, Millabur said the following about his relations with the police, the army and the media:

> "Above all, we have problems with the police, but also with the media, who have a political philosophy that obeys the economic interests of this country. In May last year four Mapuches were shot and wounded by the police. We reported the whole thing, but it was in vain: no one did anything. In Chile mayors have no influence over the police. They have to respect me nominally, because of protocol, but whenever they can complicate my life, they do so."

The Mapuche's right to demonstrate peacefully has also often been quashed by the brute force of law and order. In Temuco, in July 2001, a demonstration called by various Mapuche organisations against the repression, discrimination and arrogance of the state institutions was violently put down by police. According to a report by the left-wing *Punto Final* magazine, which, in contrast with the majority of Chile's news media, has been generally sympathetic to the Mapuche and supportive of their aspirations:

> "The Mapuches mobilised with organisation and dignity, assembling in various points of Temuco, spreading out their forces, which in turn forced the dispersion of the police. The latter's inability to deal effectively with the Mapuche tactics undoubtedly contributed to stirring up their rage, so there was no surprise at the violent repression unleashed against the demonstrators. In spite of what the government claims, "there is no new relationship for the indigenous peoples, neither a new relationship nor democracy from the *carabineros*, just abuse of power", said Domingo Rain, of the Malalhue community, in the district of Teodoro Schmidt. "Here there was humiliating treatment of everyone, brothers and sisters. They hit us like dogs. Three of them stood on me, they insulted and hit me. There is a tremendous racism and *carabineros* are waging their own war against the Mapuche." Yet Colonel Luis Torres, Prefect of Cautín, stated that his men "acted with considerable professionalism."[38]

The New Relationship alluded to in the quote from Domingo Rain is the Commission for Historical Truth and a New Relationship (*Comisión de Verdad Histórica y Nuevo Trato*), set up by President Lagos in January 2001 to look at ways of improving relations between the Chilean state and its indigenous peoples, which is discussed in chapter 8. Domingo Rain is clearly sceptical about the efficacy of the Commission.

In June 2003, 6 Mapuche students were wounded and 29 arrested when police raided the Mapuche Hogar Las Encinas student hall of residence in Temuco. Mapuche student activists believe this was a clear attempt to break up Mapuche student and support organisations, as among those arrested were Carmen Jaramillo, spokesperson of the Hogar, Juan Pichún, who acts as spokesperson for the Mapuche political prisoners of Traiguén, and is the son of *lonko* Pascual Pichún (see below), and Gabriel Meñaco, son of *lonko* Avelino Meñaco of the Pascual Coña Community (again, see below) of Lleu-Lleu. The Hogar made the news again on 8 September 2005, when 58 students occupied the nearby offices of INDAP (Institute for Farming and Stockbreeding Development), to protest at the cramped, unhealthy conditions at the hostel. They were forcibly evicted, and 26 of them charged with "illegal occupation of a public place." To protest at this treatment, on 13 September six students chained themselves inside the offices of CONADI; they in turn were arrested.

Some of the most extreme brutality has been reserved for the members of the *Lof* Pascual Coña, a community engaged in a continuing struggle with entrepreneur Osvaldo Carvajal, who plans to develop a tourist complex on the banks of Lake Lleu Lleu near Cañete, on land that the community claim as theirs.

Back in March 1999, over a hundred *carabineros* raided the community, arresting a number of Mapuches. Luis Llanquilef, at the time a member of Adolfo Millabur's staff, went to inquire about the situation of those detained, and was also arrested.

In 2001 Carvajal even claimed compensation from the state for the damage he had allegedly suffered, due to occupations and fires, but his claim was thrown out by magistrate Ana Bianchi, who stated that the protection afforded him by the authorities had been more than sufficient, and perhaps even the detriment of the rest of the community.

In January of that year young Mapuche Abraham Santi Calbullanca lost his right eye when a rubber bullet was shot at him at point blank range. He and members of the Pascual Coña community and their supporters were occupying an area of the disputed land when they were assaulted by a large number of *carabineros*. Abraham was taken to the health centre in Cañete, 30 km away, where they refused to treat him, telling him to go to Concepción, 170 km from Cañete, for an appointment the following day. He did not wait, but made his way there, and fortunately he was admitted. His right eye was surgically removed.

MP Alejandro Navarro (Socialist Party) and Mayor Alfonso Millabur sued the *carabineros* of Concepción for "unnecessary violence resulting in serious injuries." Bizarrely, Navarro has himself been accused by Carvajal of being involved in a fire bombing attack on his property in March 1999. Navarro believes that Carvajal has planned a "concerted action" against the Mapuche together with Jorge Luchsinger.[39]

In April 2001 the police raided Pascual Coña, arresting *lonko* Avelino Meñaco and his son. Young Mapuche poet and musician Lionel Lienlaf has written an angry, moving account of this raid, which, to close this section, is worth quoting in full:

"Some days ago at dawn, a hundred or so heavily armed police raided a Mapuche house in the Pascual Coña community, in the Eighth Region of Chile. They broke down the doors, pointing their weapons at the whole family, including children. After the usual racist insults, they took away and arrested the *lonko* of the community, Avelino Meñaco, and his son, not even giving them time to dress properly. The raid was ordered by a Visiting Minister (a special judge appointed to pursue the Mapuche movement, by virtue of the Law of Internal Security of the State). These events were repeated in other homes that same morning, with three people arrested and taken to Concepción jail.

Then in Chile's newspaper headlines I read "Mapuche violence", "Mapuche terrorism in the south", but nothing is said about the children hit by *carabineros*, or people woken up at midnight, with machine guns pointing at them and tear gas canisters everywhere. Nothing is said about the *peñi* who lost an eye after a *carabinero* shot him at point blank range, or about the beaten up *machi*, or about the baby suffocated by the smoke-bombs that the police criminally hurled into the houses. Nothing about the armed forestry guards either, or about the entrepreneurs who, shielding themselves behind the state (the law, they say), privatise the police.

For many long years in the south, this damp south, we Mapuches have seen silence, death and the looting of our lands, and they call us violent! Banished to the most inhospitable places of our formerly rich and fertile land, and today, thanks to the "progress" driven by the entrepreneurs, impoverished by the monocultivation of pines and eucalyptuses.

Our sacred places have been razed, as have the trees, as have the very names we have given to the places we inhabit, as have the waters. And not content with this, they spray us with insecticides and tear gas and humiliation. And they call us violent.

Every day huge trucks rumble along the dusty roads that cut through our poor lands, each time covering us with dust, noise and that penetrating stink of petroleum. And that black smoke that sticks to the clothes and the body. As though they wanted to wipe out even our faces and our homes.

They are bound to keep assaulting us each dawn,
trying to interrupt our dreams,
they are bound to keep isolating us in their jails,
they are bound to keep calling us violent.

Their judges, their lawyers, their policemen
and armed guards are bound to come.
Bound to ...

But they will not uproot our history, they will not make me forget the names of the birds, the trees, my grandmother's stories, stories of this damp land, because the territory is not what they see as an economic asset. The territory is the dreams and spirits of our ancestors. The territory is fire, it is air, it is water.
The territory is also our rage."[40]

A law unto themselves: Mapuches and the legal system

Using their rage as fuel, Mapuches have used various form of non-violent protest against the actions of the forestry companies in recent years, such as marches, demonstration, occupations and hunger strikes.

Some of them have also committed violent acts, such as stonings of police and pitched battles, as well as arson and sabotage. Acts that cannot be condoned, but can at least be understood. As is to be expected, it is such acts that provide the justification for the violence on the part of the forces of law and order that inevitably follows.

A curious and worrying legacy of the Pinochet era is that in Chile the military courts judge not only the crimes committed by members of their own institutions, but also acts committed by civilians involving aggression against uniformed officers and acts the National Security legislation defines as acts of "terrorism and internal subversion." Such as those referred to in the previous paragraph. It is very difficult to understand where the limits of military jurisdiction lie.

It is supremely ironic that anti-terrorist legislation devised by Pinochet to control opponents politically to his left is now being used by the latter, now in government, against Mapuche organisations, such as the Arauco-Malleco Mapuche Co-ordinating Committee (CAM). In February 2000 the CAM Office of Human Rights published a report into human rights abuses perpetrated against Mapuches[41], including the systematic use of torture during detention. José Omar Ancán, of the Colihuinca Tori community near Collipulli, was arrested and held in isolation in Temuco Prison on 23 December 1998. There he was interrogated about various crimes, including arson against Forestal Mininco's Fundo Rucañanco. He states that during interrogation he was beaten on the face, abdomen, legs, and his eardrums were almost burst by simultaneous blows with open hands on both ears (this form of torture is known as the "telephone"). They kept beating him until he signed a declaration confessing his involvement in the arson attack.

Alberto Coliñir Painemal of the Truf-Truf community was arrested on 16 December 1999 and detained, along with other members of his community, at the *Carabinero* Station in Padre Las Casas, near Temuco. There he was punched, kicked and hit with sticks, electricity was applied to sensitive parts of his body, and he was semi-asphyxiated with plastic bags (a technique known as the "dry submarine").

Many Mapuches fear that the torture, intimidation and imprisonment of activists and their families is part of a covert strategy on the part of the Chilean state in complicity with the business interests involved. Such concerns were voiced in a statement issued by the Mapuche Political Prisoners in Temuco Prison on Columbus Day, 12 October 2000:

> "Our imprisonment obeys the repressive policy that the Chilean government is applying against the Mapuche people and its militants today. We are not the first Mapuches, nor will we be the last, to be detained for these unjust and absurd reasons. Our imprisonment is only intended to scare the communities that are struggling at this time to recover their territories and to defend themselves against the invasion of the transnational forestry companies. History will judge us, not the oppressive Chilean state."[42]

The criminalisation of the Mapuches' struggle is achieved most effectively through the high-profile arrests and trials of Mapuche leaders.

After some of the machinery of Endesa was sabotaged in the Upper Bío-Bío in March 2002, the *Diario El Sur* newspaper began to print stories linking one of the main leaders of the Mapuche movement, Victor Ancalaf, of the Communities in Territorial Conflicts of Collipulli, with the attacks.

Ancalaf was arrested in Temuco on 6 November 2002, while he was on his way to a *Futa Trawun* (Grand Meeting) of Mapuche leaders to be held in Makewe. He was "arrested" in the sense that in the centre of Temuco, at 11am, he was violently set upon by 15 men, 6 in civilian clothing, and forcibly taken to the Second *Carabinero* Station in Temuco. There he was detained under the Law of Internal Security of the State. Ancalaf is currently serving five years in Concepción prison.

It would be naïve to claim that Mapuches do not commit violent acts; they are not a wholly innocent party. Some more militant activist would say that they are at war, so must use violence to defend themselves. Others make a more studied response to violence, seeing it as lamentable but ultimately beneficial. Tirúa Mayor Adolfo Millabur was asked his view of such tactics as the burning of trucks. Though not condoning them, he clearly understands that they serve to draw attention to the Mapuche struggle:

> "The press pigeonholes you, stigmatise you. Such acts do not make me feel either good or bad. Yet I am sure that if there had not been the burning of

the hacienda in Lleu-Lleu, if there had not been the burning of trucks in Lumaco, for which Aníbal Huichacura is now paying the price[43], then people would not be talking about the Mapuche now."[44]

On 4 March 2002, former government minister Juan Agustín Figueroa had one of his trucks burnt out near his property, the Fundo Nancahue. Subsequently *lonkos* Aniceto Norin Cetriman, of Pantano, and Pascual Pichún, of Temulemu, were arrested and held in Traiguén Prison, under the Anti-Terrorism Law, along with Pichún's young sons Rafael and Pascual, aged 21 and 19 respectively; the truck driver had initially declared that he could not recognise the truck's attackers. Other members of the Coordfinadora Arauco-Malleco were also held, as was Patricia Roxana Troncoso Robles, a theology student from Santiago, known as La Chepa.

Such was the exasperation and frustration of *lonko* Pichún's two sons that in August 2002 they embarked upon a hunger strike, which lasted over 31 days, only desisting when their physical condition became life-threatening. Pichún's sons were eventually granted parole in return for payment of compensation of 6,000,000, plus costs, but found themselves unable to pay, so were sentenced to jail in November 2003. Pascual evaded capture, but was eventually recaptured by police in July 2005.

In June 2002 Aniceto Norin and Pascual Pichún were sentenced to 800 days' imprisonment, plus a fine of $601,986. After a long and complicated series of legal proceedings, including three separate re-trials, *lonkos* Norin and Pichún were absolved by the Temuco Court in November 2004, along with La Chepa and 5 others, on the grounds of insufficient evidence presented against them, but early in 2005 the Supreme Court annulled the judgement and ordered a retrial. They are currently serving five years and a day in Angol prison for "terrorist threats" against Figueroa. Pascual Pichún has by now lost any faith he might have had in the Chilean legal process: "It makes no difference what we say or do, they have already decided to condemn us; this is not legal, but political. We believed in justice and we were wrong."[45]

On 9 September 2005, when President Lagos visited the region in implementation of his "New Relationship" policy, a group of Mapuche women including Pascual Pichún's wife, Flora Collonao, attempted to hand him a letter condemning the criminalisation of the Mapuche struggle, but were arrested and charged with public order offences. Alejandro Navarro claims that Figueroa is abusing his position of influence in order to use the justice system against the two *lonkos*: "He has succeeded in reversing a judicial process against lonkos Pascual Pichún and Aniceto Norin based on his extensive knowledge as one of the authors of the Reform of the Penal Process, taking advantage of his position close to the courts."[46]

For a time there was a glimmer of hope that at last the tide of repression and injustice was starting to turn. In May 2003 the court threw out the case against

Luis Ayllapan of the Lafkenche Territorial Council and Margarita and Catalina Marileo Lefio of the Pu Budi Lafkenche community of Puerto Saavedra, who had been accused of the offences of making death threats and minor wounding against state officials in connection with their opposition to the controversial megaproject for a coastal highway through their territory.

An even more extraordinary event, in September 2003, was the request for political asylum received - and accepted - by the London Court of Immigration from two Chilean *carabinero* officers, former sergeant Julio César Pino Ubilla, aged 29, and Myriam Alejandra Solís Fernández, aged 30, who fled Chile after allegedly receiving death threats from their superiors.[47]

Ubilla could face court martial and 20 years' imprisonment for desertion; he was forced to flee after challenging the mistreatment and unnecessary violence used by some officers against their men and civilian detainees, including members of Mapuche communities in the south of Chile. Among the cases of torture against Mapuches denounced by Sargeant Pino Ubilla is that of members of the Truf-Truf community using the "dry submarine" technique, which is discussed above.

The fact that the UK had the honour of hosting General Pinochet's lengthy sojourn a couple of years ago served to remind people here of what happened in the land of the "English of South America" thirty years earlier. Let us hope that the presence here of these two new guests will lead to the awareness that human rights abuses did not cease when Pinochet took a back seat in Chilean politics.

"Aucán President with the force of the earth"

After CAM, considered the most dangerous organisation, one of the more bothersome Mapuche figures, as far as the Chilean authorities are concerned, is Aucán Huilcamán, the charismatic international *werken* of *Aukiñ Wallmapu Ngulam*. Aucán was active in the Ad Mapu organisation, until he and others split to form *Aukiñ Wallmapu Ngulam* in 1990.

Internationally Aucán is perhaps as well known as the Quintreman sisters, partly because he has always attempted to give the Mapuche struggle an international profile, by seeking a voice for the Mapuches at the United Nations and in other international forums. Such an approach has had its critics, however; for example, Victor Ancalaf himself has said that "We must fight in our own land, not in the international forums."[48]

Having had such a high profile over a number of years, Aucán has been particularly subject to vilification and ridicule by the news media. This description of him appeared in *El Mercurio*, attributed to Rodrigo Barría:

> "Huilcamán, whose long dark hair gives him an appearance something like a sort of *Criollo* 'Pocahontas', behaves like an indigenous 'yuppie'." [49]

Heavily armed Chilean police hurry to take up a position as Mapuches protest in the background. Photo: IWGIA's archive

On 20 July 2001 the headquarters of Aukiñ Wallmapu Ngulam was raided by a large contingent of *carabineros* and police at the request of public prosecutors Alberto Chiffelle and Francisco Rojas, supposedly to seize the computer back-up of a letter sent to the Regional Governor. Subsequently, on 29 November, military prosecutor Rodolfo Kaufhold ordered the arrest and trial of Huilcamán, together with other leaders of Aukiñ Wallmapu Ngulam, Manuel Santander, Margot Collipal, Adán Ayenao, Adrián Ayenao and Sergio Marillán, and also *in absentia* of José Nain, who was away in Europe, for "ill-treatment of *carabineros*", a crime under the Code of Military Justice, denying them bail as they were considered "a danger to society."

On 11 December 2001, the UN Special Rapporteur, in a joint letter of urgent appeal with the Special Representative of the Secretary-General for Human Rights Defenders, sent a communication to the Government of Chile enquiring about the detentions, appealing to the Government to provide information about the situation of the people mentioned.

The Aukiñ Wallmapu Ngulam leaders were eventually allowed out of prison, but the trial is still pending. In January 2003 Aucán received threats to his life on his mobile phone, believed to have come from the shadowy "Trizano Squad" mentioned earlier.

Aucán's career path took an unexpected turn in September 2005, when he announced his candidacy for the Presidency of Chile, and rode 800 km on horseback to register. His slogan: "Aucán President with the force of the earth." This news was also greeted with enthusiasm by non-Mapuches from the Chilean political left. Tomás Hirsh, from the Humanist party, said "It does Chile good to have different candidatures; it does it good for there to be a diversity of proposals and for all the sectors to present their plans for the country. To hinder this is to hinder the creation of a true democracy"[50]. It seems Chile is not yet ready for a true democracy, as on 5 October the Chilean Parliament rejected the proposal of Aucán's candidature.

In memory of Alex Lemun

On 7 November 2002 the Mapuches could add a violent killing to the list of injustices committed against them, when Edmundo Alex Lemun Saavedra was shot in the head, and died from his injuries.

17-year-old Alex, of the Montutui Mapu community, was involved in a land occupation on the Fundo Santa Alicia, near Angol, owned by Forestal Mininco, when his group clashed with *carabineros*, and he was shot in the forehead by one of them. He was taken to Angol Hospital, and from there to Temuco Regional Hospital, in a critical condition. From there he was transferred to the better-equipped private German Hospital.

Alex Lemun died at 8.30 am on 12 November. The cause of death was brain trauma caused by a steel bullet. The *carabineros* deny having fired steel bullets during the incident.

The following is part of a statement issued by the Arauco Malleco Mapuche Co-ordinating Committee:

> "In our history, many Mapuches have given their lives for the dignity and freedom of their People; today we must include Alex Lemun Saavedra, who to the end demonstrated the fortitude and resistance that characterise the young Mapuches who day after day commit themselves to the recovery of their political and territorial rights as Mapuche People and Nation.
>
> We call upon all our Mapuche brothers and sisters to turn this moment of grief into strength and energy to continue struggling, to continue with the process of recovering land, to strengthen territorial control, continue resisting and advance towards Mapuche National Liberation."[51]

On 15 November between 500 and 600 people marched from the Cerro Welén to the centre of Santiago, chanting "Policía Asesinos!" When they reached Plaza de los Heroes they set up barricades. After some hours, the police succeeded in breaking up the demonstration, arresting 22. Alex Lemun is the first Mapuche martyr of the modern conflicts in Chile. Is it a vain hope that he will be the last?

The case of Alex Lemun links the present with the past, making a tragic new addition to the ranks of heroes of the *Mapu*, to Lautaro and Galvarino, Namunkurá and Pincén. The next chapter is also a bridge, as it shows that the visions that led to the colonisation of Patagonia in the 19th century are still alive in the dreams of the gold-diggers, adventurers and men of science of today.

Notes

1. These quotations by Aylwin are cited in "Los mapuches y la lucha por el reconocimiento en la sociedad chilena", by Rolf Foerster and Jorge Iván Vergara, published in: Castro, Milka (Publ.) XII Congreso Internacional. Derecho consuetudinario y pluralismo legal: desafíos en el tercer milenio (March 13-17, 2000, Arica, Chile) (2 Volumes). The text of this article is available on the website of the Rehue Foundation (www.xs4all.nl/~rehue/).
2. From an interview with Ms Paillalef in her office in Cañete, 14/12/02.
3. Cited from "Globalización y megaproyectos en territorio mapuche", by Jaime Soto Navarro (www.derechosindigenas.cl).
4. Cited by José Bengoa in an interview with Quepasa magazine, edition 1495, 13th December 1999.
5. "A Dam of Destruction", by Penny Cabot, Resurgence, March 1997.
6. Interviewed on 28/1/02.
7. Hilda Riquelme is another Mapuche activist in *Mapu Domuche Newen*.
8. *Ibidem*.
9. "Cardinal to assess Ralco conflict", quoted from CHIP News, Santiago, 12th March 2001, information held on the Ñuke Mapu website.
10. According to the report in the International Rivers Network newsletter, BIOBIO UPDATE, # 9, Volume 2, English Version June, 1998. (www.irn.org).
11. "La década indómita" by Rodrigo Barría Reyes, in El Mercurio, 3rd March 2002.
12. From an open letter from *Mapu Domuche Newen* to police chief Manuel Ugarte, 6th April 1999.
13. The report is on the Rehue Foundation website: www.xs4all.nl/~rehue/ralco/ral041a.html.
14. "Berta Quintreman protests in La Moneda against the Ralco company", Ñuke Mapu Documentation Centre, 1 September 2005 (http://www.mapuche.info/).
15. Pinochet is known by his adoring supporters as "Tata", grandpa.
16. Le Monde Diplomatique, article "Long march of Chile's mapuches" by Jaime Massardo, November 1999.
17. Le Monde Diplomatique, *op. cit*.
18. CMPC is the holding company that owns Forestal Mininco S.A. CMPC itself is part of the Matte group of companies.
19. www.ecuador.washcoll.edu/.
20. Interviewed on 20/12/01.
21. Interviewed on 1/2/02.
22. Catalán Labarías, Rodrigo y Ruperto Ramos Antiqueo, 1999, Pueblo Mapuche, bosque nativo y plantaciones forestales; Las causas subyacentes de la deforestación en el sur de Chile; Temuco: CET, CONADI, cited in "Pueblo Mapuche, Expansión Forestal y Poder Local" by David McKinnon and Sara McFall, the Spanish text of which is available on the Mapuexpress website (www.mapuexpress.net/biblioteca/).
23. Idem.
24. Cited in McKinnon and McFall, *op. cit*.
25. Interviewed on 14/12/01.
26. The information is again from the Resistencia Mapuche website.
27. Interviewed on 14/12/01.
28. *Ibidem*.
29. Article by Iván Fredes, El Mercurio, 18th June 2002.
30. Interviewed in Temuco on 9/12/01.

31 Le Monde Diplomatique, op. cit.
32 Quoted from El Diario Austral, 29/01/2001, "No queremos matanza en la Noventa Región."
33 "Controvertida vinculación mapuche zapatista", in El Diario Austral, 22nd April 2003.
34 Reported in "La Jornada", Chubut, Argentina, 6th December 1997.
35 Luchsinger made these statements to the press form his hospital bed in the German Clinic in Temuco, reported in Azkintuwe, 21 June 2005.
36 "Terrorismo en páginas Web", reported in Azkintuwe, 20 June 2005.
37 Quoted in Azkintuwe 24 August 2005.
38 "Represión al pueblo mapuche", Punto Final, 30/7/01 (www.puntofinal.cl/).
39 Quoted in Azkintuwe, 25 July 2005.
40 This text (in Spanish) is also available on the Ñuke Mapu website.
41 The Spanish text "Informe anual de derechos humanos 1999" is also available on the Ñuke Mapu website.
42 The statement (in Spanish) is available on the Rehue Foundation website.
43 Huichacura was sentenced in 1999 to three years and one day for burning and destroying three lorries belonging to Bosques Arauco. He is currently in Temuco Prison.
44 Interviewed 4/2/02.
45 Quoted in Mapuexpress, 11 May 2005 (www.mapuexpress.net).
46 Azkintuwe 15 July 2005.
47 Information from Mapuexpress (http://www.mapuexpress.net/) 17 January 2005.
48 Quoted in "El Grito Mapuche" by Aníbal Barrera, publ. by Grijalbo, 1999, p. 48.
49 "El Grito Mapuche", *op. cit*. p. 47.
50 Quoted in Azkintuwe, 23 September 2005.
51 Press Release, Temuco, 14th March 2003, available on the Mapulink website (www.mapuche-nation.org).

THIS LAND IS OUR LAND: EXPLOITATION OF THE *WALLMAPU*

Chapter eleven is in many ways a continuation of the two previous chapters, in that it considers various threats to the Mapuche's land and livelihood. Yet in a sense it is a bringing up-to-date of chapter five, "Land for Sale", as it highlights some of the pressures on the ecology of the *Wallmapu* due to interests that ignore the Mapuche's presence and perspective: gold mining, irresponsible waste disposal, the destruction of medicinal plants, the stealing of genetic information, and finally - speaking of medicine - large-scale tourism as the dubious panacea for all the region's ills.

In the previous two chapters we have looked at the clashes in Argentina and Chile between Mapuche rural communities and their various antagonists, be they multinational companies, state security forces or even courts of law. Clashes over land. This chapter is in a sense more of the same, but it will go a little deeper into two opposing visions of people's relationship with and use of the land: the Mapuche's, a deeply spiritual one whereby individual and community are part of the land and must live in balance with it, and the materialistic one whereby land is a possession, a resource to be used and exploited to generate wealth.

Due to the followers of the latter vision, in Chile and Argentina, forests have been felled, never again to grow. Sheep have been introduced in enormous numbers to provide cheap wool for export. Every use of the land has been aimed at making profit. And all the time the native people, the living demonstration that another approach is possible, have been pushed aside and away.

For five centuries no substance has highlighted the contrast between these two visions more than gold.

City of the Caesars: gold in Esquel's hills

The mid-19th century marked the beginning of the age of gold fever, with hopeful prospectors heading for California and Alaska (1849), and Australia (1851) in droves in search of gilt-edged betterment. Gold diggers, dreamers and schemers have gravitated towards Patagonia ever since the days of the search for the City of the Caesars, the mythical other El Dorado inspired by stories of a city with buildings of gold told by Francisco César, Sabastian Cabot's pilot, who journeyed inland in 1528.

In 1882 they also invaded Tierra del Fuego. By 1909 they had the heavy dredging equipment in place to be able to prospect on an industrial scale. Julius Popper, the Selk'nam hunter, used his private army to defend the island of Isla Grande for the Argentine state, and also to protect his gold extraction business, which produced 173 kilos of gold between 1886 and 1892.

Yet fortunes were generally not made. The miners could make enough to buy provisions and settle their debts before squandering the rest of their earnings on alcohol and prostitutes, only to return to search for more. They made just enough to enable the towns to grow.

Columbus said: "Of gold is treasure made, and with it he who has it does as he wills in the world and even sends souls to Paradise[1]. Though Columbus is five centuries gone, his assertion still holds true today, as gold is still the stuff of dreams.

Gold is part of a new vision for Chubut. The major ranchers and entrepreneurs of the province see their traditional livestock vocation in terminal decline, and see potential in new sources of revenue, namely tourism, oil, wind power ... and gold.

In an interview with *La Nación* newspaper on 4 May 1998, Eduardo Vidal, manager of the Estancia Santa Teresita, said:

> "I believe two Patagonias exist: an original, cattle-raising one, which will now never return to its former glories, and the new one, totally different, with promising prospects and enormous potential, to which we will have to adapt if we want this land to survive."

The same article talks about changing the iconography of the province, until now represented by sheep farms and oil wells, by the introduction of quarries for gold extraction. At the time the project concerned was Cerro Vanguardia, which today is still the main gold mine in Patagonia, with reserves of eight million ounces. The exploitation of Cerro Vanguardia did not meet with significant opposition, mainly because it is far away from centres of population.

The Esquel mine, on the other hand, to be exploited by Meridian Gold, a US/Canadian multinational, is just 5 km from the town. The initial project covers an area of 2.5 km by 500m, between Esquel and Trevelín. In July 2002 Meridian Gold acquired Brancote Holdings plc, which was 100% owner of the Esquel gold deposit. The majority shareholder in Brancote Holdings was Australian media magnate Kerry Packer.

The Esquel deposit is just the tip of an iceberg. Cerro 21, as the mountain purchased by Meridian Gold is called, which the Mapuche call *Futa Mawida* (Great Hill), has gold reserves of 3.8 million ounces. According to Meridian Gold: "Mining properties cover an area of at least 1,400 square kilometres and are located near an established infrastructure, which facilitates positive logistics for the development of the mine. So proximity to urban centres is a good thing.

Mapuche communities and organisations, environmental organisations and local residents have been united in their opposition to the mine project. Lucas Chiappe, co-ordinator of the Proyecto Lemu environmental group, condemns the mine in these terms:

> "The development planned for open-cast mining clearly means the transformation and devastation of many hills and valleys, the highly risky transportation by land and sea and subsequent use of thousands of tons of cyanide, the exposure and release of heavy metals into the atmosphere, the felling and contamination of huge tracts of native forest, the pollution and depletion of many streams, rivers and lakes; in short, the incalculable loss of quality of life and biodiversity."[2]

The main concern of environmentalists and ordinary citizens alike is undoubtedly the extensive use of cyanide envisaged, up to 180 kg per day, which will not be recoverable and will be released into the environment. The extraction will be carried out by dynamiting 30,000 tons of rock per day, 3,000 tons of which are ground to dust (70 microns). The gold is extracted by treating the ground minerals with sodium cyanide dissolved in water.

The co-operative that supplies water to Esquel and Trevelín says that water supplies will be jeopardised. And the problem will not be local, as the areas to be mined will affect both the Futaleuf river basin, which flows to the Pacific, and the sources of the River Chubut, which flows to the Atlantic. Futaleuf is inside the Los Alerces National Park, so the consequences of contamination for the growing tourist industry would also be catastrophic.

Though the project met with initial approval from the population, with the promise of jobs - the number 300 was bandied about - and prosperity for the area, public opinion gradually turned. The perception was that local politicians had acted behind people's backs. The Mayor of Esquel, Rafael Williams, justified his actions a posteriori by saying that he considered it "necessary to complete this enterprise on account of the investments that will be generated and contribute to the development of the city, and also the possibility of direct and indirect work that the mine will produce.[3] In a town with a population of 28,000, the majority of whom of Mapuche origin, with an unemployment level of around 20%, jobs are much needed. The problem is, as Noam Chomsky has often said, the word jobs is corporate code for profits.[4]

Mauro Millán is well aware of this. Mauro, *werken* of the Mapuche-Tehuelche 11 October Organisation, was interviewed by the provincial newspaper *El Oeste*, who quoted him:

"The Government plans the exploitation of the natural resources as an opportunity for jobs, but we are well aware that this will not happen. There are large numbers of indigenous people living in the neighbourhoods of Esquel and in other localities and towns, who want to return to the land, and the state does nothing to promote the idea. Quite the opposite, it acts in concert with the big entrepreneurs to prevent us from exercising this right to work the land and generate our own resources." [5]

The project falls within the framework of the "Treaty of Mining Integration, signed by officials of the Argentine and Chilean Governments in 1999, during the government of Carlos Menem, which made no provision for the environmental integrity of the provincial and national parks and reserves. The national state cannot exploit the riches under the ground, but must use private companies as intermediaries, from whom it collects a maximum annual levy of 3% of the value of the metal extracted at the mine mouth (i.e. a much lower price than the international price of the metal). If 3% was meagre, the provincial law of Chubut reduces this 2%. And according to one interpretation - which I have not been able to verify - since Patagonia has special status as an export region, then, in order to favour exports from its ports, the government actually gives a 5% remuneration to the exporting companies. If this were the case, the government would actually be paying Meridian Gold to remove its minerals, receiving only cyanide in return.

Meridian Gold rejects the accusations that the cyanide is damaging to the environment. On their website (www.meridiangold.com), they state:

"Manmade cyanide is used in the manufacture of many items in our daily lives, while thousands of natural sources of cyanide exist worldwide in the environment. In some form, we are exposed to cyanide every day. Although the fear of cyanide is well-founded, it is often exaggerated by an ever-growing volume of misinformation. With knowledge, we can overcome the effects of this misinformation."

The company is also active in Chile, in the El Peñon project, in Atacama, Northern Chile. Again according to their website: "Through the combined ownership of Esquel and El Peñon, Meridian will control mines located in two of the most prospective, highest-grade gold districts in Latin America.

Their reputation precedes them regarding their activities in the USA. Canadian mine monitoring organisation Mining Watch writes:

"Mines owned or run by Meridian have created serious toxic pollution in at least three locations in the United States. One of the largest emitters of atmospheric mercury in the U.S. is the Jerritt Canyon mine in Nevada, which was part-owned by Meridian until its recent sale. This mine emits more than 10 times the amount of mercury released by a typical U.S. power plant."[6]

Against the best advice of the "experts, local campaigning against the project increased. On 4 December 2002 a demonstration against the mine was held in Esquel, with 4,000 people turning out, converging from all over Chubut and beyond. 4000 may not sound like an enormous number, but in a town of less than 30,000 they had a major impact.

The stakes were being raised. A journalist with the national newspaper *Crónica*, Lautaro Recalde of Comodoro Rivadavia, was threatened with dismissal for criticising his newspaper's editorial line, which was favourable to the mine's development. Intimidation and telephone death threats were received by prominent members of the anti-mine campaign.

Against all expectations, the campaign forced the Esquel town council to conduct a plebiscite, and the vote against the mine was resounding - 80%, with a 75% turnout, higher than that for general elections.

Veronica Odriozola of Greenpeace Argentina greeted the result of the plebiscite with these words:

"The people of Esquel are saying today that they want and need jobs for everyone in the community - but these must be based on sustainable activities. They do not wish to pay the price of gold mining, and this is a historic decision for a poor country."[7]

Meridian Gold seems to have been taken aback by the popular rejection of its plans to develop near the town. It has now engaged the services of a PR company, Business for Social Responsibility (BSR), "to help better understand the concerns of the residents of Esquel, Argentina. It has also stated that it will "pause in the development of its Esquel Gold Project while it listens to the community and attempts to understand the issues important to the residents of Esquel. The company may be moving more cautiously in the light of the local population's clear rejection of the project, but it has not abandoned it. After all, mining is their business.

Mauro Millán explained to me the clear difference between the Mapuche vision and that of the mining company that is implicit in the Esquel conflict:

"As a fundamental principle of the *Ad Mapu* (Mapuche tradition), the Mapuche are part of the nature and not its owners. The Mapuche interact with the *Itrófilmogen* (the different elements of nature) with the responsibility of maintaining the balance. When they arrived, the *winkas* imposed another paradigm, another philosophy of relations with the land and nature, where man is above everything. So he doesn't see the forest, he doesn't see the river, he doesn't see the hill, but only resources to be exploited and economic benefits to be gained."

It is significant that a worldview that Mapuches have held for centuries chime with those of Argentine ecologists such as Lucas Chiappe, who arrived through very different routes, such as scientific analysis, at the same conclusions.

Let us now move from Argentina to Chile to consider another ecological issue seriously affecting the Mapuche, but this time not the riches taken from their land, rather the rubbish forced onto it.

Mapuche communities: Chile's dumping grounds

One would be tempted to think that rubbish dumps symbolise the Chilean authorities' attitude towards the Mapuche and their place in Chilean society, namely that the Mapuche are fair game for the dumping of rubbish, as they seem to view them as *resaca*, the dregs of society.

In Chile's Ninth Region there are no less than nineteen landfills installed directly in or beside Mapuche communities, 70% of the total. With the return to democracy, various municipalities, of the political right and left, quickly created new rubbish dumps on land designated as for Mapuche communities, to act before the promulgation of new indigenous and environmental laws. This is the case of the waste sites for Temuco (Boyeco community), Gorbea (Antonio Millaman community), Lumaco (Pililmapu), Perquenco (Llancamil), Melipeuco (Juan Meli), Pitrufquén (Cleonardo Pilquimán and Ignacio Huaiquimil communities), Loncoche (María M. Quilacán), Nueva Imperial (Hueche Huinca) and Vilcún (Jos M. Millaleo), all created between 1990 and 1993.

In 2001 the Mapuche communities of Boyeco, the waste site for Temuco, Quilaco in Purén and Ancúe in Gorbea began proceedings to demand that the authorities remove the landfills from their land, claiming that 70% of rubbish dumps in the Ninth Region are on Mapuche land.

In the same year a boy from Boyeco named Aquiles Epul died. The medical report determined that his death was due to a bacterial infection, which his family and community leaders immediately related to the existence of the landfill and the risk of infection it constituted.

That year, a series of meetings began, with the setting up of a discussion forum between various representatives of public bodies (the Health Service, the Regional Government, Conadi, the Association of Municipalities, the municipalities involved, CONAMA, Serplac) and the communities themselves. However, following a series of encounters and on-site visits, on 26 December 2001 the regional government approved the Environmental Impact Study for the extension of the term of operation of the Boyeco landfill until 2025. The Boyeco dump has been in operation since 1992 and to date some 6,700 tons of rubbish have been dumped there.

The communities denounce the following: environmental pollution, damage to health, contamination of waterways, contamination of underground water sources, alteration of life systems, impoverishment, violation of Mapuche sacred sites and cultural patrimony, with various community members feeling they had no choice but to leave.

A far-sighted ecological approach would mean a concerted effort to recycle rubbish, yet the short-termism that is so common in Latin America's version of capitalism means that the rubbish is dumped – like the communities that have to put up with it – out of sight and out of mind.[8]

However, interest is reawakened in the Mapuche when it is discovered that they have something that has acquired value, such as their knowledge of the curative powers of autochthonous flora, or special illness-resistant characteristics of their genetic make-up, dwindling "resources", precious "properties" suddenly in great demand.

Genetic property is theft: the patenting of indigenous knowledge

A recent report by a Chilean import-export company on the industrial production of medicinal plants went into great detail about the many ways that Chile's medicinal plants could be used for medical, pharmacological and cosmetic purposes, giving geographical locations, estimated quantities, average annual yields, etc. The report enthused about satisfying the developed world's currently insatiable desire for traditional remedies, such as St. John's Wort, Aloe Vera, Camomile, Rosehip and Valeriana. Yet the one element that the report failed to include was any mention of the indigenous people of Chile, without whose age-old knowledge the healing properties of these plants would never have come to the attention of the industrial producers, much less the eventual consumers abroad. Chile is in fifth position in the classification of the world's exporters of medicinal plants, which are considered - appropriately - by experts and economists to be a "growth sector for the Chilean economy. Dozens of different varieties of traditional medicinal plants are now grown for export; the very dry climate, particularly in Northern Chile, make it ideal for the preservation of plants after they have been harvested.

The awareness of the special qualities of Chile's medicinal plants is not new. The *foye (drimys winteri)* is an evergreen tree native to Argentina and Chile that is commonly found in Mapuche kitchen gardens, as the bark of this variety of cinnamon is used in cooking. It is one of the *lawen* sacred to the Mapuche, as it is used to cure a number of ailments, such as fever and stomach pains, and is diuretic, analgesic and antiseptic. When Sir Francis Drake was on an expedition through the Magellan Strait, his physician John Winter was recommended the use of the *foye* to treat the stomach pains he was suffering. He was so impressed by the plant that he took it back to Europe and claimed it as his own, which is why it is known as "Winter' Bark or "Drimys Winteri"[9]. Such "discoveries of traditional plants have since become commonplace. Today the *foye* is becoming ever scarcer.

The figure in Mapuche communities who is responsible for administering the medicinal plants, as the intermediary between the sick person and the curative divine forces, is the *machi*. The extermination of plants in many Mapuche communities and the difficulties in finding them, because much autochthonous vegetation has been destroyed by the process of forestation with introduced species such as pine and eucalyptus, have become a worry often dwelled upon by *machis* these days. María Claudina, a *machi* of Rupukura, now an octogenarian, is very concerned that the skills she learnt from her mother and honed throughout her life will be lost to future generations:

> "The remedies of the earth are very important, but they no longer exist, the *winka* has exterminated them by fire, he has also planted pine, he has planted eucalyptuses. For that reason the remedies have finished, there are no longer *lawen*, they have ended."[10]

To make things worse, added to the dangers posed to the traditional plants by forestry are the worrying investigations being conducted into the ancestral knowledge of the use and handling of medicinal plants, the results of which are not for the benefit of the communities, but for patenting by multinational drug companies. Says the *machi*:

> "We the Mapuche are concerned about this situation. Why do they try to steal our medicinal plants? Why do they keep on taking away what is ours, first our land, and now our plants? What would come of us without the plants, which are a part of our being?"

The Mapuche are not the only indigenous people that are worried about the patenting of traditional knowledge, particularly since the advent of the Agreement on Trade-Related Aspects of Intellectual Property Rights of 1994, commonly known as the TRIPS Agreement. On 25 July 1999, at the United Nations, Geneva, Switzerland, representatives of 87 different indigenous peoples' organisations and NGOs worldwide, including Aucán Huilcamán on behalf of Mapuche organisation *Auki Wallmapu Ngulam*, signed a statement drawing attention to the dangerous implications of TRIPS, and refuting the basic premise of its existence. The statement reads:

> "We know that intellectual property rights as defined in the TRIPS Agreement are monopoly rights given to individual or legal persons (e.g. transnational corporations) who can prove that the inventions or innovations they have made are novel, involve an innovative step and are capable of industrial application. The application of this form of property rights over living things as if they were mechanical or industrial inventions is inappropriate. Indigenous knowledge and cultural heritage have collectively and accretionally evolved through generations. Thus, no single person can claim invention or discovery of medicinal plants, seeds or other living things."

During 1992 the Italian geneticist Luigi Luca Cavalli-Sforza proposed the inclusion of a specific subproject among the interests of the Human Genome Organisation (HUGO): the study of genetic variations among human groups (Human Genome Diversity Project). The aim was to reconstruct the evolution and migrations of homo sapiens starting from the study of the DNA of 500 aboriginal communities, to distinguish their peculiar genetic features, those that were the most resistant or susceptible to certain illnesses.

The most high profile case in this subproject occurred in Panama. There, in 1991, Panamanian scientists, in collaboration with North American colleagues, extracted genetic material from a 26-year-old Guaym woman who was hospitalised with leukemia in a hospital in the Panamianian capital. Subsequently Doctors Jonathan E. Kaplan and Michael Dale Laimore attempted to patent a cellular line in the USA - using the dubiously obtained blood samples - arguing that a certain retrovirus that infects the Guaym could be used in future investigations into leukemia and HTLV III, given its similarity. Following a battle by the Guaym General Congress, various NGOs and indigenous organisations, in late 1993 the patent application was withdrawn.[11]

In mid-1993 a team of scientists from the Retrovirus and Leukemia unit of the New Bolton Centre (University of Pennsylvania) travelled around various provinces of Argentina on what was referred to somewhat euphemistically as a "Scientific Humanitarian Mission: to take blood samples of individuals belonging to different aboriginal communities. In Formosa, they extracted blood from groups of Chorotes and Wichís in order to detect resistant genetic sequences for the subsequent production of medicinal substances.

The last stage of the project was to take 94 blood samples from members of the Mapuche communities of Ruka Choroy, composed of 140 families a few kilometres from Lake Alumin, and Los Miches (20 families living in the north of the

Province of Neuquén), both communities with subsistence economies. Without the authorisation of the Provincial Undersecretary of Health, Argentinian Professor of Microbiology Jorge Ferrer extracted samples to investigate the presence of the retrovirus of human leukemia HTLVI and the virus of AIDS and hepatitis B and C. The unwitting donors were paid nothing for these samples. All this information was to be taken back to the USA, and the fear among the Mapuche and others was that it was to be used for the patenting of any special genotypes found.

The Mapuche see this as a uniquely modern, hi-tech form of theft of what is theirs - genetic theft. It is only the latest stage in a centuries-long process of depredation. Now *winkas* have begun to take and claim ownership of their very blood, what else can possibly be taken from them?

But after all, as Machiavelli advised his young Prince, the end justifies the means, and a little theft is a small price to pay for the sake of progress, development.

The "development of the Argentine-Chilean Lake District: Parks versus people

"How can they stand in the way of progress? "Do they really want to remain underdeveloped? These are inevitably the type of mock-surprised comments that are made by corporations and authorities when indigenous communities dare question the role they have been given in the development of the areas in which they live. When that holy mantra "development is invoked in support of a project, it is asked that our critical faculties be suspended. Just as "jobs is used to cover the unmentionable term "profits, so "development is one of those warm Newspeak words used to conceal motives that dare not speak their name.

The 300-mile stretch of the Argentine-Chilean Lake District between Lake Alumin and the Futalafken Hydroelectric Complex is the string of pearls of the two countries' tourist development. It has 8 national parks: Huerquehue and Villarica (Chilean), Lanín, Nahuel Huapi and Los Arrayanes (Argentine), Puyehue and V. Pérez Rosales (Chilean) and Los Alerces (Argentine). On the Argentine side, there are prestige ski resorts, such as La Hoya near Esquel and Cerro Catedral near Bariloche, and lakeside resorts such as Villa La Angostura and the former hippy Mecca El Bolsón. This is an area of extraordinary beauty and biodiversity, in the midst of which are a large number of Mapuche communities, in conditions of extreme poverty despite the wealth being generated around them, continually suffering "encroachment by the forces of development.

Pulmarí, near Aluminé, 350 km west of Neuquén, was for a long time the best-known case in the battle for land rights of the Mapuches of Argentina.

Following the Conquest of the Desert, the Pulmarí area had come into the possession of the English Miles family. In 1948, during the first presidency of Juán Domingo Perón, the land was expropriated by the state and handed over to the Argentine Army. At that time the Mapuche communities began their claims for the land to be returned to them.

Following the end of the last dictatorship, new President Alfonsín declared from the balcony of Neuquén City Hall, "Now, Pulmarí for the Mapuche!

The Corporación Interestatal Pulmarí (CIP) was set up to distribute the land between the inhabitants of the region, giving priority to the Mapuches. There are 7 Mapuche communities in the Pulmarí area: Aigo, Salazar, Puel, Ñorkin-ko, Catalán, Currumil and Plácido Puel.

In fact the very opposite occurred when the sales began in 1995. A large chunk of the 110,000 hectares administered by CIP President Omar Dos Santos, a choice area on the banks of Lake Pulmarí, was awarded to Domenico Panciotto, an Italian entrepreneur. There he planned the creation of an "ecological tourist complex, targeted at an élite clientele. In the area there is a Mapuche sacred burial area, to which access is prevented by a wire fence.

As a consequence of international denunciations, the European Parliament sent an observation delegation to the area. In parallel, an investigation was ordered of the actions of the director of the CIP for supposed irregularities in the sale process. In 1996, due to the intervention of the Bishop of Neuquén and Nobel prizewinner Adolfo Pérez Esquivel, and letters of support from the European Parliament, a meeting was held with new Governor Sapag, in which he promised to analyse the Mapuche proposals.

Yet the provincial justice system was heavily weighted in favour of those with influence, i.e. those with money. Since the Mapuche communities, impatient with the judicial inaction, had recovered some of the land they claimed, Judge Rubén Caro ordered the trial of a number of Mapuche *lonkos* and *werkens*.

There was clearly an air of panic in the corridors of power over the issue. On 14 January 1996, an article appeared in influential local newspaper *La Mañana del Sur* entitled: "The Government fears Mapuches will transform Pulmarí into Chiapas, with the evident intention of alarming its readers with the fear of the threat of armed rebellion. This strategy of evoking the spectre of terrorism and insurrection is common in Chile, as we have seen, but is rare in Argentina.

Since 1996, a total of 80 Mapuches have been subject to legal proceedings, and a number of cases are still pending. Problems such as Pulmarí do not go away, however. They are just put on the back burner as others come to the attention. New ones such as Cerro Chapelco.

Curruhuinca is the largest Mapuche lof in the Province of Neuquén, with over 600 members, and has the dubious privilege of being located near the Cerro Chapelco ski resort. The Curruhuinca community claim that the resort is on their land; besides using the official channels, they have also protested by occupying the offices of the National Park and blocking Provincial Highway no. 19 for several hours to distribute leaflets and increase awareness of their complaints.

The resort is run by the company Nieves del Chapelco, owned by Francisco Capozzolo. Señor Capozzolo had big plans for the resort, such as the construction of a 5-star hotel: "in two years Chapelco will be the main ski centre in South America, and for this we will invest many millions over the coming years.[12]

Responding to accusations by Mapuches that the resort is polluting the area, Capozzolo said: "We don't contaminate the hill; the contamination was already here when we arrived. Mapuches also contaminate with their animals.[13]

The authorities seem to disagree, as on 29 August 2002 the Judge of the Civil Court of Junín de los Andes, Norma González de Galván, closed down the ski centre, due to the spillage of sewerage from the commercial installations into the mointain streams.

There are nine Mapuche communities in all in the Lanín National Park: Curruhuinca, Vera, Cañicul, Cayún, Aigo, Ñorkin-ko, Lefiman, Salazar and Raquithu; there are 4,000 people (500 families) living in the nine communities, often in conditions of extreme poverty. They have had many things to protest about as regards Cerro Chapelco, not least the fact that in their view the mountain's real name is not Cerro Chapelco, but Pillan Mawida (Spirit Mountain). The mountain is used not only for winter sports, but in the summer for golf, motocross, a 4x4 circuit, horse-riding and mountain biking, all putting its ecosystem under pressure.

While most communities have opposed the tourism megaprojects, some have provided a certain level of assistance to tourists, acting as guides in the park. They have also been proactive in attempting to develop their own small-scale sustainable tourism activities. They were hoping to benefit from financing to the tune of 3 million pesos from the Spanish Government, as part of the latter's commitments made at the Environmental Conference in Rio in 1997, known as the Araucaria Project, or Liwenmapu (Dawn) Project. The implementation of the assistance, to which the Spanish International Co-operation Agency was to contribute manpower and funding to the tune of $7,000,000, was dependant on an agreement being signed by the Spanish agency, the Mapuche Co-ordinating Committee of Neuquén (CMN) and representatives of the Provincial government. Unfortunately the deadline was not met to obtain the funding for the project, because the Neuquén provincial officials did not deign to sign the agreement. This, according to Eduardo Fuentes of the Alianza Party, was because the provincial government "did not want the CMN to be party to the signing of the agreement as a member of the governing committee."[14]

Whether due to negligence or vindictiveness, this has been yet another disappointment for the Mapuche communities within the Lanín National Park. As the lonko of the lof Cañicul, Daniel Kilapán, said in a speech marking the 60th anniversary of the Argentine National Parks system:

"During these sixty years of National Parks we have suffered many injustices, many abuses; there is a lot of history, a lot of pain within the Mapuche People. For this reason I have said that it is not easy to forget, because a People that forget their roots have no life. I believe that it is our duty not to forget, but also to talk and be able to walk together as two cultures that respect each other."[15]

Indigenous organisations and NGOs are rightfully suspicious of megaprojects, and indeed, the bigger the megaproject, the more damage it seems likely to cause. The Mapuche are also all too aware that they are often used in a tokenistic way to give tourism projects a veneer of respectability; meanwhile their art, textiles, dances and music are used by tourist enterprises in the marketing of their own products.

In Bariloche, where Swiss-style, winka-owned bungalows are advertised for rent going by names in Mapudungun such as Peuma ñi (our dream) and Ruka Piren (snow house), it is hard for a tourist to contact Mapuche communities. While visiting Bariloche in 2000, I called in at the tourism office in the main square, and conducted an experiment. I asked for a leaflet with information on the local Mapuche communities, and was told by the member of staff that "they cannot be visited. When asked why, I was told that "they do not take kindly to visits by tourists. Those who control tourism in Bariloche do not take kindly to competition, would be closer to the truth. Tourism is an increasingly large and rich cake, but it is not being shared out evenly along all.

Tourism: fantasy worlds and real estate

Those responsible for tourism policy in Argentina are slowly but surely coming to the realisation that today's tourists are tired of tango, sick of steak and gauchos. In a sense the discourse has come full circle, in that the solitude that was so appealing to W.H. Hudson a hundred years ago, prior to colonisation fever, is once again being yearned for. First come the artists and explorers, and finally the tourists. Once again Patagonia is the last wilderness, the only place left to escape to.

In recent years hyper-endurance races against the elements, such as the triathlon, have come to be in vogue. Patagonia offers the perfect terrain for these. In 1998 the ultimate adventure race, the Eco-Challenge, hit Bariloche with its low environmental impact bandwagon. According to its website:

"Patagonia, the location of the 1998 Eco-Challenge, has been called "the ends of the Earth and "the beginning of the world. In this land of extremes, the terrain is both immense and virtually inaccessible, ensuring its natural diversity has remained untouched. Yet it has captured the souls of famous writers, scientists, explorers and artists."[16]

Patagonia is no longer virtually inaccessible, and is sadly far from untouched. Adventure tourists, like Hudson, are in a hurry to get there before the tide of humanity arrives. Tapping into such desires to test oneself against the elements is in a sense harkening back to the days of the great adventurers. Adventurers such as George Newbery, who in 1885, on honeymoon with his wife Fanny, took the train from Buenos Aires to Mendoza, crossed the Andes on mules, sailed from Valparaíso to Puerto Montt and from there to Nahuel Huapi on horseback; there they travelled by boat for two days, before resuming their journey on horseback to the place where they built their house.

By the Atlantic coast, Welsh teahouses have provided the best opportunity for Welsh communities, such as Gaiman, to benefit from the influx of tourists in recent decades caused by the attractions of the marine wildlife of the Peninsula Valdez. Such teahouses have been so successful that one enterprising Mapuche family has even opened one in Puerto Madryn, called *Mari Mari* (the Mapuche greeting).

The end of the millennium brought together that explosive combination of apocalypse panic and the desire to party like never before. Ever since the sixties, young people, disillusioned with the material possessions of consumer culture and not attracted by the staid rituals of the traditional religions, have been seeking a more spiritual dimension elsewhere, the arcane in the mundane.

The phenomenon has reached the *Mapu*. From 28 December 2002 to 1st January 2003, at the Aldyhana eco-village, Paso Cordova, Leufuche, a special event took place: an initiation and celebration for the beginning of the new year, organised by the Centro Experimental Yatra Expedition, part of World Awakening USA. The first day included Vedic chants, yoga, sensorama of the elements, ritual dance, meditation, Temazcal ...

David, a participant in a previous event there, in December 2000-January 2001, said this of the experience:

> "In Aldyhana a cataclysm occurred, subterranean rocks emerged of experiences erased by consciousness. I plunged into depths and came up floating every time. I felt fears and blessings. It extracted parasitic roots from me and left my whole being full of hopeful seeds. I felt the marvellous presence of the whole of existence conspiring to give us what we needed."[17]

It would perhaps be tempting to mock the flower-power theology here, but ultimately such an event probably has just as minimal an impact on the area as the Eco-Challenge. What is depressing is the fact that the participants in the event arrived, experienced their transcendental moment, then left, blissfully unaware that less than a kilometre away was the Mapuche community of Leufuche, engaged for years in a struggle for its very existence against the wishes of the authorities and business leaders of the zone.[18]

President Hipólito Yrigoyen said in 1929: "I do not fear so much those from outside who want to buy us as those from inside who want to sell us. His fears were well founded. Just as the Argentine state had been generous in the past to those to whom it owed a duty of thanks for serving it well, so it continues to be generous today to those to whom it owes money, or who help pay its debts. In 2002 major plans were afoot to sell off the most precious of family jewels - state-owned land - to obtain revenue for debt repayment. Thus we have the arrival of "property investment tourism", perhaps more insidious than adventure tourism or spiritual tourism.

The consultancy company Giacobbe y Asociados was commissioned to carry out a survey among residents of the province of Chubut on, among other things, the principle of paying debt with assets. Question 14 in the survey was: "Would you agree with selling state-owned territory in Chubut to cancel the provincial public debt? Understandably, there is strong resistance to the idea: out of the 1,201 citizens who participated in the survey, 131 answered "yes and 1,061 "no to the question, a resounding defeat for the proposition.[19]

There is no cause for rejoicing, however; eventual official policy could well begin with a seemingly innocuous survey, as part of the "softening up process. In neighbouring Río Negro Province, this is already the case. Provincial Law 3210, issued in October 1998, provides for the transfer of provincial government-owned land to the trust company "Río Negro Fiduciaria S.A. for the "realisation of [...] operations, the income from which will be used for the payment of the provincial State debts.

Lawyer Darío Rodríguez Duch, one of the Mapuche's leading advocates, has published a report on the selling-off of land in the Patagonian region, from which I quote:

> "In this region at the "end of the world, space and possibilities for development abound. There are significant extensions of land that are perfectly cultivable using modern methods. As well as all the energy sources (petroleum, gas, wind and sun), there are endless natural forests, marine fauna able to feed several countries and, a fact that is not widely known in our culture but that arouses considerable interest for those who run the world's future, it is also an inexhaustible source of drinkable water, guaranteed through countless rivers, streams, springs and even continental glaciers.
> It is no coincidence that major national and regional real estate agencies publish sections in their internet pages offering appetising plots to foreign investors who want exclusive locations to while away their leisure time. In

1997 the Argentine Secretary of Trade, Industry and Mining made an open invitation in London to buy Argentinian land "at advantageous prices."[20]

That is why the Estancias Pilcañeu, Alicura, Leleque and El Maitén were acquired by Luciano, Giuliana, Gilberto and Carlo Benetton, who own a total of nearly a million hectares in the region; the Estancia Lago Escondido, 14,000 hectares, by the Englishman Joe Lewis (former proprietor of the Hard Rock Caf and partner in Planet Hollywood with Sylvester Stallone, Bruce Willis and Arnold Schwarzenegger); the Estancia La Primavera, 4,400 hectares, today owned by North American Ted Turner (founder of CNN); the Estancia San Ramón, 35,000 hectares, belongs to Swiss Jacob Suchard (owner of Nestl). Today large properties in the Andean region belong to Jorge Acevedo (Acíndar), Francisco Pérez Companc, Diego Maradona in Villa la Angostura, Argentine media star Marcelo Tinelli in Cholila and Christopher Lambert in Villa Arelauquen (Bariloche).

Paradoxically, and despite the economic dimension represented by these major investors, many of their *estancias* owe large sums to the Provincial States as property tax. Yet this was nominally the reason why state officials often removed the indigenous occupants from state-owned lands, the problem that would supposedly be solved with the privatisation of those same lands in the hands of supposedly solvent residents.

The Van Ditmar real estate agency of Bariloche was the intermediary in a number of the above sales, and is still offering plots and estancias for sale on its website (www,camposargentina.com.ar), as indeed are many other estate agents, such as the Patagonia Land Company, whose website (www.patagonialc.com) says: "have you ever thought about owning land in Argentina or Chile? Are you looking for a good investment or just somewhere you can pass the time fishing for a trophy trout or kayaking a glacier?

George Soros, the international financial speculator, who always has an eye for a good deal, is also heavily involved in investment in Patagonia, through the IRSA investment bank; he has managed to become one of the biggest landowners in Argentina, with 500,000 hectares, and also owns some 150,000 head of cattle. He owns the Llao Llao Hotel in Bariloche, with its own spa and golf course, which he bought for six million dollars. It is where then-President Bill Clinton stayed when he visited the region with Hillary.

Ted Turner, on the other hand, is there for the trout fishing, at his Estancia La Primavera with its 11,000 acres less than 10 miles from Villa Traful in the Nahuel Huapi National Park.

Christopher Lambert is quoted by The Christian Science Monitor (27/1/1998) as saying "I want to own this paradise when he first saw Cholila, Butch Cassidy's former haunt. Sylvester Stallone also owns land in Cholila, as well as a large plot in El Foyel, 70 Km from Bariloche. Apparently Sly also likes fly-fishing, as locals have reported seeing him up to his thighs in water, searching for that elusive bite.

The phenomenon has not gone wholly unnoticed, however; indeed, many articles have been written on the selling-off of Patagonia. Rumblings of discontent have even been heard in the provincial assemblies, and a bill was presented in May 2002 in the Chubut Provincial Assembly by the Alianza UCR - Frepaso Block to halt the process under way. These were the words of warning in the bill:

> "To summarise, we believe we are facing an unknown phenomenon, we suspect, like any Patagonian, that we are facing the danger of the loss of integrity of our territories. We have still not settled our historic debt with our aborigines, when we are facing this new scenario, which obliges us to plan actions that allow convenient measures to be adopted in defence of our identity. This is the theoretical framework that has Patagonia as the recipient of interests that are not yet defined, manifested in the ways described. The deepening of these signs could provoke alterations in the relationship between population and territory, fundamental components of the state."[21]

Perhaps the Mapuche should be grateful that the business tycoons and Hollywood stars are in Patagonia, as it means that it is still sufficiently unspoiled and free from the *hoi polloi* for them to wish to remain. Their problems may really begin when Turner and Stallone decide to leave.

The tourist industry has also been developing at a pace in recent years in the Chilean Lake District and Chilean Patagonia. Both the state and private enterprises know perfectly well that what Chile has to offer in terms of tourism is its nature, its people and its traditions.

It is ironic that some of the areas that would be prime candidates for tourism development are those where the major conflicts are taking place, such as the Upper Bío-Bío. Indeed, when the Ralco Dam was being sold to the Mapuche communities in the area as an idea, the development of tourism in the zone was one of the carrots used to prompt them to relocate. To this end, Endesa commissioned Fundación Chile to prepare an Operational Plan for Sustainable Tourism in the Santa Bárbara area. Mapuches would thus theoretically be able to benefit from the tourist inflows by selling organic products and medicinal herbs and participating in the creation and operation of sports and leisure facilities, such as fishing, horse-riding, trekking and kayaking.

Judging by the number of Mapuche women in traditional clothing, headdresses and jewellery that adorn the catalogues and websites of Chilean tourist agencies, you would assume that the Mapuche were at the forefront of the country's tourism development. Sadly, this is generally not the case, indeed the images are generally used to provide local colour - a form of "brand identity for Chile.

Some Mapuche communities have attempted to claim a share of the tourism pie for themselves. In the area of Nueva Imperial, for example, small-scale agrotourism is under way involving eight Mapuche families. It is described in these terms on the website of the Regional Government of Araucanía[22]:

> "A kilometre from Chol-Chol is Huiñoco, where an agrotourism project is being developed. Here, starting from next season, tourists will be able to stay in comfortable *cabañas* that blend the style of the Mapuche construction with contemporary comfort. They will also have the possibility of boat trips, horseriding, wagon rides, enjoying typical foods, participating in field work and being part of the life of the Mapuche families. The project is also being developed in two other localities: El Peral and Rupukura, located on the banks of the river Chol-Chol."

The challenge for the authorities is to ensure that such initiatives are not just tokenism, but are part of a general development of the Mapuche economy through sustainable tourism projects. As time goes by, ever greater numbers of ecological tours are available on the market. Turismo Sur de America, for example, offers a "unique eco and cultural tour to the rainy ancestral Mapuche territory, in the mountainous region of La Araucanía, where the sounds of an ancient Indian culture emerge mixed with the lively colours of a wonderful land. I cannot comment on the merits or otherwise of such tours; it is only to be hoped that the benefits of such enterprises do more than just trickle down to the Mapuches involved in them.

In these postmodern times, it is perhaps fitting that the best hope for conservation in Patagonia should come not from the cash-strapped Chilean and Argentine governments, nor from the all too powerless Mapuche, the stewards of ecological equilibrium for a millennium, but from a couple of ultra-rich *gringo* capitalists, Doug Tompkins and Kristine McDivitt, and what is branded wildlands philanthropy.

According to Jonathan Franklin and John Vidal of the Guardian:

> "This couple, who own more than two million acres in Chile and Argentina, are "eco barons: multi-millionaires buying swathes of wild, barely inhabited land around the world to conserve some of the world's remotest places."[23]

Ms McDivitt was CEO of the Patagonia Clothing Company, until she retired in 1993; she literally retired, in that she and her husband Tompkins went to live in a remote Chilean homestead without electricity, computer, email or phone. In 2000 she founded the Patagonia Land Trust, which, according to its website[24], is "a charitable foundation by Kristine McDivitt Tompkins to raise funds in order to restore and preserve the fragile forests, grasslands and coast of South American's Patagonia, one of the last wild places on earth. The Trust has bought up huge amounts of land in Argentine Patagonia, including the 155,000-acre Monte León, north of Tierra del Fuego, which will become Argentina's first coastal national park, and 82,500 acres at Dor-Aike and 35,000 acres at the foot of Cerro San Lorenzo, which the Trust also plans to hand over to the Argentine government.

Over a number of years, Tompkins, co-founder of the North Face outdoor gear company, has gradually bought the 800,000-acre Parque Pumalin, a temperate rainforest complete with snow-capped volcanoes and glacial fjords. He plans to donate this to the Chilean government.

Tompkins has not only met with applause for delving into his very deep pockets, he has also suffered a torrent of criticism. Attempts have been made to emphasise his links with the radical ecological activists Earth First and the Deep Ecology movement. He has also been accused of driving the smallholders off the land, a charge he flatly denies: "these farmers can't make it; they want to sell their land[25]. It is true that once the word spread that a pair of rich *gringos* were buying up uninhabited - and, many say, uninhabitable - forest tracts, proposals flooded in.

The nationalists are certainly worried, particularly the Chilean military, who regard the emergence of a sort of private mini-nation as a threat to the country's sovereignty. Tompkins was attacked by a farmer neighbour, one of Pinochet's former bodyguards[26]. Even more worrying corollaries of such nationalist sentiments are conspiracy theory paranoia and the inevitable anti-semitism that goes with it. Tompkins has been accused by Chilean neo-Nazis of planning to establish a Jewish homeland, a "Zionist Empire in Southern Patagonia[27], the alleged proof of which being the fact that his mother is Jewish and that he has purportedly signed an agreement with the Israeli government to host visits by Israeli youngsters to his land following their military service.

So ends our short overview of the use and abuse of the resource that is the *Wallmapu.*, the defence of which has brought together a unique coalition of Mapuches, ecologists, concerned local citizens and even US philanthropists. In the next chapter we look at a menace that tends not to unite Mapuches and *winkas*, but rather leaves the former feeling isolated, angry and vulnerable: racism.

Notes

1   "The Log of Christopher Columbus' First Voyage to America in the Year 1492, London, W.H.Allen & Co., Ltd., cited in "The Open Veins of Latin America, by Eduardo Galeano.
2   Cited from an article by Chiappe published on Argentina's Ecoportal.net, issued no. 507, entitled "Mining: Everything or Nothing in the Lakes Region.

3   From an article "Popular consultation on mining exploitation in the Diario El Chubut, 26th November 2002.
4 ' Jobs' is Newspeak for the unpronounceable term 'profits', as increases to profits, in the name of "jobs, oddly seem to coincide with a decline in real jobs. - in "World Orders Old and New, Pluto Press, 1994.
5   El Oeste, 4th December 2002.
6   From their press release dated 24th March 2003. (www.miningwatch.ca).
7   Cf. above Mining Watch press release.
8   Information from "Basurales en Tierras Mapuche", by Alfredo Seguel, available on ecoportal (www.ecoportal.net) and Mapuexpress (www.mapuexpress.net).
9   For an analysis of Mapuche medicinal plants, see "Plantas Medicinales empleadas por los Mapuches" by Dr Jorge R. Alonso (http://www.plantasmedicinales.org/etno/etno8.htm).
10 Quote from an article by Ivonne Jelves Mella, "Intervención externa y medicina mapuche, on the Kolektivo Lientur website (www.nodo50.org/kolectivolientur/medicina_mapu.htm), March 2003.
11 Information from an article by Dr Sergio Cocchetti, "Genética, dominación e identidad cultural en el sur argentino -chileno, on the Pro Diversitas website: www.prodiversitas.bioetica.org/nota40.htm.
12 Quoted from "La Mañana del Sur, 20/12/02.
13 Idem.
14 "Vence el plazo para el proyecto Araucaria", *Río Negro* newspaper, 15/4/2003.
15 Quoted from Werken Kuruf, issue 3.
16 Idem.
17 www.yatraexpedition.org.
18 The Municipality of General Roca has given its permission for the construction, on the land of the Leufuche community, of an establishment by the Bodega Escorihuela, a wine production and distribution company from Mendoza, in return for an investment on the part of the company of $85 million and the promise of one hundred and fifty jobs. The project has meant the displacement of the community from their original site, the fencing off of the best land, and the prevention of access to the river for their animals.
19 As reported in an article by Liliana Venanzi in EcoPortal (www.ecoportal.net/articulos/patagonia.htm).
20 "Los conflictos territoriales de los pueblos indígenas en la Patagonia, by Dr Dario Rodriguez Duch.
21 Bill no. 090/02, presented by deputies Iralde and Lorenzo of the Alianza Block.
22 www.laaraucania.cl/a-2/comunas/nimperial.html.
23 "Baron Lands, published in the Guardian on 23/1/2002.
24 www.patagonialandtrust.org.
25 "Baron lands, op.cit.
26 The incident is reported in an article by Kent Black in "Travel & Leisure" from February 2000, "Mr Tompkin's Neighbourhood" (http://www.travelandleisure.com/).
27 According to a Chilean Nazi website, www.resistenciaaria.org.

"CABECITA NEGRA": STORIES OF EVERYDAY RACISM AND RELIGIOUS INTOLERANCE

"Kom xipace, fijke mojfvñ ce wixapvraley ñi kvme felen, nor felen tvfaci Fvxa Cijka mew, cumgeay rume ñi zugun, ñi wimtun, cem azgeay rume, cem kimun rume nieay."

Universal Declaration of Human Rights in *Mapudungun*, Article 2[2]

(Translation: "Everyone is entitled to all the rights and freedoms set forth in the Declaration, without distinction of any kind, such as race, colour, sex, language, religion, political or other opinion, national or social origin, property, birth or other status.")

"Aliens, we continue to look at ourselves in the distorted mirror of other cultures."
Guillermo E. Magrassi[3]

This penultimate chapter focuses on racism, one of the underlying themes of the whole book. It is about indigenous identity seen through the distorting mirror referred to by Magrassi, which embellishes the European and the North American and disfigures the indigenous. Reflected in this mirror, the Mapuche have been presented – even by world-renowned writers such as Borges - as drunk, lazy, disorganised, thieving and bellicose. Equally disparaged, their language, *Mapudungun*, has often merely been used as a medium for evangelising or the imposition of imported culture.

The consequence of the low esteem in which they have long been held, and the undermining of the cornerstones of their culture by imposed religion and education, has often been the denial of Mapuche identity, particularly by the urban Mapuche, as evinced by the results of the censuses conducted in recent years. Yet curiously, coexisting with the denigrated image of indigenousness there is another more positive one, that of the exotic, folkloric Indian, still regularly used in advertising and tourism.

The casual racism of Europeans

This chapter will deal with the painful subject of racism in Chile and Argentina. Not so much the violence and abuse that are often the expression of racism, although they too will be discussed, as the casual racism that results from the deep-seated feeling of racial superiority of those of European stock.

One European to become enchanted with Patagonia was Bruce Chatwin. His book "In Patagonia" undoubtedly contributed to the creation of Chatwin's cult status. In it he describes in great detail the encounters and conversations he has with the people he meets there. He talks about the "Araucanians" a great deal, often mentioning their bravery, but invariably qualifying this with reference to their "drunkenness":

> "An Indian came in drunk and drank through three jugs of wine. His eyes were glittering slits in the red leather shield of his face."[4]

Did Chatwin ever consider engaging this "Indian" in conversation, or indeed any of the "Indians" he encountered? Was he curious to find out why they drank? No, they were usually either serving him or providing fodder for his poetic powers, while he conversed with the eccentric European farmers who really interested him, also heavy drinkers, incidentally. Though he had abandoned a job at the Sunday Times to embark on his trip to Argentina and Chile, he never abandoned his perspective, and was always writing with an eye to an English readership. The indigenous peoples were therefore merely exotica, local colour, a backdrop.

Louis C. Faron was Emeritus Professor of Anthropology at the State University of New York at Stony Brook, Long Island, in the 60s and 70s. His book "The Mapuche Indians of Chile", published in 1968, is a seminal work for anthropologists working with the Mapuche, and is still the most widely available work in English on the Mapuche. On page 6 of his book, Prof. Faron writes:

> "I also learned that in the past twenty years of missionary work in Cautín, made up of about fifteen reservations, the Protestant group had made fewer than a dozen converts and that Mapuche religious beliefs are tenaciously maintained. As noted before, human sacrifice is still said to occur in times of great general calamity."[5]

And on page 14:

> "One-quarter million or more Mapuche, conservative and recalcitrant, continue to pose a great problem of assimilation for the Chilean government."[6]

Racism seems to be a strong word to apply to someone who was undoubtedly sympathetic towards Mapuche culture, yet when Prof. Faron uses hearsay posing as scholarship in accusing Mapuches of cannibalism while offering no evidence to support his claim, and when he criticises Mapuches of being "recalcitrant" for maintaining their religious beliefs and for resisting assimilation, it is clear that he is not *super partes*, but is speaking with the same tone of condescension that the Chilean and Argentine states have so often used in relation to their nations' indigenous populations.

The Mapuche Centre of San Carlos de Bariloche is just a short walk from the Bariloche bus station. The Centre is also used by families living out of town and in the more remote neighbourhoods as a place to stay when they have to visit the city hospital. It was founded in 1984, as a way of meeting the needs of the many Mapuches who were forced to migrate to the city because of the harsh winter of that year.

In the kitchen of the Centre I got into conversation with María, a young woman from out of town who was accompanying her disabled 10-year-old sister on a hospital visit. I told her a little about my book, and asked her how she felt about being Mapuche. "Oh, I'm not Mapuche" - she said - "I'm Argentinian." Of course she is Argentinian. Clearly having more claim to the title than the many Argentinians who prefer to wear their European roots as a badge of honour. She has no European roots, yet, either through lack of knowledge of her real ethnic origins or fear of social stigma associated with being indigenous in Argentina, she would rather be considered Argentinian than Mapuche.

It is not only the flagrant racism against indigenous people that makes them reluctant to embrace an indigenous identity, but also casual, everyday racist episodes and phenomena, such as the "*pelo de negrito*" (little Indian boy's hair) wig in the novelty shop window before carnival (Argentines often refer to people with indigenous features as "Negros", making no distinction between them and Afro-Americans, of whom there are few in Argentina, compared with, say Brazil); or the throwaway use of the word *quilombo* to indicate something noisy or messy, when *quilombos* were in fact the communities of escaped former slaves on Brazil. The framework of racism has already been formed, but it now takes a variety of subtly different forms.

The problem is that casual racism can escalate, and people die as a result. People such as Bolivian Marcelina Meneses and her 10-month-old son, who were thrown from a train near Avellaneda, Buenos Aires, because their fellow passengers did not like the colour of their skin. Prior to pushing them from the train, the guard allegedly shouted "These Bolivians causing trouble ("*haciendo quilombo*") again! They make me sick! I'll get them"[7]. Such appalling incidents are deeply worrying for Argentina's Mapuches; we saw in chapter one that Mapuches themselves are often referred to as Bolivians by those who will not let concern for accuracy of ethnic identity ruin a good insult.

In Chile Mapuche women often wear their traditional dress when in the city; a dangerous act, considering the sometimes dire consequences. In January 1999 Clara Antinao was walking along the street in Santiago, wearing traditional Mapuche clothing, when she was abruptly stopped by *Carabineros*. They told her that she must leave the area immediately, as access to the area around La Moneda, the presidential palace, was not permitted to people dressed as Mapuches.

The consequences for *lonko* Juana Calfunao of the Paillaleff community were far worse:

> "I was arrested in the Temuco bus station just for being a Mapuche, for wearing my traditional clothing. They dragged me by my braids and handcuffed me. My son tried to defend me, but he was also beaten and cuffed. My husband was also arrested. My other children and my fellow Mapuche brothers tried to help me, but couldn't do a thing ... As a result of the beating I received, I lost my unborn child. I was stripped naked and left in a cell overnight. They strangled me with my braids, let me catch my breath and then strangled me again. They stood on my stomach, they spat on my face, they beat me all over."[8]

Since that attack, Lonko Juana has suffered 3 arson attacks against her property, the third of which - on 22 July 2005 - reduced her home to rubble. She earned notoriety among the *winkas* (and some kudos among her fellow Mapuches) when she hit the director of Conadi, Rodrigo González, in 1999 (see note 9, chapter 8).

As the episode mentioned above demonstrates, Mapuche women are doubly victimised, as victims of both racism and sexism, *machismo*. Elisa Manuel, of the Leufuche community, Río Negro, Argentina, tells of her "education":

> "I was born in 1923 in a place just outside El Cuy, in the Province of Río Negro. My mother died when I was a baby and my father when I was eight. An aunt took me to live in the house of the Justice of the Peace, in the town called El Cuy. I never went to school, because the judge said that reading is not necessary for women, as it teaches them bad things. That is why I and another girl brought up by the judge and his family never learnt to read."[9]

It is not uncommon for the élites in a society to harbour a grudging respect for other cultures; in certain historical moments, this respect can even reach the point of adoration, as in the case of Czarist Russia's love of France and the French language, or the English Romantics' attraction to all things Italian. Yet these two examples do not even come close to matching the level of centrality that Europe has had and continues to have for the dominant class in Argentina, and consequently for those subject to the latter's influence.

Some time ago I happened to be listening to a talk radio station in Buenos Aires[10], and caught popular shock jock "Baby" Echecobar talking about the Peronist politician Ruckauf. I jotted down the following jaw-dropping words: "what we need are modern politicians, politicians like Ruckauf who look to Europe, and not to Formosa." In Argentina the problem is that for three centuries "modern politicians" have looked to Europe, and Formosa and the rest of Argentina's provinces have paid the price.

Argentina's most famous and revered writer, Jorge Luis Borges, was also an incurable Europhile, but more specifically a champion of northern Europeans. His disdain for the Spanish was only exceeded by his utter contempt for the Mapuche. The following is an extract from an interview with Borges that was published in Buenos Aires magazine "7 Dias" in April 1973, recovered from the archive of writer Norberto Galasso[11]:

> **Journalist:** And do you justify the extermination of the Indians? The way your grandfather proceeded?
> **Borges:** Well, I believe that we did the right thing to get rid of the Spaniards. Spain was a decadent country and the English invasions demonstrated that we could govern ourselves: the war of independence is therefore justified. Something similar happened with the Indians. They attacked the ranches and they needed to be defended. Look at my grandfather, he was boss of the three frontiers: North and West of Buenos Aires, and South of Santa Fe. My grandmother accompanied him for four years and she had the opportunity to converse with Catriel, with Pincén, with many caciques: they were barbarians; they didn't know how to count beyond four. The war against the Indians was very cruel on both sides. But the Spaniards first and those who conquered the desert later, represented culture.
> **Journalist:** So, would there exist a permitted violence (for example, that used against the Indians) and another condemnable one, such as that which you attribute to your enemies?
> **Borges:** If violence is used for the sake of culture, I allow it. If not, no. For that reason I believe that, all things considered, the soldiers of the conquest of the desert fought for a fairer cause than the Indians, who did it for nothing. But, I wonder, why do you insist so much on discussing such an exotic topic as that of the Indians. You sound like Bolivians!

Chileans too have a self-image that is – or at least yearns to be – European. The British presence in Chile since before the founding of the nation state has contributed towards the creation of this self-image, which to a large extent denies its indigenous roots. José Aylwin, of the University of La Frontera, Temuco, explains this in the following terms:

> "Chile has historically denied its ethnic and cultural diversity. The country's ruling class has been able to build and internalise in the minds of the people the idea that ours is a racially homogenous society, basically of European origin. This idea, which for centuries has been promoted through different means, including family, school, and literature, became dominant during the republican period, giving birth to the myth, still believed by many, of the Chileans as the "English of South America.""[12]

This is the Janus-faced view of many of Chile and Argentina's elite, to gaze adoringly at Europe and identify themselves with Europeans, while looking down in disdain on their indigenous peoples. Ammunition for their scorn is provided by a vast repertoire of racist stereotypes.

Racist stereotypes

Mapulink, the UK-based Mapuche support group, prepared a press release about the insulting treatment some Mapuche-Lafkenches had received from a Chilean government minister, and sent it to all those on their e-mail list. It mistakenly reached a recipient who could not by any stretch of the imagination be called a sympathiser. To spare his shame, we will not give his name here, but this is the translation of his reply:

> "Perhaps if they got jobs, instead of taking land, things would go better for this unintelligent, dirty and thieving people, who did not even leave the slightest relic of their culture, and did not even learn to write. Mapuches are worthless. They should stop messing about and get to work like everybody else does."

This remarkable little paragraph manages to concentrate in a few lines virtually all the racist clichés that circulate about the Mapuche in Chile. But they apply equally to Argentina, and to indigenous people generally. And racist slurs are no less common coming from the mouths of the supposedly cultured; leading Chilean historian Sergio Villalobos believes that the Mapuche are inferior and so deserved to be dominated, as we saw in chapter five. His Argentine counterpart, Rodolfo Casamiquela believes that Mapuches and Tehuelches rarely have "analytical capacity", and they have a "particular incapacity […] for abstractions and generalisations."[13]

In the lines that follow we will look at a few of the clichés often used to denigrate indigenous people.

The idea that the Indian is a thief, for instance, was even espoused by that defender of the gaucho, José Hernández, in his classic "Martín Fierro":

"The Indian is an Indian and does not wish
to cause pity with his condition
he was born a thieving Indian
and a thieving Indian he will die."[14]

Mapuches are lazy, and don't use their land. A people with centuries' experience of small-scale agriculture are assumed to be inept, incapable of cultivating the land because their methods are less invasive than heavy machinery. José Ignacio Letamendi, of the Corporación Chilena de la Madera (CORMA), is reported to have said: "On no pretext and under no circumstances will we return the land to the Mapuches, who are incapable of cultivating it."[15]

The same accusation was made by Jorge Luchsinger, the landowner of Swiss origin: "It is not possible to hand over land to the Mapuches... there is going to be absolute destitution, because they don't work. […] Have you seen how the fields are that were bought for them by the State through CONADI? Nothing is left there, not even a tree left standing, they don't produce a thing!"[16]

A similar slight, regularly used by media and politicians, is that the Mapuches are incapable of organising themselves, and need to be trained by foreigners or left-wing parties. A report in *La Tercera* newspaper in April 1999, referring to a land occupation near Temulemu, Traiguén, stated "In this action three foreigners were stopped (one French, one North American and one Spanish), whom Governor Isaac Vergara Torres ordered to be expelled from Chile."

Alihuén Antileo and Pedro Cayuqueo, then members of the Mapuche organisation Coordinadora Mapuche de la Región Metropolitana, were incensed by the implication that they were incompetent if left to their own devices, and wrote to the newspaper:

"It bothers us that there is talk of infiltrators, believing that we are not capable of taking our own decisions, having our own successes and making our own mistakes."[17]

As well as being thieving, lazy and disorganised, they are also factious. The stereotype is still commonly resorted to today, particularly by journalists looking for an easy angle for the many conflicts over land title that exist today. One representative example is a news item that appeared in *La Tercera* newspaper on 3 February 2002. The headline "One thousand hectares of hatred in San Juan de la Costa" had the following paragraph below it: "An ancestral dispute has brought about a lethal brawl between the Mapuche-Williche families Cumilef and Lefián. Not even the five deaths recorded on Wednesday between the two factions have succeeded in placating the hatred and resentment that exists between the two families." Five deaths are of course a tragedy, and there can be no excuse for the killings, but the journalist chose not to dig too deeply into the murky details of agreements reached with CONADI over the purchasing of the land, claimed by both families, and the involvement of the forestry companies interested in exploiting the land.

Responding to the article, and the approach of the press generally, the Resistencia Mapuche organisation identified more sinister strategies than simple journalistic laziness, the age-old ones of "divide and rule" and the carrot and the stick:

> "This strategy, within the sphere of the Mapuche/Chilean conflict, is clearly manifested in the persistent mania of the authorities to classify our organisations as either "violent" or "peaceful", as either "bad" Mapuches or "good" Mapuches, as leaders who either opt for the "anti-system" route or the "institutional" route, as those deserving carrots and projects, or those who can only expect sticks and police persecution as a response to their demands."[18]

The separation of Mapuches into "good" and "bad" Indians would be bad enough, but it is aggravated by the fact that Mapuches' various land claims and protests exist within a climate of what is referred to as "insecurity" ("inseguridad") by the panic-stirring media, namely the catch-all category in which various forms of crime and social unrest are all lumped together. The good citizens are urged to worry about everything from petty theft to terrorism at the same time as they consume brain-numbing trivia. The "good" Indians are compliant and offer no cause for concern, but the "bad" ones are likely to be among the many delinquents and terrorists in our midst.

How does one become a good Indian? Going to church is a very good start. One of the best tools for engendering compliance among the "uppity" Indians is religion.

"And the word was good": The Bible and Mapudungun

Over the last couple of decades, the Southern Cone of South America, as much of the rest of the continent, has undergone a new invasion, this time by evangelical Christians, bringing the message of Christ to those who, in the evangelists' view, had previously lived in spiritual limbo.

> "Temuco, Chile - At the end of March the Mapuche people of central Chile observed a two-day celebration to mark the official presentation and dedication of the first Mapudungun New Testament - a fitting tribute for nearly 20 years of translation work."[19]

So begins an enthusiastic report by the United Bible Societies from May 1997, which goes on to say ominously that this is 'just the beginning'. The ambitious translation project was carried out by two members of SIL International.

On its website (www.sil.org), SIL International states that its purpose is to "work with language communities worldwide to facilitate language-based development through research, translation, and literacy." Estimable aims indeed, yet a report on the organisation by the Interhemispheric Resource Center says: "SIL teams use native languages to teach the Bible in a fundamentalist fashion that the North America Congress on Latin America (NACLA), in its 1973 study, concluded diminished the way natives felt about the traditions of their own cultures."[20]

Considering the translation of the New Testament into Mapudungun, and leaving aside the motives of the translators, what of the quality of the translation? The famous passage from John 1:1 "In the beginning was the Word, and the Word was with God, and the Word was God" has been rendered in Mapudungun as:

> "We llitualu mew dew mülewiyekey tati Dungun, fey tati Dungun mülekey Ngünechen engu, fey kisu ta Ngünechen ürke."

To translate "God", the word *Ngünechen* (a variant of *Ngenechen)* has been chosen. *Ngenechen* is just one god from the Mapuche pantheon; the Mapuche, like many other indigenous peoples of the Americas, have an essentially animist religiosity, attributing divinity (*newen*, or divine forces) to all aspects of life. These *newen* are generally embodied in four main deities. According to Sonia Montecino:

> "In almost all cases the divinities appear with the terms *fuchá* and *kuché*, that is to say, old man and old woman respectively, in this way simultaneously bearing an attribute of gender (male, female) and another of age (they are old). In some places, these main organisers of sex and age make up a nuclear "family" structured into four divinities: the old man and old woman gods (*fuchá* and *kusé,* respectively) and young male and female gods (*weche wentru* and *ulcha domo*)."[21]

Yet John's verse, if back-translated, means "In the beginning was the Word, and the Word was with *Ngenechen*, and ONLY *Ngenechen*." So the translators have not just promoted *Ngenechen* to the position of unchallenged number one, but have eliminated the other deities altogether. They have been silenced. From pantheism to monotheism in a word.

The New Testament translation comes at a time when increasing numbers of young urban Mapuches are keen to learn their mother tongue, as part of an attempt to reconnect with their history, traditions and spirituality. When seeking someone to teach them, they often find themselves having to resort to evangelical Christians, whose zeal in wishing to learn Mapudungun perhaps exceeds even their own, though obviously not for the same reasons.[22]

The latest episode in the saga of the Mapuche language came with the announcement by Microsoft that they have been working on a Windows operating system in Mapudungun, which should be ready by the end of 2005; In November 2003 Microsoft signed a protocol of cooperation with the Chilean Government's Ministry of Education, the University of the Frontier and CONADI. If Bill Gates was expecting applause from all quarters, the reception among Mapuches was mixed, to say the least. Aucán Huilcaman, of *Aukiñ Wallmapu Ngulam*, is unhappy that the azünchefe alphabet was chosen, as although this is approved by the Ministry of Education and CONADI, it is not popular with Mapuche users, who prefer Ragileo; in any case, he resents the lack of consultation, classing the Microsoft exercise as "piracy", cleverly measuring the irony of his choice of words. The debate continues.

This is not the first time in the history of the Mapuche people that their own language has been used to favour the imposition of an extraneous culture. Eliseo Cañulef, a Mapuche academic at the Universidad de la Frontera, Temuco, in a study on the socio-linguistic situation of Mapudungun, cites Bernard Pottier's account of an earlier incursion, by the colonial Spanish, into indigenous languages[23]:

> "With the territorial occupation, the Hispanic invader attempted from the very start to impose a language and a culture that were superior, in their own evaluation, to the languages and cultures of the peoples they invaded. This was carried out mainly through the process of evangelisation, a process that in its initial stage needed to be carried out in the mother tongue of the conquered people, and so the first attempts were made to write down the indigenous languages, with the creation of grammars and dictionaries to be used by the missionaries."

The history of the written form of Mapudungun fits this model perfectly (see chapter one). Later the need arose for the use of a single language, Spanish, to consolidate the Spanish domination. After the Conquest/Pacification, with their incorporation in the new states, the Mapuches lost not only their territorial independence, but also their linguistic autonomy.

About half of the Mapuches in Chile (some 400,000) are speakers of Mapudungun. A much smaller percentage of Argentina's Mapuches speak the language actively, a few thousands at most. Mauro Millán estimates that 70% of Mapuches in Argentina do not speak Mapudungun at all. Almost all literate Mapuches in Chile (some 40% of active speakers) are living in a state of diglossia, that is, speaking Mapudungun at home, but using the Spanish language outside and for almost all written purposes. Until very recently, 'learning how to write' meant 'learning written Spanish'.

According to Eliseo Cañulef, the bilingualism of Spanish and Mapudungun is one in which the former holds all the aces: "In our case it is relatively easy to confirm that Spanish, as a social language, has much more power and prestige than Mapudungun, which is confined to a domestic and ritual use."[24]

I discussed this with José Bengoa, suggesting to him that in Argentina, where very few Mapuches speak Mapudungun, it has come to be a little like the Latin mass for Roman Catholics, taking on mystical, spiritual qualities when they hear it spoken, but often without their being able to understand more than but a few words, words which have a great resonance for them. According to Bengoa:

> "In Chile, of course, many Mapuches speak Mapudungun, perhaps as many as 50%. It is like Latin mass, it is true; the indigenous language has survived because of its very link with the religious ceremony, the *nguillatún*, and in the *nguillatún* if you do not understand Mapudungun, then you are outside of the ritual community. There is a link between religion and language; the *nguillatún* is a place where people speak the "perfect" language, the traditional language, whereas at home they mix it with many Spanish words in their ordinary language. In ceremonial moments, when the *lonko* speaks, we have the ancient Mapudungun."[25]

Bengoa's estimate of 50% might perhaps be a little high[26], but it is difficult to confirm or deny, as speaking Mapudungun is often a private, rather than a public activity. In a climate of prejudice, and even of fear, to speak Mapudungun openly can itself be a political action. At his trial in 2002, Lonko Pichún addressed the court in Mapudungun, offering the traditional greetings and evoking the Mapuche divinities, and an interpreter was used to translate his words for the court's benefit.

At the Mapuche Centre in Bariloche, the activists recently began to run classes on Mapuche language and culture for the youngsters of the city's poor neighbourhoods, and were surprised and delighted to find that many of the children already knew many words and phrases, which their parents, or more often their grandparents, used at home, without saying that they were Mapudungun.

According to José Bengoa, in Chile it is not uncommon for children to speak Mapudungun better than their parents, particularly in rural areas, where the in-

Young urban Mapuches taking part in lessons in Mapuche language and culture at the Mapuche Centre in San Carlos de Bariloche, January 2001. Photo: Leslie Ray

fluence of grandparents is very strong. Very often it is the grandparents who are in charge of children, as the parents are at work in the city; maybe the mother is in Santiago working as a domestic help, and only visits for holidays. So a skipping of a generation occurs, the parents', in the passing down of traditional culture and language.

When Mapuche families live in the city - and, sadly, to a lesser extent even in the communities themselves - there may often be a voluntary abandonment of their culture and language, on account of the poor self-image that *winka* society encourages them to have. Mapuche art historian José Ancán Jara goes into this in a study on urban Mapuches:

> "The most dramatic of the strategies of "protection" employed by the parents of city-born Mapuches is the abandonment of the Mapuche language and the most visible aspects of Mapuche customs. We've heard it so many times that the justification for this is now common knowledge: "I didn't teach my children to speak Mapuche so that they wouldn't be made fun of like I was." This strategy is reinforced by the desire to climb the social ladder, the desire of migrants to send their children to receive formal education, "so they'll be better off than we were.""[27]

It is an unfortunate fact that Mapuches have often felt obliged to deny their Mapuche identity as a means of getting on in *winka* society. This perceived need has emerged in stark relief through the issue of the census.

The numbers game: Mapuches and the census

1992 was a pivotal year for the reawakening of Mapuche identity, as it marked the celebrations-cum-lamentations of 500 years of European presence in the Americas. It was also the year when Chile discovered its urban Mapuche, through the census that was conducted that year. Until that date, according to José Ancán Jara and Margarita Calfio Montalva of the Liwen Mapuche Studies and Documentation Centre, the general view was that "Mapuches are basically small-scale *campesinos*, exclusively inhabiting the *reducciones* of the south - the favourite subject of traditional anthropological field studies - also the version of ethnicity that was easiest to digest and understand for the Chilean public at large, and even for certain Mapuche sectors."[28]

The 1992 census swept that view away, as it demonstrated that around 400,000 Mapuches (44% of the 928,000 people aged over 14 who identified themselves as Mapuche) lived in Santiago. This result even surprised the leaders of the Mapuche movement, particularly those who saw the creation of Mapuche identity as only possible in the traditional rural community.

Ten years later, another census was conducted, showing that the Mapuche population had fallen by over 300,000, with the number of Mapuches being given as 604,340. Even in the restored democracy, Mapuches still seemed to be dropping like flies! How was this possible?

As in any questionnaire, the formulation of the question dictates the results of the answer. The question had simply been changed. The question in the 1992 census was "If you are Chilean, do you consider yourself to belong to one of the following cultures?", whereas in 2002 the question was "Do you belong to one of the following Original or Indigenous Peoples?" The 1992 question encouraged Mapuches to admit their identity more readily, as it was made clear that this would not exclude them from being Chilean; in the 2002 question, however, anyone affected by the social stigma associated with being indigenous would be reluctant to own up to this.

A further element of confusion was the fact that in 1992 the possible answers were: Mapuche, Aymara, Rapanui, none of the above, while in 2002 there were eight different ethnicities offered as possible answers to choose from: Alacalufe, Atacameño, Aymara, Kolla, Mapuche, Quechua, Rapanui and Yamana. How would someone considering themselves Kolla or Quechua have responded in 1992? Would they deny their indigenousness, or associate themselves with another indigenous people, such as the Mapuche?

Marcos Valdés has written a thoughtful article on this issue[29], in which he looks in detail at the methodological problems associated with the two censuses and the significance of their different wordings. Among other things, he points out that when the 2002 census asks people of they "belong" to an Original People, many Mapuches may have disqualified themselves, as they fact that they do not speak Mapudungun or attend a *Nguillatún* may make them feel that they are not entitled to consider themselves as belonging to the Mapuche.

What is more, in neither of the censuses was the whole question of *mestizo* identity broached at all. All of which goes to prove what an imperfect tool the census can be. In any event, the 2002 census was certainly more imperfect than the 1992 one.

The census-takers, as representatives of the state, only venture into the areas where Mapuches live intermittently. Evangelists, on the other hand, are a more committed and more permanent presence.

Evangelists and the urban Mapuche

The Mapuches living and working in the cities are in a vulnerable position, separated from the source of their traditions, and it is in the margins of the cities that they come into contact with the evangelists. In his "Faces of Latin America"[30], Duncan Green describes this vulnerability of the new urban poor:

> "Protestant preachers and TV broadcasts tap into the anxieties of life in modern Latin America - health, jobs, crime and family breakdown. Many authors connect the rise of Protestantism to urbanisation. Peasant migration to the cities severs an individual's links to the community, resulting in isolation and confusion. In such circumstances, Evangelism can offer both a supportive community and a strong sense of purpose and identity. The emphasis on sobriety is particularly attractive to many women whose partners have alcohol problems."

I received a moving confirmation of the damage being done to Mapuche religiosity by evangelical Christians from a surprising source, a Mapuche woman studying English in Santiago called Lorena Norín, who had read an article of mine in *The Linguist* magazine. I quote from Lorena's letter to me:

> "The Mapuche have great resentment because we continue to suffer from social discrimination and great poverty, factors that force us to emigrate and hide their identity. Besides, our ancestral land is threatened by powerful commercial interests, both Chilean and foreign. But, even worse, new religious groups of evangelical inspiration are doing great cultural harm

because those who join them lose touch and are made to forget our own religiosity and are also prevented from following our old traditions, like the *nguillatún*."

Lorena was surprised and pleased to find such interest in the Mapuche in a UK publication, interest that she found sadly lacking in Chilean mainstream media.

Among the evangelical sects, it is the Pentecostals who are meeting with the most significant success in converting Mapuches. Pentecostalism has been present in Chile as far back as the 1950s, and its popularity has increased as traditional Catholicism and Protestantism have declined. The influence has spread over the Andes, and the Pentecostal church has significant success in Patagonian cities such as Bahía Blanca. In an article on this phenomenon[31], Argentine sociologist Graciela Hernández affirms that part of this church's success is that it provides a support network for the poor that is not available from the state:

"The evangelical churches frequently become venues for Adult Schools and Municipal Literacy Centres, which are mostly attended by migrant women; this happens because some neighbourhoods have nowhere to house a public structure, in others the institutions are not prepared to provide their halls as classrooms. In short, in our experience, in many cases these churches end up fulfilling the functions that civil society claims to fulfil, but for which it does not take responsibility; that is to say, the churches are not just a spiritual refuge, but also a material one."

The danger to Mapuches does not come from the fact that the Pentecostal church replaces the state, as in this sense it is clearly valuable and necessary, but rather that it replaces their own religion. Pentecostalism is attractive to Mapuches precisely because many of its practices, such as spiritual healing and the trance-like states attained during its religious ceremonies, have affinities with the behaviour of the *machi* and the conducting of the *nguillatún*. In this sense at least the transition may be a smooth one. Lorena Norín's concern is well placed.

Petrona Pichiñan, of the Mapuche organisation Puel Pvjv, of Neuquén, has her own theory as to why Mapuches are so vulnerable to conversion: "Who are the best Christians that the church has today? The Mapuches. Why is this? The spiritual part has always been of great importance for the Mapuche People, and that is why it is so easy to convince them and to impose another belief system, because Mapuches devote great importance to their spirituality."[32]

The threat to the survival of the Mapuche belief system posed by Pentecostalism is due to the fact that, whereas the Catholic Church is and has been prepared to tolerate certain elements of indigenous spirituality, perhaps the key to its survival over the centuries, the Pentecostal church most categorically does not. According to anthropologist Roger Y. Kellner, who has studied the effect of evangelism on Mapuche belief systems:

> "Unlike the accommodation shown by the Catholic Church in their attempts to convert Mapuche, Pentecostals vehemently deny any connection between the Christian God, and *Ngenechen*, the indigenous name of God, or *Chau Dios*, the now more widely diffused quasi-Christian name, or any other lesser spirits. As could be expected, given Pentecostal insistence that all non-Pentecostal beliefs of whatever nature are inherently evil, the truth value of these indigenous entities is rejected, and they are made to appear not merely illegitimate, but profoundly damning and deceptive as well. Erected in their place are the concepts of *Dios, Jesucristo* and *el Espíritu Santo*."[33]

So with the advent of Pentecostalism, the prospects of survival for Mapuche spirituality, already bleak, are becoming ever bleaker. Yet it would be unfair to claim that the influence of the church on the Mapuches has been wholly negative. Many Christians have in fact worked tirelessly to improve the lives of the poor and the dispossessed. One such figure was Don Jaime de Nevares, who was Bishop of the Diocese of Neuquén until his death in 1995. Monseñor De Nevares, like the practitioners of liberation theology, believed the church should stand beside the poor. He supported the workers of the El Chocón Hydroelectric Dam, who in 1969 occupied the plant to claim unpaid salaries. He refused to share a stage with the Military Junta when they organised a function in his city, and he gave refuge to Chileans who had escaped from Pinochet's Chile. "God is not neutral", he famously said. His habit of wearing a poncho over his robes endeared him to the indigenous people in his flock, including a number of Mapuches who are now in key positions in Neuquén's Mapuche organisations, such as Jorge Nahuel.

Similar voices have occasionally spoken out from the pulpits of Chubut. Recently the Bishop of Comodoro Rivadavia, Monseñor Pedro Ronchino, also aligned himself with the cause of equal rights for the indigenous communities:

> "Only when the aboriginal communities of our region are protected against all possible plundering, will a necessary step have been taken to achieve the ideal of a Province consolidated in solidarity, brotherhood and peace."[34]

Unfortunately, remarkable people such as Monseñores De Nevares and Ronchino are the exception that confirms the rule, and the rule of Christianity has rarely been beneficial to the Mapuche. It is unfortunately the case that hundreds of Mapuche children have been forcibly taken away from their parents by the Salesians to be placed in their colleges, using poverty and the accusation of alcoholism as the pretext. In Bahía Blanca I met Beatriz Curriche, now in her twenties, a member of the recently formed organisation *Kumelen Newen Mapu*, who told me that her attempt the reclaim her Mapuche identity is associated with her search for her natural parents. When just a baby, Beatriz was taken away from both her parents, who had separated, and was placed with an adoptive *winka* family.

As a child Petrona Pichiñan was also taken from her parents, in the Chiquilihuin community, 50 km from Junín de los Andes, to be placed in a religious boarding school (*internado*) in Junín, where she says she had to pray from when she got up till when she went to bed. Chilean rural families, both Mapuche and non-, often send their children to *internados* in the cities, in order to guarantee that they continue their education after elementary school. Here Mapuche children are particularly vulnerable to discrimination and forced assimilation. In a report to the "Encuentro de la Juventud Mapuche de Europa", held in Rouen, France, in April 2002, Elsa Pepin tells of an *internado* in Tirúa, run by a Mormon couple whom she interviewed, who stated that their aim in the classes was to enable the young Mapuches to "rediscover their identity", this of course through reading Mormon scriptures.[35]

In 1884, the year of the founding of the Museum of Natural Sciences in La Plata, and of the last battles in the Conquest of the Desert, primary education became obligatory in Argentina. This considerably assisted "Castellanisation" - the imposition of Spanish as the replacement for Mapudungun. Single-language Spanish schools were established in areas where Mapudungun was the mother tongue, as a form of peacetime continuance of the military campaign.

This would have been slightly more defensible if sufficient resources had been made available to assist this wholesale linguistic transformation of a society. Yet attending schools is still often a major struggle in the rural communities today; we saw in chapter 9 how the community school in Futa Huau, Chubut, was almost casually handed over to a local landowner, forcing the community's children to attend a boarding school 70 km away from the community. Such situations are also not uncommon in Chile, such as in the province of Osorno, where schools tend to be concentrated in the towns, or the Lautaro area, where the communities living near the Andes must make long, expensive journeys for the sake of their education. In the winter, communities which are only accessible by dirt tracks are cut off due to flooding or rendered impassable by the mud. Even in the warmer months, children often have to set off while it is still dark to make long, hazardous journeys to school.

Together with bad weather, another cause of absenteeism is the harvesting season, when the communities often work together, and the children are required to stay and help. This is not taken into account by the schools, who mark this down as unauthorised absences. If they manage to reach school, Mapuche children are at a distinct disadvantage if their first language is Mapudungun, as they find the lessons difficult to follow. This in turn exacerbates absenteeism, and also reinforces the old stereotype that Mapuches are dumb dullards.

Courses in catechism are obligatory even in Chilean state schools, and any reluctance by parents to have their children receive these lessons may well be interpreted as ignorance, since many teachers are unlikely to have any in-depth knowledge of Mapuche spirituality.

In any event, what the school does not do, the radio will. Most Mapuche homes have a radio, if not a TV, and these of course serve to reinforce the Castellanisation begun in the schools, with programmes not only exclusively in Spanish, but also reflecting the established view of Chilean or Argentine society and the Mapuches' role within them.

Estimable initiatives are taking place in Chile, particularly in Santiago, to re-establish the connection between urban Mapuches and their language and culture, such as the programme for the teaching of Mapudungun sponsored by the Chilean National Library, which has been running since 1995. Despite these, the report card says "could do much better." According to educationalist Marcela Villarroel, in an article for the Kolektivo Lientur website[36], despite the various educational reforms, schooling in Chile continues to move the ethnic minorities away from their reality. There are still hundreds of children coming from ethnic minorities spread throughout Chile who are taught in *winka* rural or urban schools without an ad hoc programme "to reflect their socio-cultural reality."

Education should be the means to enable Mapuches to take their rightful seat at the table at the state banquet, but for now it would seem that their allotted role is to stand at the door, in costume, to be photographed.

The exotic, folkloric Indian

To learn their place, this is the duty of the Indian in Chile and Argentina, the folkloric Indian that Eduardo Galeano describes ironically thus: "The cultures of non-European origin are not cultures, they are ignorances, at most useful to prove the impotence of the inferior races, to attract tourists and provide a typical note at the parties at the end of courses and on national holidays."[37]

Mapuche organisations are often scathing about indigenous people who lend themselves to activities providing ethnic colour but no substance, such as the re-enactment of the arrival of the Welsh in Patagonia, discussed in chapter 5. They refer to this as the presence of "the indigenous face" ("*la cara indígena*"), a token presence to give the impression of a tolerant society.

In Chubut, Tehuelche Rosa Chiquichano has often been the target of such criticism. It is she who has taken part in the re-enactments referred to above. She is not the passive, unassuming Indian, but a successful politician, not averse to using her indigenousness to her advantage, such as being photographed in traditional dress astride a horse for her local election campaign, to attract the indigenous vote. She has made certain accommodating compromises that raise the hackles of her more intransigent fellows; such as swearing "by God and the Fatherland" when she received her diploma as the first Tehuelche lawyer.

The Argentina newspaper La Nación describes the scene:

"The emotion was palpable. Among those who approached to embrace her were not only her family, but also a woman whose presence had a great significance: Luisa Calcumil, singer, actress (*"La nave de los locos"*) and, above all, representative of the culture of the Mapuche people. Reflected in the embrace of the two was the sentiment of unity of two cultures that were formerly set against each other."[38]

Such gestures are comforting. Even more so inasmuch as this one paragraph manages to both invent a conflict and resolve it in one fell swoop. All is well and everyone is in their place.

A similar occasion was when the elderly Mercedes Nahuelpan, of the Nahuel Pan Reservation, was honoured as an "Illustrious Citizen" by the Municipality of Trevelin in April 1996. Such honours do not put food on anyone's table, or provide education for anyone's children, but they make the bestowers feel good about themselves, while preserving the status quo. As we saw in chapter 9, the Nahuel Pan community are the "good" Indians, being compliant with the requirements of the holders of power in Chubut province, and as such they must be seen to achieve some reward for this, in contrast with troublesome "bad" Indians, such as the Prane family and others active in the 11 October Organisation, who merit no reward, only chastisement.

"Good" Indians do not mind when the elements that make up their language and culture are pilfered. A further threat to the health of their identity is the way the body of knowledge that helps compose it is raided seemingly at random to meet the needs of advertising and marketing. Whilst Mapuche culture is not accorded any semblance of parity with Western culture, it does provide a useful source of lexical resources for the dominant society to dip into and pick out the bits it likes.

If you travel around the areas with a Mapuche presence, then you notice the abundance of shops, restaurants, hotels and *cabañas* with names in Mapudungun, chosen presumably because the marketing people like the exotic yet unthreatening connotations. In Chile there is "Puelche S.A.", producers of plant products in Los Angeles, and the Pehuenche S.A. hydroelectric company; in Argentine Patagonia there is the "Maputur" travel agency in El Bolsón, the "Cumelen" hotel in San Martín de los Andes, and also the "Cumelen" drug addiction charity in Olavarría. Revealingly, the website of the charity[39] states that "'Cumelen' is a word in the Araucanian Indian dialect that means 'be well'." They like the word, but they are not concerned that the Mapuche do not wish to be known as Araucanians and that theirs is a language, not a dialect.

This is nothing new: there was the Tehuelche beer produced by the Azul brewery, and Moss y Cia. Ltda, producers of Bols gin, showed their sensitivity to indigenous alcoholism problems by using the image of elderly Tehuelche drunkard K'chorro to advertise the product with the slogan "even old Indians knew the excellent qualities of Bols gin!"

The comic book character Patoruzú, the giant Tehuelche, known and loved by generations of Argentine children, was created in 1928 by the *Crítica* newspaper. In his first appearance, he asked his master, Don Gil Contento, "Are you my guardian, *che*? Curugua-Curigüigua salutes you." Don Gilito replied, sensitively: "You have finally arrived Patoruzú. I christen you with this name because yours dislocates my jaw." Did the Tehuelches find this funny?

Chileans often pride themselves on being "the English of South America" or "the Switzerland of South America", yet in the football stadiums and fanzines their Bolivian and Peruvian call them "Mapochos", a pejorative corruption of Mapuches. This is in a sense the Chilean - and to lesser degree the Argentinian - dilemma, to crave the European identity yet be identified by others with the autochthonous, indigenous one. Could racism against indigenous people therefore be a projection of a self-loathing? In an illuminating essay, "Inocencia y neocolonialismo: un caso de dominio ideológico en la literatura infantil"[40], Chilean writer Ariel Dorfman analyses the way that through cartoons and comic books children absorb the values of the society into which they are to grow up, comparing this process with that whereby colonised countries - like children - adopt the values of the paternalistic colonisers. Dorfman quotes from chapter one of Franz Fanon's "The Wretched of the Earth":

> "Every colonized people - in other words, every people in whose soul an inferiority complex has been created by the death and burial of its local cultural originality - finds itself face to face with the language of the civilizing nation; that is, with the culture of the mother country. The colonized is elevated above his jungle status in proportion to his adoption of the mother country's cultural standards."

This may be the case, but today it seems to me to be more likely that the "colonized" are losing the capacity to even distinguish what their own culture is, as off-the-peg consumerism means all cultural artefacts can be acquired at little cost or effort. An art student at the University of Lanús in Gran Buenos Aires told me that she and some fellow students they are working on a project to renovate and paint an old abandoned railway carriage from the Gloucester Railway Carriage & Wagon Company on the premises of the former workshops of Ferrocarril Sud in Remedios de Escalada that are now used by the university. Their plan is to create a mural depicting the *kultrun*, representing southern culture, divided into four by railway lines, representing northern Celtic [sic] culture. Their motives are certainly positive, the embracing of two distant cultures, but they seem to be unaware that to use a powerful Mapuche symbol, and then paint on it the railway line, inevitably associated with the campaign of the Desert and the Mapuche's defeat, is deeply offensive, even if the offence is unintentional.

Lying on my bed to keep out of the afternoon heat in a dirt-roaded *barrio* of Neuquén, I heard a street vendor moving slowly down the street shouting out his wares for sale: "*Hay mote y ñaco casero*" ("there's mote and home-made ñaco"). *Mote* (wheat boiled with sugar and honey) and *ñaco* (toasted and ground wheat) are two staples that would have been made in every Mapuche home, which have now made their way to the poor neighbourhoods of the cities, sold by microenterprises such as the street vendor I heard. *Mote* and *ñaco* represent a culture that exists within another culture, almost imperceptibly, but confidently nevertheless. Such small affirmations of Mapuche identity that have not been suppressed or appropriated, despite the odds. In the final chapter I will look at other confident affirmations of Mapuche identity, success stories to provide the antidote to the pessimism of the last few chapters.

Notes

1. Literally "little black head", a racist expression used to refer to indigenous people in Argentina.
2. Translated into *Mapudungun* by Fresia Mellico (www.unhcr.ch/udhr/lang/aru.htm).
3. Giullermo E. Magrassi, "Los Aborigenes de la Argentina", p. 5, Galerna, Buenos Aires, 2000.
4. "In Patagonia", p. 27, publ. by Vintage, 1998.
5. "The Mapuche Indians of Chile", Louis C. Faron, Holt Rinehart and Winston, Inc. 1968.
6. Idem.
7. Reported in Página 12, 1/6/01. The murder took place on 10th January 2001.
8. Interviewed by the Santiago Times, "The Nation through the eyes of a Mapuche leader",14/2/2001.
9. Interviewed in Werken Kuruf, issue 2.
10. Radio 10, 10/7/01.
11. The essayist Mario Tesler also published the interview in 'Pregón', 29-IX, 1985, Jujuy. It also appeared in: "America was conquered. Heirs and victims" (1992) 83 pp. Almagesto. Buenos Aires.
12. José Aylwin, Institute of Indigenous Studies, University of La Frontera, Temuco, Chile, "Indigenous Peoples' Rights in Chile." Paper presented at the Canadian Association for Latin American and Caribbean Studies (CALACS) XXVIII Congress, Simon Fraser University, Vancouver, B.C., March 19-21, 1998.
13. Cited by Julio Vezub in "El museo leleque, los científicos y los mapuche-tehuelche", Azkintuwe, 26 September 2005.
14. "El indio es indio y no quiere / apiar de su condición / ha nacido indio ladrón / y como indio ladrón muere." Martín Fierro, IV, 493.
15. Le Monde Diplomatique, "Long march of Chile's Mapuches" by Jaime Massardo, November 1999.
16. Published in the magazine *Qué Pasa*, June 2005, quoted in Azkintuwe, 21 June 2005.
17. Declaration to La Tercera newspaper on 13/4/99; it is contained in a report by the Aukache organisation (available on the Rehue Foundation website).
18. "Las consecuencias de una estrategia maldita", press release dated 5/2/02.

19 www.biblesociety.org.
20 www.namebase.org/gw/sil.txt.
21 Sonia Montecino, "Sol Viejo, Sol Vieja. Lo feminine en las representaciones mapuche", chapter 2 (rehue.csociales.uchile.cl/rehuehome/facultad/publicaciones/Excerpta/excerpta7/soltapa.htm).
22 For example, Mapuches wishing to learn Mapudungun in Esquel must go to classes run by Antonio, an evangelical Christian who teaches Mapudungun.
23 Bernard Pottier, America Latina en su Lengua Indigena, UNESCO, Monte Aguila Editores, Caracas-Venezuela, 1983, pp. 19-39, cited in Eliseo Cañulef, "Hacia una caracterización de la situación sociolingüística del Mapudungun como paso previo a una planificación lingüística", p. 54, in "Sociedad y Cultura Mapuche. El Cambio y la Resistencia Cultural" by the Sociedad Mapuche Lonko Kilipan, Temuco 1992. The history of the written forms of Mapudungun is discussed in Chapter 1 of this book.
24 Eliseo Cañulef, *op. cit*, pp. 56-7.
25 Interviewed in Cambridge, 5/5/03.
26 R. Croese of the Summer Institute of Linguists confirmed the 50% figure in 1982 (see chapter one), but gave the total Mapuche population in Chile as 400,000, and active users of Mapudungun as 200,000. We now know that there are at least twice that many self-identified Mapuche in Chile.
27 "Urban Mapuches: reflections on a Modern Reality", on the Ñuke Mapu Documentation Centre website.
28 "El retorno al país mapuche: reflexiones preliminares para una utopía por construir", by José Ancán Jara and Margarita Calfio Montalva, available on www.mapuexpress.net.
29 "Reflexiones metodológicas en torno a los censos de 1992 - 2002 y la cuestión Mapuche" (http://www.mapuche.cl/documentos/).
30 Latin America Bureau, 1991, p. 212.
31 "Entre la adscripción étnica, la cultura u la supervivencia en contextos de pobreza", paper presented at the symposium "La Cuestión Indígena Hoy", Fourth Chilean Anthropology Congress, Chile, November 2001.
32 Interviewed in Neuquén, 2/6/2003.
33 Quoted from "Christian Gods and Mapuche Witches: The Retention of Indigenous Concepts of Evil among Mapuche Pentecostals", by Roger Y. Kellner, in "Popular Use of Popular Religion in Latin America", Susanna Rostas and Andre Droogers, CEDLA 1993.
34 Quoted from Diaro El Chubut, 23rd October 2003.
35 Educación Chilena y negación de la historia Mapuche" (http://www.mapuche.nl/publ/elsap.htm).
36 "Gulumapu: ¿Educación para "matarle el indio" al mapuche?, 10th July 2003, on argentina.indymedia.org.
37 Eduardo Galeano, "Patas Arriba", Siglo XXI, Spain, 1998, p. 58.
38 La Nación, "La primera abogada tehuelche" 1/9/99.
39 www.olavarria.com/archivos/organismos/ ongs/cumelen/indcx.php.
40 The essay is available at http://www.nombrefalso.com.ar/.

SEEDS OF HOPE: MAPUCHE SUCCESS STORIES TODAY

*We don't want them to give us a hand,
we want them to take their hands off us."*
Mapuche saying

The previous few chapters have inevitably tended to dwell on the injustices to which the Mapuche have fallen and are falling victim. To remedy this tendency, this final chapter is intended to leave the reader with a more positive sense of where they are as a people today, by outlining some inspirational stories of Mapuche success.

Mapuche culture is going through something of a renaissance, with increasing interest being shown in their traditional arts and crafts, their music and medicine, in learning their language, and even their "national" sport, palín, by Mapuche and *winka* alike. Whether they choose to seek success in society's terms, as in the case of politician Francisco Huenchumilla or model Ximena Huilipán, or opt for a more independent path, as in the case of the *Warriache* urban poets, the Mapuche are increasingly being seen as a force to be reckoned with.

"Returning to our roots from the cement"[1]: rediscovery of Mapuche culture

For many Argentinians, it came as a complete surprise to discover that Mapuches existed in their country when, in 1985, Luisa Calcumil played the title role in the film "Gerónima", about a Mapuche woman struggling against poverty and abuse in a wind-swept Patagonia.

Today, Argentina's cultural élite would not deny its existence. In 2001 a prestigious coffee-table book was published by Luz Editora of Buenos Aires, "Mapuches del Neuquén, Arte y cultura en la Patagonia argentina." The book contains 269 pages of photos of Mapuche art objects, artefacts, textiles, silverware, etc. Mapuche culture has clearly taken its rightful place as part of the culture of the Argentine nation. Sadly, at the price of $95 hardback and $75 paperback, very few Mapuches will be able to afford to possess a copy of this inventory of their culture.

Fortunately, affordable art that is by the Mapuche for the Mapuche does exist. As I mentioned in the introduction to this book, my own first contact with the Mapuche came through a visit by three Mapuche women, to talk about their struggle and run a number of pottery workshops. One of these women was Evis Millán. For Evis and many other *warriache* (urban Mapuche), political struggle and the strengthening and dissemination of their cultural traditions are inseparable. When Evis conducts her pottery classes, she teaches not only the traditional techniques, but also the worldview that underpins them.

In the past Mapuche pottery was used on a massive scale and were of very high quality. The most significant varieties are the *kitra* (pipe), used to smoke and also to "incense" during religious ceremonies, *challas* (pots) of various shapes and sizes, various types of *metawe* and *pitrén* (pitchers) used for holding liquid. These items were often anthropomorphic or zoomorphic, and were also used for ritual purposes. Particularly characteristic pieces are the *ketru metawe*, in the shape of a duck, representing motherhood. One piece that speaks volumes of the importance of diplomacy is the jug with two spouts, to enable two guests to be served at the same time, thus ensuring equality and the absence of hierarchy.

Evis' brother Mauro is a *retrafe*, a silversmith. For Mauro making silver objects is not only a means of paying the bills, it is also a political act, an affirmation of his culture. Silversmithery is in fact one of the cultural manifestations that best represents the Mapuche people. Their whole symbolic world is expressed in the silver plates and the engravings on them. Silverwork among the Mapuche dates back several centuries, and seems to have developed particularly after the availability of silver coins obtained from trade with the Spaniards.

Mauro makes *chaway*, the silver earrings that are presented to girls during the initiation ceremony of *katan pilún*, when their ears are pierced. An ancient basic form of the *chaway* is the flat trapezium; these large shapes were traditionally used as earrings, but now tend to be for hair decoration, as they are too heavy for the ears to bear their weight; over time earrings have tended to become smaller. Mauro also makes *sikil*, used by women to adorn their chests; these consist of a number of silver plates with different designs and motifs, depending on the woman concerned and her characteristics of birth, place of origin and community, hinged together to represent the division of vertical space between the *wenu mapu* (celestial world) and the lower worlds.

Until the early decades of the 20th century, Mapuches' lives were still populated with objects made from vegetable fibres, where various everyday needs were resolved using basketwork items. Current basketwork practice, as regards raw materials and techniques, has not changed substantially from the past. On the coast of Cautín, objects made with vegetable fibres are still important in domestic life and in fishing, hunting, gathering and horticulture.

Mapuche textile work, usually performed by women, was and is not only the production of items for clothing and furnishing, but also a sophisticated religious and social language, expressing in the choice of colours and designs a symbology only known by the great weavers, or *duwekafe*. Knowledge of textiles and their recreation is linked to the cosmovision and to religious meaning. A set of techniques, designs and types of clothing are the result of an inheritance and a memory that has been transmitted over time and defines a part of Mapuche being.[2]

Along with traditional crafts, Mapuche music is also alive and well. Beatriz Pichi Malen is Argentina's best-known Mapuche singer. She is the great granddaughter of Coliqueo, the 19th-century *lonko*. Since 1984 she has been active in disseminating Mapuche culture and history, collaborating with many educational institutions all over Argentina, and conducting workshops on Mapuche song and dance. In 2000 she released the CD "Plata", which has met with considerable success in South America. Beatriz sings in Mapudungun, although she cannot speak the language fluently.

Beatriz describes her "discovery" of her Mapuche identity:

"When I was a young girl, I was very far away from my people. I even lived for a time with some Germans, who had planned for me to be a pianist. Later my mother was able to rescue me, that is why, as a teenager, I needed to go out and search to find out what we Mapuche were like. This I did, and with it I found myself."[3]

Another musical voyage of discovery is "Feley", a CD of Mapuche songs released in 2004. The CD is a collaboration between the rock group Superpatria and the Mapuche-Tehuelche communities that are part of the 11 October Mapuche-Tehuelche Organisation. The sleeve notes explain the rationale behind the project:

"For the people of the 11 October Mapuche Tehuelche Organisation, this commitment is important in terms of cultural continuity: the vast majority of the interpreters of the music that is shared here are grey-haired and are inexorably approaching their re-encounter with the *newens* that brought them into existence. It is therefore fundamental for all these *tayúl* (songs) to be conserved, so the young Mapuches who are forced by circumstances to migrate to the cities and move away from the wisdom of their elders can link up with it once again and, if possible, assist in its recovery and new development."

In Chile the Mapuche cultural identity is now shouted out accompanied by the pulsating rhythms of rock: "five centuries dominated, for five centuries they've lied to us, five centuries oppressed us, confounded us." The six-piece band from Villarica, *Meli Weichafe* (Four Warriors) claim that their reason for existing is "to build and boost the expression of Mapuche culture and the marginal art of the shanty-towns"[4]. Another band, *Purilonko* (Wormhead), have put poems by Elicura Chihuailaf to music.

The proliferation of Mapuche music is only part of a general resurgence of Mapuche culture among the people's young, thanks to whose energy the *rukas* are being built again. In the Prane community, they signify their intention to remain despite the menacing presence of the Argentine army. In Valle de Elicura, near Cañete, where Manuel Maribur says "we have a project for a *ruka*, a cultural centre, with a meeting hall and computers, to teach the people in the community everything about our culture."[5]

In Esquel there is an ambitious project to build a cultural centre along the lines of the one planned in Valle de Elicura, except that this one is well on the way towards becoming a reality. The plot of land has already been purchased, and the architectural plans have been drawn up. The project is known as *Petú Mogelein* (we are still alive). Its objectives are to build a physical space to facilitate the development and recovery of Mapuche and Tehuelche culture in Esquel, but also to create a suitable atmosphere for the *peñis* who have left their communities and now live in Esquel to participate in cultural activities. It is also hoped to gain the participation of the community at large, as well as generating ways to secure the long-term viability of the cultural centre by financing the costs through regional, national and international tourism.

Another key aspect of the resurgence of Mapuche culture is the increase in interest in learning Mapudungun. On 15 October 2000 the newspaper *Clarín* announced that Provincial School no. 319 in Aucapán Abajo, near Junín de los Andes, had been allocated a teacher of Mapudungun, following the demand by the Mapuche community in the area to have their constitutional right to bilingual education respected. By March 2001 no less than 39 teachers of the Mapuche language had been appointed by the Neuquén province as part of their Bilingual Education Programme, to work at the schools on the Mapuche "reservations" in the province.

There are also initiatives to promote the teaching of Mapudungun privately. For example, the Mapuche Education Team is running classes in the Mapuche language in Neuquén and Buenos Aires, with courses going by the name of *Mapuncezugulekayayiñ* ("We will continue speaking the language of the land").

Chile is noticeably behind Argentina in this respect, with plenty of talk - such as an international seminar-workshop on "The Teaching of the Indigenous Languages in School" held in Santiago in November/December 2001 - but little concrete action by the state. Mapudungun is still regarded for the most part by the educational establishment as a sociolect (the 'dialect' of a social group), and so far there are only a couple of pilot bilingual elementary schools in Temuco.

Mapudungun is now also alive and well on the Internet, with a section devoted to it on the Italian Logos online dictionary project[6], enabling visitors to translate words between Mapudungun and a host of other languages; this is thanks to the endeavours of Chilean living in Italy, Rodrigo Vergara, whose ambition is "to incorporate all the languages and all the dialects" of the world.

Another ambitious intention in the *Puel Mapu* is to prepare young urban Mapuches for a return to the land. As there are no Mapuche *lofs* in the Province of Buenos Aires, the urban Mapuches from the province who are interested in learning about their traditional wisdom, religiosity and social structures have had to recreate the *lof* on a short-term basis, with a view to an eventual future return to the land.

For this reason, as guests of the Puel community of Neuquén, in October 2001 members of urban Mapuche organisations formed a *campamento* - a short-term community - in which they chose their own *lonko*, *werken* and *weipife*. The year before a similar experiment took place in the Ñorkin-co community.

Anahí Meli of *Kumelen Newen Mapu* of Bahía Blanca told me about the experience:

"The event was very good for all of us who participated. We were joined by people from the province of Buenos Aires generally, (Olavarría, Carmen de Patagones, Capital Federal and other organisations from here, Bahía Blanca). The meeting had a lot to do with recovering lost identity, because it concentrated on Mapuche philosophy, trying to clean it up from all those western ideas and concepts that have been imposed on us throughout our history, such as the idea of a *futa chau*, a single, all-powerful creator god who governs people's destinies. We saw the importance that it had above all in this province, because, being the first Mapuche region over which the *winkas* advanced, we lost many *konas* and there are now no *lofs* functioning as such, nor do we have original authorities to guide us with their *kimun* (knowledge), and there is a great deal of confusion. This is a first step, but it has helped us clarify many things."[7]

Prompted and galvanised by the experience, Daniel Navarrete of *Kumelen Newen Mapu* has begun to construct and play traditional Mapuche instruments, *kultrun* and *trutruka*, to accompany the group as they re-learn their Mapuche songs and dances, such as the *choikepurún*.

Music, community, ritual, spiritual and physical well-being, all are interrelated. Awareness of this is essential to the ethos of the Mapuche hospital in Makewe, near Temuco.

Makewe: medicine the Mapuche way

The Makewe-Pelale Rural Hospital came about in 1895 as a health dispensary, but by 1925 it had been transformed by missionaries into a hospital to meet the increasing health care needs of the communities around Padre las Casas and Freire, but also Temuco, Nueva Imperial and Puerto Saavedra.

In 1962 it began to receive subsidies from the Ministry of Health, but over time, as the missionaries pulled out from working there, it suffered increasing financial problems, which came to a head in 1993. In 1999 it came under the control of the "Makewe-Pelale Indigenous Health Association", resulting from the support of 92 Mapuche communities.

The Association has designed its own "Intercultural Health Care Model", which it describes as follows:

> "The goal that the Association has set itself is to participate in the improvement of the quality of life of the population in the area, through the implementation of an intercultural health model. This means strengthening local resources, considering the different conceptions of health/illness and strengthening an approach that is complementary with biomedical medicine. This intercultural health model falls within a general project of ethnic development, tending towards the recovery of sociocultural control by the Mapuche people."[8]

In practical terms, this means a more holistic approach to medicine than is common in hospital structures in the "developed" world. As hospital director Carlos Zuñiga explains:

> "For the Mapuche, a disease is not just something that strikes an isolated individual, but occurs within the context of the family, the community and the environment. A patient who visits the Makewe hospital is asked a series of questions about family, neighbours, the year's harvest, and what the patient believes about why he or she is sick. A patient can choose to be seen by one of the two doctors on staff, or be treated by one of the eleven *machis*, who work out of their homes in the neighbouring area. In western medicine, a doctor will give the patient something to treat the pain. In Mapuche medicine, a *machi* treats the disease as an entity, and establishes a dialogue with it to find out what the original transgression was and re-establish a balance."[9]

The healing process would involve the gathering and administering of traditional Mapuche curative plants, *lawen*, and often the conducting of a healing ceremony, the *machitun*, in which a ritual battle is fought against the disease.

The hospital is still thriving, despite attempts to destabilise it, such as anonymous letters of accusation of malpractice published in the newspaper *Austral* in June 2002, which were immediately repudiated by Makewe's supporters in the medical profession from as far afield as Mexico and Australia. For indigenous struggles, such as the defence of Makewe hospital, the Internet is indeed a blessing, as it enables worldwide campaigns to be mobilised at incredibly short notice.

Talking across boundaries: Mapuches and the Internet

At the World Social Forum in Porto Alegre, international solidarity for the Mapuche cause took a surprising direction, as police brutality was "laid bare." According to the report in UK Indymedia:

> "WSF Ends With Brutal Police Repression February 1, 2003 Police did what police do best when they violently attacked protesters and bystanders on the last day of the World Social Forum. It started when a Mapuche woman who was attending the WSF and staying at the international youth camp was arrested with charges of "obscene acts" for bathing nude in a river. Activists saw this and organised over 400 people to protest by non-violently taking their clothes off in solidarity. When the nude protest left the youth camp to march downtown, the police attacked. After injuring and arresting some of the nude protesters, the police lashed out at journalists and bystanders. An unknown number of people were hospitalised or arrested as a result of the police assault."[10]

The photographs of the brutality against naked protesters were quickly posted on the web by the many photographers at the event. Thanks to e-mail and the Internet, there is a real hope that the Mapuche will never again be as isolated as they were when they were decimated by the armies and dictators of Argentina and Chile.

When in January 2000 the Prane community in Chubut challenged the right of the Argentine army to conduct military exercises on their land, the camera of Andrés Kudacki was there to photograph this very unequal contest between horses and tanks. The camera is not neutral; by revealing realities, it takes sides. The digital camera and the laptop mean that photos such as this can be on the other side of the world before any government can intervene. This is an age in which alternative visions, alternative representations, can flourish. "A world where there is room for many worlds", to quote the Zapatistas.[11]

The Internet has meant that NGOs such as "Equipo Nizkor"[12], the Spanish human rights organisation, have been able to monitor events in the far-flung areas of Chile and expose them to the international gaze.

It has meant that the "Fundación desde America"[13], which presents itself as "a bridge between indigenous cultures in America and new paradigms in the West", is able to consolidate the bridge's structure and increase its span. The Foundation's director, Carlos Martínez Sarasola, is not immune to the potential of the Internet, citing the Zapatistas as an example:

> "Globalisation is producing effects that were not wanted by its main instigators, since people are taking advantage of this phenomenon to contact each other in a way that was not possible before. This is also taking place among the aboriginal groups, albeit in a subtle way. At the moment, many of the websites created by indigenous groups in Chile, Brazil, Mexico and the United States are amazing, because of the high quality of the contents and the communication potential they generate. In fact, the Zapatista uprising in Chiapas in May 1994 survived thanks to the help computers offered in allowing it to transmit the characteristics of this rebellion quickly to the world."[14]

The Internet has enabled the Mapuches in Chile and the Cree People in Canada to meet, to exchange and transfer knowledge. As a consequence, they have identified similar traditions and similar needs:

> "Our brothers of Canada have spoken of things that they have in common with us, the Mapuche. They have spoken of the creator, the family, our ancestors, women, men, children, of the mother, the earth, fire, the living beings - of water as an element that accompanies man whether it be clean or, as it is today, contaminated."[15]

These are the words of José Rain, *lonko* of Chol-Chol, speaking at the International Development Research Centre symposium in Ottawa, November 1992, on "First Nations Adopt Southern Technologies for Health." The Cree have passed their testing system for monitoring the safety of drinking water systems on to the Mapuche.

The bond between the two peoples goes beyond nationality. According to Cree writer and activist Doug Cuthand:

> "In our languages there are no words to define the nationality of a group of people. The name of a tribe or nation is simply translated as "the people." When I was in South America I visited a Mapuche community in Chile. My host introduced me as "a Mapuche from Canada." They had no words for other tribes and considered everyone a part of them."[16]

Another activity that Cree and Mapuche have in common is the ball game. The Cree play and played lacrosse, the Mapuche *palín*. The European colonisers were suspicious of these games, as they believed them to serve as training for war.

Palín: war minus the shooting[17]

Played by Mapuche, Tehuelche, Rankulche, Pewenche, as well as by the peoples of the Chaco in North Argentina (Wichí, Toba), *palín* or *paílin*, also known as *chueca*, might well have been considered Argentina's national sport.

A game with a stick and ball, similar to hockey, as indeed are many other traditional sports played in Mesoamerica, it also arose as a means of resolving disputes without conflict; it is played by two teams of 15 players, without shoes. Along with Mapudungun and the *nguillatun*, it could be considered one of the pillars of Mapuche culture, and could lay title to being the most important aboriginal game in South America, in view of its cultural content and geographical extent.

In contrast with football, with its local and national rivalries, *palín* is a community game whose objective is to strengthen the friendship between *lofs*. The whole *lof* participates in it, recreating the sense of community as regards its religiosity, values, historical origin, social organisation, which are expressed in the different parts of the celebration.

The *lonkos* of the communities agree on the rules and characteristics of the game. Rogatory ceremonies and dances are held around the *rewe*, to give thanks for the celebration and ask for the *palín* to be successful. The host community solemnly receive their guests, according to ancient tradition. The *palín* is played for the agreed period of time, with team numbers and *raya* (goals) as agreed. The *palife* (players) try to hit the ball into the opposing *raya*. If the defenders manage to knock it off, then the play begins again in the centre of the *paliwe* (pitch). The end of the game is followed by a feast.

Palín matches are another tangible sign of a resurgence of Mapuche culture among the young; they have been played between Mapuche and *winka* students on the sports fields of the Universidad de la Frontera in Temuco and the Universidad Nacional del Comahue in Neuquén; a complete tournament took place in Loncoche between 24 teams in October 2002. A new rival for the World Cup? The sport that was originally devised as a form of conflict resolution is perhaps needed now more than ever.

Zanón under workers' control: the unthinkable in action

The political upheaval following the *Cacerolazo* of December 2001 in Argentina has also reaped fruits of positive change. The neighbourhood assemblies made people believe - at least for a while - that an alternative form of conducting politics was possible.

Another form of social interaction born out of financial necessity is *trueque*, local systems of exchange of goods without money, which flourish when hard cash is at a premium. In exchange for other goods, a service or a commitment, food can be put on the table. Mapuches had long practised this activity before it became fashionable due to the economic crisis; they refer to it in Mapudungun as *trafkin*, the mutual exchange of gifts. The needs of the present cause the re-emergence of the practices of the past.

Perhaps the most interesting new paradigm to emerge from the crisis has been the unique collaboration between the Mapuche communities of the province of Neuquén and Zanón, the ceramics factory under workers' control in Neuquén. When the Italian owner of Zanón fled the country in October 2001, leaving huge debts in his wake, the factory workers decided that, rather than give up their jobs, they would attempt to run the factory themselves.

Despite the staunch resistance of the judicial authorities and creditors, suppliers and clients, many of whom were on good terms with the departed factory owner, they succeeded, and have now celebrated the fourth anniversary as a factory under workers' control.

The Mapuches' role in this is that they have now become the preferential suppliers of the factory, which has now even created a line of tiles with motifs from traditional Mapuche textiles.

On 11 January 2003 Hernán Scandizzo and I interviewed the general secretary of the factory workers' union, the SOECN, Raúl Godoy, and we asked him how this collaboration with the Mapuches worked:

> "Several of the quarries that Zanón used were in the territory of the Mapuche People. For years Zanón exploited them; they exploited not only the quarries, but the Mapuche People as well. They took their clay without paying them a cent, nothing. We met with them many times on demonstrations, we had a quite a good relationship of solidarity with them, but starting from the occupation of the factory, all this became deeper, because we could also make agreements with them. So for the first time they began to be paid something, respecting their culture and their land, their habitat. And we think that this is an important detail. It generated relationships and links based on another history, based on another way of operating; it is no longer plundering by a company, but rather we, the workers, in unison with the communities and with the People, having another way of seeing things, and things are done differently."[18]

It will not reverse several hundred years of history, but it is a start. The first few bricks in the construction of a new egalitarian relationship between Mapuche and *winka*.

But is it possible for Mapuches to become successful on *winka* society's terms, without losing the essential aspects of their Mapuche identity, without selling out, in other words? The case of Ximenita Huilipán would seem to suggest that it is.

Ximenita and the assimilation issue: if you can't beat 'em ...

In an article for *Kolektivo Lientur*[19], Marcela Villarroel discusses Mapuches who have become assimilated, that is, those who have acquired the values and codes of behaviour of the *winka* culture. She is dismissive of those who excel in the terms of the dominant society, and traces their attitude back to the school context:

> "The school welcomes the pupil with a pedagogical device that produces and reproduces the dominant *winka* culture and transforms or sublimates minority cultures, whether they are ethnic or not. To deal with this new world, the schoolchildren considered "successful" are the ones who "assimilate" the new cultural reality, making it their own without questioning it. This option of cultural accommodation generally exacts a high emotional price, since these schoolchildren tend to reject their roots."

This judgement might be seen as unduly harsh. There are only a handful of Mapuches who have become household names in Chile, such as Ximena Huilipán the model or Marcelo Salas Melinao the footballer, fewer still in Argentina. They have achieved success along the few avenues that the hierarchical societies in which they live have allowed them, but who among us would deny them their right to such success? In any case, does success necessarily mean that they have turned their back on their roots?

In the previous chapter we looked at the risks that Mapuche women can run if they dare to wear their traditional dress in the city. Paradoxically, this is at the very time when international designers have deemed what is called the "ethnic look" to be highly fashionable and desirable. Attempting to divest itself of its image as élitist and superficial, in recent years the fashion industry has embraced ethnic dress and attempted to show it has a heart and a concern for the state of the planet. In its search for the exotic, it has been plucking indigenous girls from their "natural" environments to place them on the catwalk, alongside the usual boyish, anorexic models.

One such indigenous girl is Ximena Huilipán, who was "discovered" as a 14-year-old by Dominican designer Oscar de la Renta, who chose her to model his collections. Ximena was presented to De la Renta by Chilean designer Rubén Campos, for whom Ximena's mother worked as a seamstress.

Frenchman Jean Pierre Begon, European representative of the French model agency Élite Model, who organised the model contest in Tunis in which Ximena took part, Élite Model Look, has been glowing in his praise of her: "She is the most exotic, on account of her Mapuche origin, because she has an unusual face and very pretty green eyes. In the contest we do not look for a certain type, but beauty and personality. Ximena will do very well"[20]. Begon goes on to say: "People find unique features very important, the pure race, not mixtures, and Ximena has sophisticated Araucanian features."[21]

For such a young girl (she is now 17) in an environment where she is bound to be surrounded by the wily and the predatory - and increasingly so, as she is now moving into a movie career – Ximena has shown that she is wise beyond her years. Born in Nueva Imperial, Ximena grew up in Santiago. She says that when her grandmother died, the family were in danger of losing touch with their Mapuche traditions, but she is determined not to let that happen. In June 2003 she was photographed attending the *We Tripantu* celebrations in Peñalolén, near Santiago. By choosing so publicly and willingly to participate in a traditional Mapuche celebration, Ximena perhaps gave Mapuche religious belief more credibility among young Chileans than any number of worthy statements by militant organisations could.

In the southern hemisphere the winter solstice falls in late June, and this is when the Mapuche hold their own festival, *Wiñoy Tripantu* (*We Tripantu* in the *Gulu Mapu*), meaning the return of the year. This is a ceremony to which circularity is central, and is the ritual in which the renewal of the forces of nature and the universe is symbolised. In this ceremony, as in the *nguillatun*, the people of the *lof* renew their commitment to the rest of the *newen* of nature and take responsibility for preserving the balance between them. With *Wiñoy Tripantu* the cycle of nature, of being born, growing, reproducing and dying, closes, to then be reborn, thanks to the presence of the sun, the generator of life.

With the first light of dawn, the rogation begins, accompanied by the beat of the *kultrún*. The celebrations go on throughout the day till sunset.

As the event took place, Ximena was asked if there is still discrimination against her race; she replied "Yes, but I have not experienced it. You have to make sure you're respected and know how to answer back, because there will always be ignorant people around who are going to bother you because you're Mapuche. I feel very proud of my race and I believe we should all be."[22]

Mapuche professionals and entrepreneurs break through the glass ceiling

Although Mapuches have now reached the pinnacle of success in such areas as sport and fashion, it will perhaps not be until they occupy some of the key positions in Chilean and Argentine society that they will see themselves as having achieved true equality. When I interviewed him in 2003, José Bengoa was optimistic about the prospects of access to professional and political careers for Mapuches:

> "There are now many schoolteachers, and now there is a big wave studying at university. There are many, many university students, particularly at the University of the Frontier in Temuco; there are anthropologists, law-

yers. In government, now one of the most important ministers is a Mapuche, Francisco Huenchumilla, who is a lawyer, a Christian Democrat. There are scholarships from the government for indigenous students, over a thousand. The University of Arica is now practically an Aymara university."[23]

Francisco Huenchumilla, who was a government minister until he retired in 1991 following his failure to regain his seat in the Senate, was a member of parliament for three periods from 1989 onwards, and chaired the parliamentary commission that drafted the Indigenous Law. Huenchumilla says he was not particularly committed to the Mapuche issue until he gained a seat in Congress: "When I studied it was more important to have links with Chilean society and the struggle against the dictatorship. When I was elected a deputy I realised that I had to 'learn to be Huenchumilla'"[24]. General Secretary of the Presidency in Lagos' Government from February 2003, Huenchumilla resigned in June 2004 to present his candidacy for the post of Mayor of Temuco, and was duly elected in October 2004.

For politicians and successful professionals the story is similar to that of sports stars in the respect that their higher profile means that they have to tread a difficult path between the expectations of their fellow Mapuches and those of society at large.

For professional Mapuche women, it is even tougher to make headway in a chosen career in a Chilean society that is very *machista*, and that has passed on these values to Mapuche men. So these women have learned to be combative. One grouping of such women is *Aukiñko Zomo* (Voice of Women), an organisation of professional women in Temuco formed in 1996, working to defend and support Mapuche women in their struggles, such as the *ñañas* in their battle against the construction of the Ralco Dam. A member of *Aukiñko Zomo*, María Isabel Curihuentro, talked about their work:

"At this moment there is a lack of participation by women, so we are trying to do something about it. The political parties and the church have pushed women into the background, and this has made Mapuche men adopt customs and values that are not traditionally theirs, attitudes such as 'man is the provider, the man commands'. This organisation works so that women have parity with men in the struggle, working with other women's organisations.

There are eleven of us, teachers, IT engineers, agronomists, social workers, agricultural technicians; it is a very interdisciplinary group. Our task is to promote the role of women in Mapuche society, to strengthen the technical and organisational capacities of Mapuche women, so they can control their own destinies. We have come to Temuco from different Mapuche communities; we are mostly bilingual. There cannot be development of our culture until they let us be what we are."[25]

Another piece in the mosaic of Mapuche organisations is the Asociación Ñancucheu, of Lumaco, which is active in supporting the communities in the area, and in promoting Mapuche medicine and education. In contrast with *Aukiñko Zomo*, the Asociación Ñancucheu is almost rigorously non-professional, but no less committed for this. This is explained by Alfonso Reiman, the association's high-profile president:

> "Here we are characterised by not having professionals. For example, I personally only finished the 4th grade. In Temuco you'll find Mapuche doctors, agronomists, and so on. Here you sometimes find Mapuches with only basic Spanish; they can't express themselves well because they speak with different codes. Pedro Rain[26], for example, was a militant in the Communist party, so he learned his political discourse from this experience. Political clarity varies from community to community.
>
> When Patricio Aylwin became President, I was in prison, I have been in prison several times - there have been seven legal proceedings against me - because I have never wanted others to do my fighting for me; as the leader, I have had to take the responsibility for my actions."[27]

Reiman is also actively involved in a Mapuche commercial enterprise, the Comercializadora de Productos Silvoagropecuarios Wagvlen S.A.. The company brings together a large number of Mapuche smallholders in the areas of Lumaco and Traiguén, to grow, market and sell certain niche agricultural products. Wagvlen's brochure presents the company in these terms:

> "Wagvlen S.A. was launched in 1995 by native Mapuche producers who sought to create marketing alternatives for the native farmers of Lumaco, Traiguén and surrounding areas. Wagvlen S.A.'s 11 partners represent over 270 native families from throughout the region. Members grow grass peas (*Lathyrus sativus*), rose hip (*Rosa rubiginosa* L.) and St. John's Wort (*Hypericum perforatum*). New investment in infrastructure makes it possible for Wagvlen S.A. to custom-harvest, process, pack and ship its products to buyers."[28]

This is just one of a large number of projects by Mapuches, in Chile and Argentina, to go beyond subsistence agriculture and work together to compete in the marketplace, both domestic and international.

Yes, there are some success stories of Mapuches in entertainment and in business, but we should not allow these to cause us to lose sight of the reality of most Mapuches today, the reality of poverty, anger and alienation in the city. We looked at the issue of the urban Mapuche in chapter one, and we are returning to it now, but with a more positive slant. Young urban Mapuches are asserting their identity and finding creative channels for their anger.

The young urban Mapuche: the *Warriache*

Throughout the book we have referred to the Mapuches of the communities and the cities, often seeing how the community life is the ideal that is strived for, the "natural" condition of being Mapuche. Yet something is stirring, changing. Young urban Mapuches are rejecting this idealisation of the traditional *lof*, and affirming their own identity as urban Mapuches, *Warriache*.

Lorena Cañuqueo, aged 22, is from *Fiske Menuko*, the Mapuche name for the town of General Roca. She defines the word for us:

> "*Warriache* is something created, one of those words that are incorporated through the new processes we Mapuche are experiencing. It refers to the Mapuches who live in the cities, where we were born and have our place, where we move every day; the place we know is the city."[29]

Lorena's town is *Fiske Menuko*. She and her friends could not bear such unpalatable compounding of injustices as the name General Roca - the mass murderer of the Conquest of the Desert - standing proud on maps of Río Negro province, yet the original Mapuche name for the settlement, *Fiske Menuko*, being officially obliterated. Now the old name is beginning to be heard again, as more and more local Mapuche groups refuse to employ the name imposed upon their town, hoping that critical mass will eventually be reached and the shameful name General Roca consigned to history's overflowing dustbin.

Another manifestation of Warriache identity is "Resistencia Mapuche", the urban Mapuche organisation of Temuco. In the "Mapuche Cultural Centre", a squatted property, Pedro Cayuqueo, director of Resistencia Mapuche - and editor-in-chief of the new Mapuche magazine Azkintuwe, which was first published in October 2003, and went online in February 2004 - talked about the meaning of being an urban Mapuche. There are more than a thousand Mapuche students involved in Resistencia Mapuche. They have been evicted from their premises a number of times over the last five years, but it seems that they have been given leave to remain by Mideplan, mainly because it is a cultural centre, for music, dance, language, history and art. Cayuqueo himself has been arrested on more than one occasion, in Collipulli on 9 September 2003, and again in Temuco on 22 January 2005.

We asked him if his organisation has links with the communities:

> "We have few links with the communities. The struggle of the communities is important, but limited. The struggle is the same, but work needs to be done in the city, educating, instigating. That is why we set up the web page, "Resistencia Mapuche", to support the communities' struggle. By mixing with *winkas* we become *winkas*, through acculturation; we need to

mix more with our own people. We need to maintain links with communities, with our culture, our religion, our music, but in an urban way. For us to develop rural practices would be ridiculous. That is why phenomena such as Mapuche urban rock, "hard core", are important; all cultures are evolving, developing, transforming."

– What are your relations like with the other Mapuche organisations?
"The "Coordinadora"[30], for example, has a very campesinist, rural approach to the Mapuches[31]; they are anti-rock, anti-Internet, they are very fundamentalist, 'the Taliban of the Mapuche world'. Aucán Huilcamán and *Aukiñ Wallmapu Ngulam* also have this traditional vision of Mapuches, that of the countryside. That is why we chose a different path. They are another generation; there is a generational change taking place. We are also connected with many other struggles, such as against the multinationals, the anti-capitalist struggle. We do not think the political struggle of our people should lead to the formation of a Mapuche state, because our vision is more influenced by libertarian ideas. It is not possible for the whole of a people to think the same way, as that would be fascism. There is a place for Mapuche atheists too. We in the city do not like the view *'winkas* bad - Mapuches good'; this is too closed a view. There must be an integration that respects differences."

– How do Chileans see you?
"The Chilean authorities see Mapuches as a problem of security and economics, but most Chileans support us; they are sympathetic. Some sectors of the population are against us, but they are in the minority, the ones with the power, the entrepreneurs, the armed forces. We want certain freedoms, but also for the *winkas* who live here. We want a multicultural, multiethnic territory. The Chilean state is very long, but very centralised, with everything concentrated in Santiago, so the *winkas* here also want more power in the south. If we leave them out, they will not support us; many of them are *mestizos*. The state presents our struggle as radical, fundamentalist, terrorist, in order to create fear in the local population, the same way that Bush demonises the Muslims. So we need to build bridges.

Previously the struggle was very closed, with the exclusion of *winkas* from ceremonies. We wish to be open, to students, with our music, also to foreigners, to enable *winka* society to get to know us, our music, our art, so they will not believe the official discourse. When the police wanted to throw us out, thousands of students from the "Universidad de la Frontera" came to march on our behalf; like in Chiapas, where their strength comes from popular support.

We are trying to generate our own media - radio, TV, Internet - to get our message across. Such as filming videos, which are then distributed.

There are many divisions between the Mapuche organisations, all criticising each other. We want an inclusive discourse. We are optimistic, because the new generations have our mentality, with fewer divisions."

The influence of music and libertarian politics on urban Mapuches emerges clearly from the interview with Pedro Cayuqueo, as does the generation gap between young Mapuches and the members of the established Mapuche organisations. The rebellion of the punk movement from the late seventies onwards, and also heavy metal, have struck a chord with young Mapuches. 17-year-old Fakundo Wala from Bariloche explains:

"Of course we are rebels against the system that our parents were forced to enter, where they were forced to be workers, to leave the countryside when they were kids. So we're not going to be happy and contented, and we identify with the attitude of punk. In the city, what else is there to do?"[32]

Oskar Moreno, aged 22, also from Bariloche, runs a radio programme, "*Grito Suburbano*" (Suburban Shout), on a community radio in Bariloche, *Gente de Radio*:

"Many people don't see us as an expression of the Mapuche People, but these days we are another form of expression of our people. These are processes that are under way, realities, however much they deny them. We are here, we are the product of living in the city and not wanting the way of life the city offers. Many Mapuches reject us, discriminate against us or overlook us because we think this way, because we dress this way. Because we reflect what we think in our clothes, in what we say, constantly questioning."[33]

A *Warriache* group in *Fiske Menuko* have set up their own fanzine, "Mapurbe", to address the concerns of young urban Mapuches. Lorena Cañuqueo, one of those involved in the publication, explains its purpose:

"We use it as a way of reaching the young Mapuches who live in the different neighbourhoods, in *Furilofche* (Bariloche), *Fiske Menuko*, any city. And I think it is a way of communicating the possibility that, even if you are living in the Villa Obrera neighbourhood of *Fiske Menuko*, today, you are Mapuche, you have an identity, an immediate origin, here in this place. You have your roots here, and that entails a lot of things. You're living in the city and you're here because there's a process implemented by the State, a system that forced the expulsion and extermination of all the Original Peoples."[34]

Of all the recent forms of expression of Mapuche life in the city, the voices of the Warriache poets have been the most powerful and effective.

Mapuche poets: the pen is mightier

Rolf Foerster, one of the most renowned experts on Mapuche culture, sees the radical poets as playing a central role in reinforcing a positive sense of Mapuche identity today. He is quoted in the book by Alejandro Saavedra Peláez, "Los Mapuche en la sociedad chilena actual"[35]:

> "The importance of this poetry also lies in the fact that it creates a symbolism for the Mapuche that is more suited to the reality of thousands of Mapuches who live in the city; the urban Mapuche experience finds in this poetry a language that not only can conjugate their aspirations but can also rid them of their malaise and resentment."

The young urban Mapuches have not only been influenced by anarcho-punk, but also by the new generation of Mapuche poets that have emerged in recent years, writing in Mapudungun, but also developing their own vernacular in Spanish. A key influence is David Añiñir, a poet and construction worker from Cerro Navia, Santiago; it is his poem "Mapurbe" that has provided the title for the fanzine and a sense of identity for the *Warriache*. The poem traces a line between the ecological destruction of the Ralco Dam and the disease of the city. This is an extract:

Mapurbe

Y me kedo parado akí
entre pewenes elektrokutados
infektándome del káncer
ke erosiona la tierra.

Y me kedo parado akí,
mirando a uno y ningún lado
ahogando kon verdades
a los títeres de la repre-salia.
La urbe gime;
ácidos llantos
kaen de las negras nubes
y kuajan en el pensamiento.

Mapurbe

And I stand here motionless
among elektrokuted pewens
infekting me with kancer
that erodes the land.

And I stand here motionless
looking somewhere and nowhere
drowning with truths
the puppets of the dam reprisal.
The metropolis moans;
acid tears
fall from the blak klouds
and kongeal into thought.

Among the most combative Mapuche poets are Lionel Lienlaf and Elicura Chihuailaf. In this poem extract below, Lionel Lienlaf invokes the spirit of Lautaro, thus expressing the continuity between the great *toki* and those fighting for the Mapuche cause today:

Lefxaru ñi pvji	**The Spirit of Lautaro**
Miawy kacil xayen	He goes by the spring
Pvtokopelu bifko	drinking fresh water
Wirarvmelekey mawidapvle	and shouts in the mountains
Muxvmpelu ñi pu kona.	calling his warriors.
Lefxaru ñi pvji	The spirit of Lautaro
Miawy ñipiukepvle	walks close to my heart
Adkintuyawi	watching
Ajkvtuyawi	listening
Mvxvmkenew kom liwen.[36]	calling me every morning.

Elicura Chihuailaf too is deeply attached to Mapuche spirituality, the ecological message of which makes him very relevant today. Beatriz Pichi Malen says he is her favourite Mapuche poet; in her words, he "writes of blue, the colour of mystery and of revelation of life. He uses it in very concrete verses. The biodiversity of the Mother Earth is very present in his thought and this is very *Mapu*, very contemporary." In this extract, which again invokes the ancients, in their guise as inhabitants of the world above, the rhythm of the verses reflect the pace and excitement of the galloping horses of the *troya*: during the *nguillatún*

Nvtramkaleyiñ tain pu wenu mapu che	**Talking with the people from above**
Wiraf, wirafgen, pewmantulen amun	Galloping, galloping, dreaming I go
Wenu Mapu rupu mew	along the paths of the sky
Wallke pule chalipaenew ti pu wagulen.[37]	From all sides the stars come to greet me.

Among the other leading Mapuche poets in Chile are María Teresa Panchillo Neculhual, Bernardo Colipán, Jaime Luis Huenún, Graciela Huinao, Ricardo Loncón and César Pailahueque. A web portal has recently been opened, where samples of their verse are available online, in Mapudungun and Spanish (www.ulmapu.cl). In Argentina, where Mapuche poets have not yet joined the frontline, perhaps the best known is Liliana Ancalao, a secondary school teacher from Comodoro Rivadavia, and a member of the Ñankulawen Mapuche-Tehuelche community, whose collection "Tejido con Lana Cruda" was published in 2001.[38]

Mapuche youth in Bariloche. Photo: Pablo Lasansky

The Mapuche are famous for their 350 years of resistance against the Spanish and then the Chilean and Argentinian states. Yet their *konas* no longer do battle, at least not in the traditional sense. They are activists, not warriors, and their struggle now is for hearts and minds. They are still proud and not cowed, and the last decade has seen a new generation of *konas* emerge, eager to claim their rights and denounce the injustices committed against them and their beloved *Mapu*.

In the words of David Añanir:

"Somos mapuche de hormigón.
Debajo del asfalto duerme nuestra madre,
Explotada por un cabrón"[39]

("We are Mapuches of concrete.
Below the asphalt sleeps our mother,
Exploited by a *cabrón*")

Notes

1 Fakundo Wala, aged 16, from the interview on 4/5/03.
2 Extensive information on Mapuche culture and art is available on the Rehue Foundation website (http://www.xs4all.nl/~rehue/cult.html).
3 Interviewed 17th May 2003.

4   "Suena el rock mapuche" by Yerko Bocic, Punto Final, September 1999.
5   Interviewed Valle de Elicura, 19/12/01.
6   www.logosdictionary.com.
7   Interviewed 1/11/2001.
8   Quoted from the Association's "Course in Mapuche Health and Thought" (available on the Rehue Foundation website).
9   Quoted from "Keeping the Balance", an article by Lisa Garrigues in "Yes" magazine, Spring 2003.
10 www.indymedia.org.uk/en/2003/01/107039.html.
11 I am using Dinah Livingstone's translation of "Un mundo donde quepan muchos mundos" ("Zapatista Stories", by Subcomandante Marcos, translated by Dinah Livingstone, pp. 7-8. Published by Katabasis, 2001).
12 www.derechos.org/nizkor/.
13 www.desdeamerica.org.ar.
14 Sarasola interviewed by Nicolás Hellers on "La cuestión indígena" in Espéculo, issue 16.
15 www.idrc.ca/books/reports/V211/path.html.
16 Assembly of Manitoba Chiefs news brief, "What's in a name, everything", 22/7/2002. (available on www.manitobachiefs.com).
17 This is the famous quote from George Orwell, referring to sport.
18 Information (in Spanish) on Zanón can be obtained from the factory workers' own website: http://www.obrerosdezanon.org/.
19 "Gulumapu: ¿Educación para "matarle el indio" al mapuche?" 10 July 2003, on argentina.indymedia.org.
20 The quotes on Ximena Huilipán come from a number of articles gathered together on the following webpage: www.mapuche.nl/publ/interv_ximena.htm.
21 Idem.
22 Idem.
23 Interviewed 5/5/03.
24 Interview with Huenchumilla in "Estado de derecho" de burla del mapuche", by Hernán Soto, available on www.mapuexpress.net.
25 Interview recorded in Temuco, 9/12/02.
26 A leading member of the association, a Mapuche activist for many years.
27 The interview with Alfonso Reiman was recorded in Lumaco on 1/2/02.
28 Wagvlen S.A.'s products are promoted by the ProChile Export Promotion Bureau (www.prochile.cl).
29 Interviewed 1/6/03.
30 Coordinadora de comunidades Mapuche en Conflicto Arauko-Malleko.
31 The Coordinadora in fact justify this on the following grounds: "The fact that the Coordinadora focuses its work in the communities is motivated by two reasons. The first is that they consider the communities to be the only sector of the Mapuche people that could provide the fight with the cultural, philosophical, political and religious Mapuche elements that the process would need to develop and to grow. And the second is that they consider that it is the sector from where it is most effective in hitting at the system of dominance, represented economically by the transnational forestry companies." (http://webs.demasiado.com/arauko_malleko/comunidades.htm).
32 Fakundo Wala is an urban Mapuche from Bariloche. The quote comes from an interview with Hernán Scandizzo on 4/5/03.
33 Also interviewed on 4/5/03.
34 Interviewed 1/6/03.
35 LOM, Santiago, 2002.
36 Published in Werken Kuruf, issue 1.
37 Published in Zyzzyva online magazine, Fall 1998 #53 Vol. XIV, No. 2, "The Blue that sustains the song" by John Oliver Simon (http://www.zyzzyva.org/f98-jos.htm).
38 Some of Liliana's poems from this collection are available online at http://www.poeticas.com.ar/Antologias/Antologia_de_Chubut/frame.html.
39 From the poem "Mapurbe, venganza a raíz", cited in Azkintuwe, 11/11/2005.

CONCLUSION

EL LENGUARAZ

The title of this book is "Language of the Land." The importance of the latter noun to the Mapuche is without dispute: their name means People of the Land and land is central to their identity, to their view of themselves, as we have seen throughout the book.

Yet the first noun of the book's title is perhaps equally important, as it is through their language that a people such as the Mapuche express their identity, and their very continuity as a people, through their stories, songs and rituals. It is through language that we give names to ourselves and to each other: for themselves they are *Mapuche*, but many *winkas* refer to them as Araucanians (from the Quechua term for barbarian, *auca*, that the Incas used to refer to them), as Indians, savages, and using far worse insults. *Winka* is the Mapuche word for non-Mapuche, with all its connotations of robber and invader, and may well have derived from *we inca* (new Inca) in *Mapudungun*. Meanings of words change, sometimes for the worse, sometimes for the better. When I first came to meet members of Mapuche organisations, I was a *winka* or a *gringo*. Now, as a result of years of friendship and shared experience, I feel honoured that I am considered by some Mapuches at least to be a *peñi*, a brother.

Through this book I hope to have used my function as the writer of the first work in English to provide an overview of the Mapuche people in order to change the meaning of another word, *lenguaraz*. This Spanish word, meaning talkative or foul-mouthed, is also used to refer to the profession of translator or interpreter. When indigenous people were employed in manual labour on plantations and farms (as indeed they still are), the *lenguaraz* was a speaker of both the indigenous language (usually his own) and Spanish, who transmitted the orders from the bosses to the workers, in what was very much a one-way process.

In his concluding remarks at the "Patagonia: Myths and Realities" Conference held in Manchester in September 2005, Cristian Aliaga, writer and poet, of the Universidad Nacional de la Patagonia, pointed out that *lenguaraces* had always been at the service of those arriving in Patagonia to the detriment of the region's original inhabitants; he said it was necessary to change the *lenguaraz*'s role to reverse the process of understanding.

Through this book I hope to have succeeded in turning the meaning, the process and the power dynamics of the *lenguaraz*'s role around, by presenting the Mapuche in their own terms, by translating the views and aspirations of Mapuches into English, providing their mouthpiece in a language in which they have not been able to express themselves in the past.

The language of the land is not dead, it exists, and it is growing and developing.

EPILOGUE

EPILOGUE

In the period of time between a manuscript being submitted to a publisher and the book eventually being published, things will inevitably happen. If the book concerned is about the Mapuche and their relations with the Chilean and Argentine states, then it is all the more likely that things will happen, as the situation in question is a highly dynamic, even volatile one, as we have seen. So imagine my frustration to find that while my manuscript on the Mapuche was with the publisher, and the months slowly ticked by, history was moving on relentless and regardless. This is not the place for me to go into why it has taken two long years for the manuscript concerned to go to print, except to express my eternal gratitude to IWGIA for taking up the mantle concerned so enthusiastically and efficiently, for finally bringing this book into the world.

History never stands still, and today's news is tomorrow's history. Perhaps the events of the last two years will not assume an enormous significance when set against the context of the over 460 years that have elapsed since the Mapuche's first contact with Europeans in the person of Pedro de Valdivia. This is not for us to say, certainly not so soon, as not everything that appears in today's newspapers will prove to have any lasting importance tomorrow. This is a roundabout way of saying that it is necessary to conclude this book by offering an overview of the events of last two years of relations between the Mapuche and the Chilean and Argentine states, to identify tendencies, to see how they augur.

When Michelle Bachelet became the first female President in Chile's history, many Mapuches felt they had good reason to expect an improvement in their relations with the Chilean state. After all, before becoming President in March 2006 Ms Bachelet had expressed her commitment, and that of her coalition, to promoting the recognition of the rights of the country's indigenous peoples in the legal system and to ratifying international treaties. Yet fine words butter no parsnips, and a year later little has changed: the persecution of Mapuche leaders through the judicial system continues, and Mapuche leaders' calls for Ms Bachelet to act on a whole series of issues have gone conspicuously unheeded. When the Chilean Premier was in Europe for a summit, Nobel Prizewinner José Saramago humbly suggested that she might "take a look at the Mapuche." As I write, although there are reports that Ms Bachelet is "working to have Congress ratify a convention recognising the collective rights of indigenous peoples", Convention 169 has still not been ratified.

Against the background of this inaction within the Chilean *Concertación* government, the situation of Mapuche political prisoners has shown anything but signs of improvement. Waikilaf Cadin Calfunao, son of *Lonko* Juana Calfunao (see chapter 12), has been incarcerated without trial in Santiago's High Security Prison since July 2006 and, along with other Mapuche political prisoners, he has been on hunger strike intermittently since October to draw attention to their plight; in Waikilaf's words: "It is not by filling prisons with Mapuches that they will break my people, quite the opposite."

In a separate development, in December 2005 Pascual Pichún, the son of the *lonko* of the same name (see chapter 10), after succeeding in crossing the Chilean/Argentine border in secret, formally requested political asylum in Argentina. His request is still awaiting a decision.

A gloomy panorama, then? No, not entirely. In chapter 9 we referred to the offer made by Benetton in July 2005 to donate 11,000 hectares of land to the Provincial Government of Chubut to be used by the communities in the province claiming entitlement to other, more fertile land. A year later came the Government's decision to reject the donation, "due to the meagre productive receptiveness of the land concerned and the disproportionate investment that would be necessary to render it useful." Ostensibly this would seem to be a rare example of a government standing up to big business. The Curiñanco family, who have been engaged in a long-standing battle with Benetton over entitlement to land in Santa Rosa, are wary of this rejection, suspecting there may be some hidden deal behind it. In the game of mirrors that is politics, only time will tell.

In June 2006 came the news that, following the successful experience of joint management of Parque Lanín between the National Parks Administration and seven of the Mapuche communities in the Lanín area (referred to in chapter 11), the experiment will be extended to nine other Argentine national parks. Here too it remains to be seen whether this will be a success, but it is undoubtedly promising.

In chapter 4 I mentioned a visit I made to the museum in Carmen de Patagones, and a conversation with the curator, who told me how police had been asked to "recover" the reproductions of weapons that had been removed from the museum by local Mapuche-Tehuelche organisations. In April 2007 I returned to the same town, and to the same museum, to find the latter completely transformed. What had previously been a rather shoddy assembly presenting the Tehuelche in the early 19th century as solely engaged in war and hunting activities, soon to be overwhelmed by a supposedly superior culture, has now been revamped, with a series of new displays attempting to explain the complexity of the commercial exchanges that took place in that period in the Pampa and Northern Patagonia between indigenous peoples and settlers, two cultures becoming mutually dependent. I asked our guide about this, and he told me that he and the other staff members had been encouraged by their management to develop this first section of the museum, as there had been some negative comments received about it from visitors. It would seem that tourists visiting the museum are no longer content with swallowing that old chestnut about civilisation defeating barbarism. Tourism can be a force for positive change.

So the story of the Mapuche has been told. How can I conclude? It is my hope that in writing a book that definitely needed writing I have contributed in some way to increasing the knowledge among English speakers of the way of life and history of the Mapuche people. Now in a sense it is time to pass on the baton, because, in the words of Sven Lindqvist in his seminal book "Exterminate all the Brutes": "You already know enough. So do I. It is not knowledge we lack. What is missing is the courage to understand what we know and to draw conclusions."

GLOSSARY

GLOSSARY OF MAPUDUNGUN

Mapudungun	English
Ad mapu	Set of Mapuche traditions
Ad mongen	Relations between natural elements
Antu	Sun
Aukiñ Wallmapu Ngulam	Council of All the Lands
Aukiñko Zomo	Voice of Women
Awun	The ritual space during the *nguillatún*, marked by fast horse-riding in circuits
Butalmapu	Region of the *Mapu*
Catuto	Wheat-cake
Challa	Pot
Chau	Father
Chavalongo	Typhus
Chaway	Girl's silver earrings, received during the ceremony of *katan pilún*.
Chaziche	People of salt
Che	People
Chenke	Mapuche tomb or cemetery
Chiliweke	Guanaco
Chiñura	Mixed-race woman
Choikepurún	The dance of the rhea. The *choike* (rhea americana), which is widespread in the Pampa and Patagonia, was hunted by the Tehuelche and the Mapuche east of the Andes. During the *nguillatún* the *choike purún* is performed, in which the feather-wearing participants dance in circular movements, nodding their

	heads and flapping their ponchos, simulating the movements of the ostrich-like bird.
Curru	Black
Duwekafe	Weaver, well-versed in the knowledge of the shapes and patterns symbolising the Mapuche cosmovision.
Eltún	Burial place, cemetery
Eluwún	The Mapuche burial ceremony
Epew	Educational, fictional narratives. Like the Greek and Latin fables, they often have animals as protagonists, typically the fox and the puma, with the former representing cunning and the latter strength. Alternatively, they may be of a mythical nature, with supernatural beings, such as the serpent *tren tren*.
Futa chau	The name given in *Mapudungun* to the Christian God
Futa Malón	Great Uprising (1881)
Futa Trawún	Grand Meeting
Geyu	Apple
Gulu Mapu	The western land of the Mapuche, currently controlled by the Chilean state
Itrófilmogen	Biodiversity, all the elements of the ecosystem
Kamarikún	Also known was *kamaruko*, this is the name given in the *Puel Mapu* to the *nguillatún*.
Kantún	Song
Katan pilún	Ceremony of perforation of the girl's ears
Ketru metawe	Pitcher in the shape of a duck, representing motherhood
Kimún	Knowledge
Kiltro	Dog
Kiñe rewe mapu	The alliance of 9 *lofs* in times of war.
Kinwa	Quinoa
Kitra	Pipe
Kona	Traditionally a Mapuche warrior; now also used to refer to political activists.
Killíñ	Livestock, currency
Kultrun	Mapuche ceremonial drum, which plays an important part, along with the *trutruka*, in ceremonies such as *Nguillatún*.

	For the Mapuche the *kultrun* is not just an instrument, its beat is the heartbeat of the Earth and is the basis of their ceremonies; it is such an important element for Mapuche *kimun* (knowledge) that it appears on the flag that has been adopted by the Mapuche people. The drawings on the top are symbols representing the Mapuche universe: a cross divides the drum into four quadrants, the vertical line represents the cosmos and the horizontal the earth. The intersection between the two is the centre of the earth, the sacred space from which the *machi* comes into contact with gods and ancestors, assisted by the sound of the *kultrun*. In preparing the instrument, the *machi* "places her song" inside it by singing into it before tensing the skin, leaving part of her soul inside. She also introduces small sacred objects (stones, feathers, medicinal herbs), which when shaken sound like a rattle. The wood of the cinnamon or the laurel, trees sacred to the Mapuche, are traditionally used to make the sound box of the *kultrun*. The skin may come from the colt, guanaco or sheep. In each of the sectors different *newen* are represented. In one of them *Antu*, the Sun, appears; in another, *Kuyen*, the Moon, and in the others, *pu wagelen*, the stars.
Kupalme	The family and ancestry of each member of the *lof*.
Kurá	Stone
Kuyen	Moon
Lafkenche	People of the shore
Lakutún	Ceremony marking the reaching of maturity for Mapuche boy
Lamguen	Mapuche sister/brother (used by female)
Lawen	Medicinal plant used by the *machi*
Lelfunche	Lowlanders
Lemu	Forest
Leufu	River

Leufún	In the *Puel Mapu*, the name of a flat terrain where the *kamarikún* is held
Liwen	Dawn
Lof	The traditional Mapuche community. The *lof* consists of a set of families, an extended family structure, settled in a well-defined territorial space.
Lonko	Community leader, literally "head". The *lonko* is often mistakenly referred to using the word "cacique", which the Spanish borrowed from Arawak and adopted to represent indigenous leaders. As well as representing the *lof*, the *lonko* must also administer justice.

The position of the *lonko* is not hereditary, but is decided by the *lof*; the *lonko* must prove his merits and ability to manoeuvre to deal with the circumstances affecting the life of the community and its relations with the outside world. |
| Machi | Mapuche spiritual leader. The depository of great knowledge, is a very influential figure in the Mapuche community, and is charged with offering guidance to her people and using *lawen* (medicinal plants) and curative techniques against illness and the forces of evil, the malicious power of *Wekufe*. *Machis* possess esoteric knowledge of the sacred codes and standards that safeguard the well-being of the community; they officiate during important ceremonies.

More than 80% of *machis* are women. Their political role has increased since the beginning of the 20th century, when the impact of the "reducciones" system (discussed in Chapter 6) diminished the power of the *lonkos*. |
Machitún	Healing ceremony conducted by *machi*
Mamulche	Carved funereal statue; people of the wood
Mari mari	Mapuche greeting, literally meaning "ten ten". It is the verbal expression of ten fingers touching ten fingers ("gimme five" times two).
Mapudungun	The Mapuche language

Mapugetuy	The transmutation of the person from the state of *che* to the new state of *mapu*, becoming earth, when they die.
Marici Weu!	We will win ten times over! Mapuche battle cry.
Mawida	Mountain
Meli Witram Mapu	Four corners of the land
Metawe	Type of pitcher, often anthropomorphic or zoomorphic.
Minche mapu	Underground level of Mapuche cosmos. The lower level is where the supernatural beings that govern the depths of the earth live and seek to free themselves through volcanoes.
Meli	Four. The number four is also sacred, representing equilibrium and harmony. This knowledge is symbolised in the sacred instrument, the *kultrun,* the skin of which is divided into four parts, and which also represents the circular movement of the universe and life. The designs on the four quadrants of the *kultrun* are painted on during the *Wiñoy Tripantu* ceremony.
Muday	A "chicha" made from fermented *pewen* nuts
Multrun	Wheat-cake
Nagche	Lowlanders
Nag mapu	The earthly platform of the Mapuche cosmos, where the *che* resides. Here both the forces of good and evil manifest themselves, affecting human conduct.
Newen	Force of nature. All the parts of nature have their own *newen*, or force. When a *newen* ceases to exist, nature becomes imbalanced and events occur that have negative repercussions upon us all. The purpose of ritual is to seek to mediate between the supernatural and the human, to reconcile complementary opposites, regulate their mutual relations and thus maintain and re-establish the equilibrium. All this is not so alien to us in Britain, as we have our own traditions of "pagan" propitiatory and rogatory rites, such as wassailing, bonfires at Halloween and corn dollies at the end of the harvest. Indeed, today's ecologists could well find some resonance between the Mapuche cosmovision and their own

	theoretical frameworks; for example, scientist James Lovelock's concept of the Earth as a self-regulating whole constantly seeking equilibrium seems to have correspondences with the Mapuche idea of *newen* and the *itrófilmogen*. Likewise, deep ecologists' adoption of Jung's "anima mundi" to explain the bond between human psychology and the changing Earth.
Ngenechen	The god of life and creation. Whether *Ngenechen* is conceived as the same or different from the Christian God, the dominant position of *Ngenechen* in the pantheon of gods may be the result of a Christian influence, yet this supremacy, in the Christian sense of the divinity, is incompatible with most Mapuche beliefs. *Ngenechen* is not considered omniscient or omnipotent; he is denominated "god of the Mapuches", "governor of the Mapuches". Often during ceremonial recitation, prefixes such as *chau* (father) or *kume* (good) are used when *Ngenechen* is invoked. There are other gods that are sometimes identified with him, although this is not usual. When there is identification, the qualities of these minor or regional deities appear as attributes of *Ngenechen* or else they themselves may be raised to the same level, when the rationale is that these qualities are simply different names for the same god. There are occasions when any deity may be described as *Ngenechen*.
Ngenechen Kusha	Wife of *Ngenechen*. Mapuche gods have wives and children. In many cases Mapuche logic seems to attribute patriarchal qualities to the gods, since the wives and children are not outstanding figures in their myths or ceremonies. *Ngenechen* is considered the first male ancestor or the Mapuches, who, together with *Ngenechen Kusha* (his wife) gave origin to the Mapuche people.
Nguillatue	Carved anthropomorphic figure
Nguillatún	The main Mapuche rogatory ceremony
Nguillatuwe	The sacred space where the *nguillatún* takes place

Nguru	Fox
Ngutram	Historical narratives told by the *Weupife*
Nor feleal	The body of justice of a Mapuche community. It considers misdemeanours in the community and decides upon reparations.
Nor mogen	The system of rules governing both the family and the set of families that make up the community
Ñaña	Elder sister
Ñuke Mapu	Mother Earth
Ñorkin	An instrument, similar to the *trutruka*, but coiled like a hosepipe
Palife	A player of *palín*
Palín	Mapuche sport, similar to hockey, played to establish good relations between communities and avoid conflict
Paliwe	Pitch for playing *palín*
Papay	Mother, old lady
Peñi	Mapuche brother/sister (used by male)
Petú Mogeleiñ	We are still alive
Pewen	Araucaria, monkey-puzzle tree, and its nut
Pewenche	The people of the *pewen*, who live in the mountain regions in the east of the *Gulu Mapu*
Pewma	Dreams. These are of great importance for *machis*; they are analysed and interpreted when they wake up and many of their decisions are made as a result of the insight that has been revealed through the dream. In dreams the Mapuche often visit the *wenu mapu*, the place of extraordinary beauty where their ancestors and gods reside. Dreams are viewed by most Mapuche as being journeys taken by the soul while the person is asleep, and are considered to be important to the dreamers because of the contact with the sacred. These dreams are proudly narrated in rituals and social gatherings.
Pikunche	People of the north
Pillan	Spirit

Pillankuse	In the *Puel Mapu* the *pillankuse* performs a similar role to the *machi*, such as conducting ceremonies, but without the ability to enter a trance state. The knowledge of healing techniques and medicinal herbs is also general exclusive to *machis*. Most of the *machis* disappeared from Argentina with the Conquest of he Desert.
Piren	Snow
Pitrén	Type of pitcher, often anthropomorphic or zoomorphic
Piuchen	Person who represents a *newen* during ceremonies
Puel	East. For the Mapuche the east, not the north, is the main cardinal point, as it is seen as the mystical and spiritual place from which life arises. It is of course the direction of the sunrise, and Mapuche women give birth facing that way. The *rewe* (altar) is inclined in that direction, and many rituals are enacted facing it. The principle of orientation is from right to left, following the universal movement of things, which we see in the path of the sun from the *Puel Mapu* to the *Gulu Mapu*. This circular movement is also represented when *purún* (dances) are performed.
Puelche	People of the east
Puel Mapu	The eastern land of the Mapuche, currently controlled by the Argentine state
Pura pagaw	The constellation in the southern hemisphere known as the "Siete Cabritos" (Seven Kids), the sighting of which marks the new year.
Rakizuam	Thought, reason
Rankulche	People of the reed
Raya	Goal in *palín*
Retrafe	Silversmith
Rewe	The ceremonial centre of the *lof*, the social and ritual community, is the *rewe*. Yet whereas a church, the heart of any village in the UK, is a permanent structure, the *rewe* takes shape during the preparation for a ceremony. The word *rewe* has been translated variously as sacred

	place, trunk, altar and ladder, and may in fact be some or all of these. In the *Gulu Mapu* it is a sacred tree (often cinnamon) or a *prawe* (stair/ladder), or a variant of these, whereas in the *Puel Mapu* it is made of branches of the colihue, lenga, maitén and other trees of the area.
Ruka	Mapuche dwelling. Historically it was between 28 and 56 metres in length, with between two and eight doors. It was made of wood and straw and could be rectangular or circular in shape. Its construction culminated with a feast lasting several days (*rukatun*). There was no division into rooms inside, but there were different compartments used for specific functions. There were no clusters of *rukas*, as those of a community were built at a certain distance from each other, near to rivers, streams or lakes. *Rukas* are quite rare nowadays, as they have been superseded by the conventionally imposed model of house.
Sikil	Ornate Mapuche woman's silver jewellery, representing the division of vertical space of the *wallmapu*.
Tayúl	Song
Toki	Mapuche wartime leader. A council of *lonkos* consisting of representatives of all *butalmapu* would choose a *toki*, who was in charge of the army and had authority for the period strictly necessary. It is important to emphasise that there was no centralised, permanent institutionalised power, but political unity was sought whenever prompted by an external threat.
Toki-kurá	Stone of command. These were often meteorites, and their falling was taken to represent a positive omen for the Mapuche, which is why their presence is often associated with events of great import.
Trafkin	The mutual exchange of gifts
Trapelakucha	Ornate Mapuche woman's silver jewellery, representing duality
Trawun	Meeting

Troya	The circling of the *awun* at high speed on horseback by men carrying the flags of the communities participating in the *nguillatún*.
Truftrufn	Smoke lodge
Trutruka	A wind instrument, used in all social and religious ceremonies. It is made from the colihue (chusquea culeu, the Patagonian cane). It is variable in size, from two to five metres, with a sound box at the end that is normally a cow's horn. The colihue is split in half and the pith removed, and it is then put back together, bound with decorative thread.
Tuwun	The place of origin of each member of the *lof*, a key element of their identity, along with the *kupalme*.
Ulmen	Wise man. The *lof* were not isolated bodies, but were traditionally united along patrilineal lines up to a total of nine. The most capable *lonko* was chosen from among the nine, and was considered the *ulmen* (wise man); this figure directed the affairs of the *kiñe rewe mapu* (the alliance of 9 *lof*), and wielded military, economic and political power. The *ad mapu* was dispensed and interpreted by the *ulmen*. As well as offering the benefit of their wisdom, the *ulmen* also acted as negotiators in the prevention and resolution of disputes, or the formation of alliances with other regions in times of war.
Wa	Maize
Wachi	Bird-trap
Wagelen	Star
Warriache	Urban Mapuche
Weichafe	Warrior
Weke	Llama
Wekufu	Evil spirit, god of death and destruction. There is a platform of evil between the earthly platform and the beneficent ones, where the *Wekufu* or maleficent reside. In the eyes of the Mapuche people, the world is delicately balanced between the positive god of life and creation,

	Ngenechen, and the god of death and destruction, *Wekufu*. These powers express themselves in either chaos, destruction and uncertainty or order and harmony, thereby supporting or punishing man and nature. They explain the arrival of Christopher Columbus in the Americas and the destruction and suffering that followed for the indigenous peoples as the overpowering influence of *Wekufu*.
Wenu mapu	The sky. For the Mapuche the cosmos is divided into various levels that are superimposed on each other vertically in space. The upper platforms, known as the *wenu mapu*, are inhabited by divinities, ancestors and beneficent spirits.
Werken	These are the *lonko*'s messengers; their training begins when they are children. The *werken* have the full trust of the *lonko*, who send them to visit other *lof* to maintain communications and strategic alliances. In Mapuche society each child is prepared as a potential future *werken*; in reality, within a community all can be considered *werkens*, but in matters of importance only one person formally takes on this position. Today Mapuche communities and organisations have *werkens* dealing with media activities and what would be known as PR in modern parlance.
Wentru	Man
Weupife	This is the community's historian, possessing knowedge of the most relevant facts of the past, which they transmit through oral storytelling. They are responsible for gathering all the information that is gradually transmitted from generation to generation, the knowledge of those who were the founding fathers of the lineage that began the *lof*, the relations held with other *lof*, and who the heroes of the culture are. In the past competitions were held to choose the best *weupife*, and one is famously said to have continued to speak of his knowledge for three days without stopping, and he claimed to have three days still to go.

Weupiñ	The occasion when the *weupife* talks. This is usually during meetings, conferences and ceremonies, but also during family visits.
Winka	Non-Mapuche
Wallmapu	Literally "whole world", the whole of Mapuche territory, also in its spiritual dimension. According to the Articles of Association of the "Katrauletuaiñ" Mapuche Community, the *Wallmapu* "is not only a right, but IS the Mapuche, it is the language, it is biodiversity, it is our most authentic cultural essence. For our culture the *Wallmapu* is not something that can be purchased or transferred".
Wenteche	Uplanders
We Tripantu	Expression used in *Gulu Mapu* for *Wiñoy Tripantu*
Williche	People of the south
Wiñoy Tripantu	Mapuche New Year, 24 June